SINUHE,
THE BIBLE,
AND THE PATRIARCHS

Foreword by Thomas E. Levy

*This publication was made possible through
the financial support from UNIS Ltd, and institutional support from
the Ministry of Education of the Czech Republic
(Project LN 00A064, Czech National Centre for Egyptology)
and the Grant Agency of the Czech Academy of Sciences (Grant No. 242001)*

*Text © Miroslav Bárta
Foreword © T. E. Levy
Photography © Miroslav Bárta, Milan Zemina, Roman Míšek
Translation © Renata Landgráfová
Line Drawings © Lucie Vařeková, Jolana Malátková and Petra Vlčková
Layout Set Out
Praha 2003
ISBN 80-86277-31-3*

SINUHE, THE BIBLE, AND THE PATRIARCHS

Foreword by Thomas E. Levy

Miroslav Bárta

SET OUT 2003

DT
87.38
.B37
2003

Table of Contents

Foreword   5

Introduction   9

Sinuhe's Narrative and its Background   13
    Sinuhe's flight from Egypt   31
    Sinuhe's duel   49
    Sinuhe's return to Egypt   57
    Sinuhe's returns to the palace   74

Egypt in the Time of Sinuhe's Flight   77

Egypt and Syria-Palestine in the Time of Sinuhe's Flight   139

Sinuhe's Afterlife   197

Afterword   273

Selected Bibliography   275

Chronological Table   280

Credits   281

Index   282

Cedars of Lebanon

Foreword

It is extremely rare when ancient history, archaeology and environment meet to give scholars a snapshot of the life and times of an ancient people, let alone an individual. We know about Sinuhe, a well-to-do Egyptian administrator, from a document about the royal court of Egypt, called the Tale of Sinuhe. It is dated to the Middle Kingdom, during the 12th dynasty (1938–1756 B. C. E.). Sinuhe was allegedly an official for the harem of Amenemhat I. On learning of the Pharaoh's assassination (1908 B. C. E.), that he may or may not have played a part in, he made a hasty escape over a circuitous route northward from the Nile Delta toward Syria. The Tale of Sinuhe may have served as a leit motif for other ancient Near Eastern literatures such as the Hebrew Bible. Sinuhe's story is remarkably similar to that of Moses who fled Egypt after killing an Egyptian to the desert region of northern Arabia to live with the Midianites (Exodus 2:11–12) and marry one of their daughters, Zipporah (Exodus 2:15–22) enabling him to ascend to prominence. Similarly, on escaping to the desert zone of the southern Levant, Sinuhe was adopted by a nomadic chief and then married his daughter, which thus enabled him to rise to power and prestige. After years of odyssey around the southern Levant, Sinuhe was invited to return to Egypt by Senwosret I, his alleged crimes were forgiven and a tomb was built in his honor. As archaeological research has failed to find the tomb of Sinuhe, his story has become a legend and his biographical short story, recorded in the Tale of Sinuhe, was transmitted for centuries during the Middle Kingdom times.

It is a story of intrigue, adventure, loyalty and redemption. In many respects, it could be considered one of the earliest short stories in human history. The Tale of Sinuhe represents one of those unique epigraphic discoveries that allow us to penetrate the thinking, culture and times of an individual who may have lived more than 4,000 years ago. In Miroslav Bárta's magisterial study of the Tale of Sinuhe presented here, he contends that Sinuhe was a fictitious character, but provides an idealized composite of historical, cultural and Middle Eastern environmental facts that underlie the tale and provide a unifying picture of socio-cultural developments in the region during the Middle Kingdom times. The Tale of Sinuhe has been preserved on numerous fragments of papyri such as the Amherst fragments, the Ramesside papyrus, Papyrus Buenos Aires, and on limestone ostraca such as those at the Ashmolean museum, the Berlin ostracon, Borchardt's Ostracon, and others. The care, in which the Middle Kingdom Egyptians took to preserve this story, highlights its importance as a kind of morality or perhaps propaganda tale for their culture during the 21st to

19th centuries B. C. E., giving us a rare glimpse of some three centuries of Egyptian history from the First Intermediate Period that followed the era of the great pyramid builders, until the end of the Middle Kingdom and the reign of Amenemhat III.

Even since the first translation of the Tale of Sinuhe by Sir Alan H. Gardiner (Gardiner 1916), there have been numerous studies of its significance as a literary document, travelogue, geographic itinerary, a judicial treatise, and other aspects of ancient Near Eastern literatures (Baines 1982, Derchain 1970, Fischer 1976, Foster 1982, Goedicke 1986, Goedicke 1992, Purdy 1977, Theodoridès 1984). However, Bárta goes beyond anything published before by integrating a wide spectrum of ancient Egyptian documents, archaeological data from both Egypt and the Southern Levant, and the Biblical record, he uses the story of Sinuhe, an event in the parlance of the Annales historians (Braudel 1976, Levy and Holl 1998), to study some of the larger social processes of the moyen durée that characterized the eastern Mediterranean during the Early and Middle Bronze Age. Bárta's detailed knowledge of the Egyptian texts, Egyptology, ancient history and the environment of the eastern Mediterranean work together to produce a profound new look at one of the world's earliest civilizations.

Thomas E. Levy
Department of Anthropology, University of California, San Diego

References

Baines, J. 1982. Interpreting Sinuhe. *Journal of Egyptian Archaeology* 68:31 – 44.
Braudel, F. 1976. *The Mediterranean and the Mediterranean world in the age of Philip II.* New York: Harper & Row.
Derchain, P. 1970. La reception de Sinouhé à la cour de Sesostris I, 22. *RdÉ* 22:79–83.
Fischer, H. G. 1976. Milk in Everything Cooked (Sinuhe B 91–92). *Egyptian Studies* 1:97–99.
Foster, J. L. 1982. Cleaning Up Sinuhe. *JSSEA* 12:81 – 85.
Gardiner, A. H. 1916. *Notes on the Story of Sinuhe.* Paris.

Goedicke, H. 1986. Three Passages in the Story of Sinuhe. *JARCE* 23:167–174.
Idem, 1992. Where did Sinuhe stay in 'Asia'? (Sinuhe B 29–31). *CdÉ* 67:28 – 40.
Levy, T. E., and A. Holl. 1998. Social Change and the Archaeology of the Holy Land, in *The Archaeology of Society in the Holy Land*. Edited by T. E. Levy, pp. 2 – 8. London: Leicester University Press.
Purdy, S. 1977. Sinuhe and the Question of Literary Types. *ZÄS* 104:112–127.
Theodoridès, A. 1984. L'amnistie et la raison d'état dans les 'Aventures de Sinouhé' (debut du IIe millenaire av. J.–C.). *RIDA* 31 31:75–144.

Introduction

The name Sinuhe is known to most readers from the famous novel of the Finnish writer Mika Waltari, entitled *Sinuhe the Egyptian*, which was first published in 1945. This fictitious account of a physician from the time of Akhenaten has an ancient precursor of the same name, who lived at the beginning of the twentieth century BC, i.e. more than half a millennium earlier. This ancient Sinuhe was, just as his more famous counterpart from the novel, also fictitious, but his destiny, narrated in the context of the events that took place almost four thousand years ago, is no less thrilling.

Sinuhe's fictitious account – we still possess no evidence that he was an actual individual – is dated to the beginning of the second millennium BC. Its author is unknown, which is typical for ancient Egyptian literature, in which authorship was not considered an important issue. Sinuhe's story may be summarised as follows: the first king of the Middle Kingdom, Amenemhat I, is assassinated while his son Senwosret I is off leading a military campaign against the Bedouin in the Western Desert. After the king's death, messengers are despatched to his son in order to inform him about the circumstances of his father's demise. Senwosret leaves the army, which is on its way back to Egypt, without hesitation and speeds to Egypt to suppress the potential revolt in the capital. The high courtier Sinuhe overhears the message of the royal envoys and, out of fear of being considered among those responsible for the assassination, sets to flight. He eventually leaves Egypt and joins the south Levantine Bedouin to the northeast of the Egyptian frontier. The Bedouin chieftain develops an affection for Sinuhe, marries his daughter to him, gives him part of his tribe, and assigns territory to him. Sinuhe spends most of his life here, surrounded by his new family. However, he is also compelled to defend his position at the head of his tribe. Thus, one day a giant arrives, the hero of the land of Retjenu, to challenge Sinuhe to battle in order to take possession of his property. The following day Sinuhe fights an almost hopeless duel, in the end, however, he manages to win. This story was, according to some scholars, the inspiration of the account of the duel of David and Goliath, dating to almost a millennium later. In the end Sinuhe, encouraged by the king, returns to Egypt in his old age, where he is welcomed as a close friend of the king, who takes care of him and has a tomb built for him in the necropolis. Thus Sinuhe's existence in the afterlife is guaranteed.

Sinuhe's account is narrated in the context of the early Middle Bronze Age Period in the area of Syria-Palestine, i.e. in the time considered contemporaneous with the Old Testament Patriarchs headed by Abraham. Sinuhe's lifestyle outside Egypt corresponds to that of the Biblical Patriarchs at the time of their arrival in Syria-Palestine. This is one of the reasons why Sinuhe is sometimes connected with the migration of Abraham and his tribe, although even now it is impossible to determine precisely the time of Abraham's appearance on the scene (it is most often dated to the twentieth – seventieth century BC).

Despite the fact that the story is fictitious, many descriptions and events included in it correspond to the conditions and environment that we know from the contemporary archaeological and written evidence from Syria-Palestine. Sinuhe's story takes place in the context of the political, economic and human events of ancient Egypt and Syria-Palestine during the twentieth and nineteenth centuries BC. The present work therefore includes, in addition to the translation of the text and commentary in the first chapter, two chapters explaining the political history of Egypt and Syria-Palestine, which may help us to elucidate the background of Sinuhe's flight. The final part focuses on the religious concepts of the ancient Egyptians connected with life after death. The individual chapters incorporate the most recent developments in archaeological exploration, both in Egypt and in the area of Syria-Palestine. The same emphasis is put on contemporary epigraphic sources and their interpretation in the light of various scholarly disciplines covering the individual problems (such as Egyptology, cuneiform studies, archaeology of the Ancient Near East, anthropology of nomadic populations, etc.). The citations of original epigraphic sources should assist the reader in creating his or her own independent concept of the problem. The indvidual chapters also include selected bibliographies with the main relevant secondary sources.

Sinuhe's story was conceived by its author(s) above all as a political composition, on the basis of which Amenemhat's son and successor was to be cleared of all charges concerning his possible participation in the assassination of his father or its organisation. This is also attested by the passages celebrating king Senwosret I (once in a hymn, the second time in a letter of Sinuhe to the king). At the same time, however, Sinuhe's account is also a description of the life of a loyal Egyptian official, who, despite his flight from Egypt (as a consequence of the 'intention of God,' as he himself makes it clear), remains true to the principles characterising the Egyptian official, i.e. loyalty to the Egyptian king, religiosity – Sinuhe never conceived of worshipping foreign gods despite his lengthy stay abroad – and the desire to be buried in the Egyptian homeland in the vicinity of his lord. To an extent, Sinuhe's text gives an impression of an ethical treatise. It is thus even now extremely difficult to determine its genre; it is a fairy tale and at the same time a political manifesto with typical biographical elements.

Sinuhe's account, one of the most interesting works of ancient Egyptian literature, remains one of the most discussed literary sources from the Middle Kingdom. By this term, Egyptologists mean the period between the years 1991 – 1783 BC, the reigns of the rulers of the Twelfth Egyptian Dynasty. After a period of internal disorder following the end of the Old Kingdom, these kings revived the traditions from the age of the famous pyramid builders. Sinuhe's account was

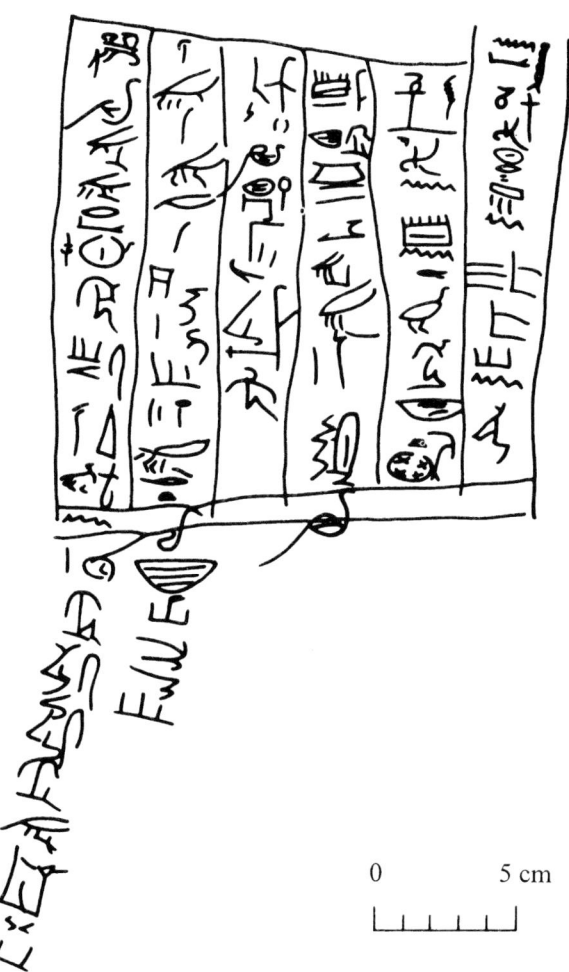

Rock-cut inscription of Dedusobek in Wadi el-Hol mentioning the gods enumerated in Sinuhe's account (Wadi el-Hol, Thebes; after J. C. Darnell, D. Darnell, Theban Desert Road Survey in the Egyptian Western Desert, Volume 1: Gebel Tjauti Rock Inscriptions 1-45 and Wadi el-Hôl Rock Inscriptions 1-45, Chicago 2002, p. 99)

preserved on several Middle Kingdom papyri, most of which come from the time of Amenemhat III. From this era two partially damaged papyri with the composition are preserved, namely Papyrus Berlin 3022 (abbreviated in Egyptological literature as B), which has a damaged beginning and contains altogether 311 lines, and Papyrus Berlin 10499 (abbreviated as R), which contains 203 lines and a preserved beginning. The translation in the present study is based on the hieroglyphic transcriptions of these two papyri. They were acquired in Egypt in the middle of the nineteenth century by the founder of German Egyptology K. R. Lepsius during a three-year expedition to Egypt undertaken in 1842 – 1845.

Fragments of this text are preserved on another four papyri. The popularity of Sinuhe's account is attested by the fact that it continued to be copied for several subsequent centuries. In this context it is interesting to mention the 2002 publication of the inscriptions from Wadi el-Hol in the Western Desert near Thebes by American Egyptologists John and Deborah Darnell. One of the inscriptions (number 4), composed by Dedusobek and dated to the reign of Amenemhat III enumerates the same gods as does Sinuhe in his letter addressed to his Lord, King Senwosret I. It seems feasible to suppose that these were the gods considered most worth mentioning by any Egyptian leaving the country. From the time of the New Kingdom (1539–1292 BC), esp. from the Ramesside Period (Nineteenth Dynasty) come almost thirty ostraca (inscribed limestone chips or pottery sherds) with parts of Sinuhe's tale, originating from the scribal school of Deir el-Medineh. The most famous copy of this text is inscribed on an ostracon now in the Ashmolean Museum in Oxford; a similar but slightly smaller ostracon is preserved in the Egyptian Museum in Cairo (No. 27419).

Having finished the draft of the book for the English speaking audience (a revised and extended version of a Czech monograph that was published in Prague in 1999) I have to thank many friends and colleagues, although it is impossible to name them all here. Those most essential for the book's production include: Renata Landgráfová who translated the book into English, Vivienne G. Callender and Jane Jakeman who painstakingly checked the text and contributed many ideas and suggestions, Roman Míšek, Hana Navrátilová and SET OUT staff, who produced the book and saw it through all stages of the publication process. My thanks go also to UNIS, whose financial assistance allowed the book to see the light of the day.

Sinuhe's Narrative and its Background

(R, 1) *Hereditary noble and prince,*
governor of royal estates in the lands of the Asiatics,
true and beloved friend of the king,
the attendant Sinuhe, says:
I was an attendant who followed his lord,
a servant in the royal chambers,
and (a servant) of the princess, one greatly praised,
the royal wife of Senwosret in Khenemisut,
(R, 5) *the daughter of King Amenemhat in Kaneferu,*
the praised lady Neferu.

In regnal year 30, third month of the inundation season, day 7,
the god ascended to his horizon.
The King of Upper and Lower Egypt, Sehetepibre,
he flew up to the sky,
and joined the sun-disc,
the divine body, uniting with its creator.
The royal residence was silent,
hearts grieved,
the great portals were closed.
(R, 10) *The heads of the courtiers were on their laps,*
and the nobles moaned.

But His Majesty had dispatched an army to the land of Tjehenu,
with his eldest son as its commander,
the perfect god, Senwosret.
He was sent to destroy foreign lands,
(R, 15) *and to smite the inhabitants of Tjehenu.*
Now he was returning, bringing captives from Tjehenu,
and all cattle without limit.
The officials of the royal palace
sent to the western border
to inform the king's son about the situation
that had come about in the audience hall.

The messengers found him on the road,
(R, 20) they reached him at night time.
He did not hesitate a moment:
The falcon flew up with his followers,
without informing his army.
The royal children who were with the army
were also sent for.
(B, 1) One of them was informed
while I was in service.
I heard his voice, as he spoke
while I was near.
My heart grew confused,
my arms spread out,
trembling befell all my limbs.

I removed myself in haste,
to search out a concealed place for myself,
(B, 5) to hide between the bushes,
and leave the road to its traveller.

I set out southward,
not even thinking of going to the residence.
I thought that a revolt had broken out,
and I did not believe I would survive it.
I travelled over the Lake of Maat in the vicinity of the Sycamore,
and reached the Island of Sneferu.
(B, 10) I spent the day at the edge of the field.
I set out at dawn, when the (new) day came,
I encountered a man standing at the mouth of the road.
He greeted me, (but) I was afraid of him.
At supper-time, I reached the cattle-ford
and crossed over in a boat, which had no rudder,
by the force of the west wind.
I passed to the east of the stone-quarry,
(B, 15) at the height of the Mistress of the Red Mountain.
I set out on the road again, going northwards,
I reached the Walls of the Ruler
which were built to ward off the Asiatics and trample the Bedouin.
I crouched behind a bush out of fear
that the watch of the day standing on the battlements would see me.

(B, 20) I set out at night time
and when dawn came, I reached Peten.
I descended to the island of Kemwer.

Fig. 1.1 Sinuhe's name can be translated as a 'Son of the Sycamore tree'; the sycamore was venerated by the Egyptians for the shade and recreation it provided during hot days. Sennedjem and his wife are represented praying to the tree and receiving refreshing offerings as a reward (Tomb of Sennedjem, Deir el-Medineh, Nineteenth Dynasty)

Then thirst overtook me; I was parched,
and my throat was dry.
I thought: 'This is the taste of death!'
When I raised up my heart and pulled together my limbs,
(B, 25) I heard the sound of cattle and caught sight of Asiatics.
One of their chiefs, who had been in Egypt, recognised me.

Then he gave me water and boiled (some) milk for me.
I followed him to his tribe, and
what they did for me was good.
I travelled from one foreign land to another,
I set out for Byblos, I reached Qedem,
(B, 30) where I spent a year and a half.
Then Amunenshi, the sovereign of Upper Retjenu,
brought me away
and told me: 'You will feel good with me; you will hear the language of Egypt.'
He said this because he knew my character,

*and had heard of my wisdom,
since the Egyptians who were with him
testified about me.*

(B, 35) *Then he said to me: 'Why have you come here?
Has something happened in the residence?'
Then I told him:
'The King of Upper and Lower Egypt went to the horizon, and it is not known why.'
– I said this as a misstatement –
'When I came with an army from the land of Tjehenu,
it was reported to me.*
(B, 40) *My heart quivered and carried me away on the roads of flight.
I had not been talked about, neither had anyone spat into my face,
and I had not heard a reproach.
My name was not heard from the mouth of the herald.
I do not know what brought me to this land,
it was like the plan of a god.
As if a man from the Delta saw himself in Yebu, a man from the marshes in Nubia.'
Then he told me: 'What is that land like without that beneficent god,*
(B, 45) *the fear of whom pervaded foreign lands
like Sekhmet in the year of pestilence?'
I told him thus, answering him:
'Assuredly, his son has entered the palace
and taken the heritage of his father.
He is a god who has no equal,
there is none who is before him.
He is the lord of wisdom, one excellent of plans
and effective of commands.*
(B, 50) *One comes and goes by his will.
It is he who conquered foreign lands,
while his father was in his palace,
reporting to him on the execution of what he had commanded.*

*He is a strong man who acts with his mighty arm,
a hero who has no equal
when he is seen attacking foreigners and approaching opponents.
He is a bender of horns, one who makes arms turn weak,*
(B, 55) *his enemies are unable to control their ranks.
He is an avenger who crushes foreheads,
one can not rise in his presence.
He is one wide of stride, who smites the ones who flee,
there is no hope for those on whom he turns his back.
One strong of heart in time of attack,
he turns around, (but) he never flees.*

He is bold when he sees the multitudes,
(B, 60) *he lets not slackness fill his heart.*

He is belligerent when he descends on the easterners,
it is his joy to attack the barbarians,
he lifts up his shield and tramples enemies.
He does not repeat (the act of) his arm to kill.
There is no escape from his arrows,
his bow cannot be diverted.
The barbarians flee,
for his arms are like the might of (the goddess) Wereret.
Fighting, he can foresee the goal,
(B, 65) *concerned with nothing, (since) nothing else exists.*

He is the lord of charm, one great of grace.
He seizes love.
His city loves him more than its inhabitants,
(and) rejoices over him more than over its god.
Men outdo women in praising him,
for he is the ruler who had been attacking even when in the egg.
His face had existed from the time of birth.
(B, 70) *A multiplier of those who had been born together with him,*
he is unique, created by the god.

Fig. 1.2 Lisht, the burial place of Amenemhat I

May this land which he rules rejoice!
He is the extender of borders.

He will conquer southern lands, not thinking about northern ones.
He was conceived to smite the Asiatics and trample the Bedouin.
Send to him, let him know your name
as one, who is asking far away from His Majesty!
(B, 75) He shall not fail to do good
to the country, which is loyal to him!'

He spoke to me thus: 'Indeed, Egypt is happy
knowing that he is firm.
Look, you are here and will stay with me,
what I will do for you is good.'
He placed me at the head of his children,
and married to me his eldest daughter.
He let me choose from his countries
(B, 80) from the choice ones in his possession,
at the border with another country.
This country was good,
its name was Yaa.
There were figs there and grapes,
it had more wine than water,
a lot of honey and oil beyond measure.
All kinds of fruit were growing on its trees;
there was barley and wheat,
(B, 85) and all kinds of cattle without limit.
Great was, moreover, what was given to me because of the love of me;
for he made me chief of a tribe
in the best part of his country.

One prepared for me daily rations of bread,
and drinks of wine for the course of the day,
cooked meat,
roast fowl, as well as desert game.
(B, 90) Someone was spearing for me, and presenting to me (food)
apart from the catch of my hounds.
One prepared for me a large number of dairy dishes
in every manner of cooking.

Thus I spent many years,
my children grew strong,
each one controlling his own tribe.
The messenger travelling north or south to the residence

*stayed with me. I let everyone stay with me.
I gave water to the thirsty,
placed the one who went astray on the road,
I rescued the robbed one.
When the Asiatics had to mobilize
to oppose the rulers of the hill-countries,
I gave them advice in their proceeding.
(B, 100) This ruler of Retjenu made
me to spend numerous years
as a commander of his army.
Every foreign country against which I marched,
I assaulted its inhabitants and drove them away from its pastures and wells.
I seized its cattle, carried off its inhabitants,
(B, 105) took their food and killed its people by my strong arm,
by my bow, by my stride and by my excellent plans.*

*I was esteemed in his heart.
He loved me because he knew I was courageous.
He placed me at the head of his children and he saw
that my arms were strong.
Then came the strongman of Retjenu
(B, 110) and challenged me in my tent.
He was a hero without equal, he had subdued the entire land.
He said he would fight with me.
He thought he would defeat me,
and planned to seize my cattle for the benefit of his tribe.
That ruler took counsel with me.
I said: 'I do not know him, I am not his ally,
(B, 115) that I could walk about his encampment.
Have I ever burst open his border
or overstepped his fences?
It is envy, for he sees me acting in your matters,
indeed, I am like a stray bull
in the midst of a different herd,
assaulted by the wild bull of the herd,
(B, 120) attacked by the longhorn.
Is a commoner beloved
when he becomes a master?
No barbarian would make friends with a man from the Delta.
What can hold a papyrus on a mountain?
If a bull loves to fight,
does a victorious bull prefer to retreat for fear
that he might equal him?
(B, 125) If he wants to fight, let him express his wish!*

Doesn't god know what he had ordained,
And (doesn't he) recognise how things will be?'

I spent the night stretching my bow and preparing my arrows.
I sharpened my dagger and polished my weapons.
At dawn, the people of Retjenu came.
(B, 130) It assembled its tribes,
its lands gathered up themselves from both sides
thinking of this combat.
[(R, 156) He came toward me, while I was standing and he appeared close to me.]
All hearts fluttered for me,
men and women were afraid,
and all hearts suffered for me,
saying: 'Is there another strongman who could fight him?'

After he lay down his shield, his axe
(B, 135) and an armful of his javelins,
I avoided his weapons
and let his arrows pass me by,
one after the other,
until none of them remained.
When he attacked me,
I shot him; my arrow stuck in his neck.
He screamed and fell on his nose (and)
(B, 140) I slew him with his own axe.
I raised a war cry on his back,
while all the Asiatics were shouting with pleasure.
While his people were mourning him,
I gave praise to Montu.
The ruler Amunenshi embraced me.

Then I carried away his possessions
and seized his cattle –
that which he had planned to do to me,
(B, 145) I did to him.
I seized what was in his tent,
I destroyed his encampment.
Thus, I became great, my possessions were plentiful and my cattle numerous.

It was god who satisfied the one,
with whom he had been angry,
(the one) whom he had driven off to a foreign country.
Today, his heart is appeased.
(B, 150) The fugitive flees from his surroundings,

but my fame is in the residence.
He who is plodding along is hindered by hunger,
but I am giving bread to my neighbour.
A man is leaving his country naked,
but I have white clothes and fine linen.
A man runs for the lack of someone else he could send,
(B, 155) but I have numerous underlings.
My house is beautiful, and my dwelling is spacious.
My thoughts, however, are in the palace.
You god, who have ordained this flight for me,
have mercy!
Bring me back home!
Surely, you will let me see the place
where my heart dwells!
For what is more important than to bury my body
(B, 160) in the land where I was born?
Come to my aid!
What happened was good.
May god have mercy on me!
May he make good the end of him,
whom he had been punishing!
May he show mercy over him,
whom he had expelled to live in a foreign country.
If he is satisfied today,
may he listen to his prayer!
May he let the one whom he let roam the earth
return to the place from where he had taken him!

(B, 165) May the king of Egypt have mercy with me,
may I live within his favour!
May I welcome the Mistress of the land
who is in his palace!
May I obey the commands of her children!
I wish my members were young,
for old age has come
and weakness has overtaken me.
My eyes are heavy, my arms feeble,
(B, 170) my legs are unable to follow.
The heart is weary, I am close to death.
May I be carried to the City of Eternity!
May I serve the Lady of the Universe!
May she speak well of me to her children!
May she bring me eternity!

Now, when His Majesty,
King of Upper and Lower Egypt, Kheperkare, justified,
was informed about the state I was in,
he sent royal gifts to me,
in order to please the heart of his humble servant
just like (that of) any ruler of a foreign land.
The royal children, who were in his palace,
made me hear their dispatch.

Copy of the decree delivered to the humble servant concerning his return to Egypt:

'Horus: Ankhmesut
The Two Ladies: Ankhmesut
King of Upper and Lower Egypt: Kheperkare,
(B, 180) Son of Ra: Senwosret,
may he live for all eternity.
Royal decree to the attendant Sinuhe:
Look, this royal decree has been brought to you
to let you know that when you travelled to foreign lands,
going out from Qedem to Retjenu,
one land giving you to the other,
you were following the advice of your own heart.
What had you done, that one should act against you?
You had not spoken ill, so that one would reprove your words.
You had not spoken in the council hall,
so that one would reject your speech.
(B, 185) This plan, it was conceived by your own heart,
it was not in my heart against you.
This your heaven, she who is in the palace,
now persists and prospers.
Her head is adorned with the kingship of the land.
Her children are in the reception hall.

You will accumulate the wealth, which they shall give to you,
you will live from their gifts.
Come back to Egypt!
You will see the residence where you had grown up!
You shall kiss the ground at the Great Gate!
Join the officials!
(B, 190) Today you have begun to grow old,
you have lost virility.
Consider the day of your burial,
when you shall join the revered ones!

*Fig. 1.3 Relief of Senwosret I being embraced by the god Ptah
(Lisht, now in Egyptian Museum, Cairo)*

*The night is assigned to you
with oils and bandages from the hands of Taiet.
The burial procession will be prepared for you on the day of death.
Your mummy will be covered with gold,
the head with lapis lazuli,
the sky above, facing you.
You will (also) be given a sarcophagus.
Cattle will drag (you)
and singers will go in front of you.
(B, 195) The muu-dancers will be made to dance at the entrance of your tomb.
One will recite the ritual, giving sacrifices to you.
One will make offerings for you in front of the entrance to your chapel.
Your pillars will be made of white limestone
among the pillars of the royal children.
Do not die in a foreign country!
Do not let yourself be buried by the Asiatics!
Do not let a sheep-skin become your primitive grave!
The dragging through this land has been long enough!
Think of your body and come back!'
(B, 200) This decree reached me while I was in the midst of my tribe.
When it had been read to me,
I lay down, I touched the ground.
I smeared it over my breast
and walked around the encampment full of joy,
calling:
'Was ever the like of this done for a servant,
whom his heart brought to the foreign lands?
Indeed, good is the graciousness
that saved me from death!
Your ka will let me reach my end,
being at home!'*

*A copy of the response to this document:
(B, 205) The servant of the palace, Sinuhe, says:
'In very beautiful peace!
As for this flight,
which this humble servant made in his ignorance.
It is your ka, perfect god,
Lord of the Two Lands, beloved of Ra,
praised by Montu, Lord of Waset,
and by Amun, Lord of the throne of the Two Lands.
Sebek-Ra, Horus, Hathor,
Atum with his Divine Ennead,
Sopdu-Neferbau-Semsher-Eastern Horus,*

Lord of Imhet who protects your head,
the council upon the water,
Min-Horus in the midst of foreign countries,
(B, 210) Wereret, Lady of Punt,
Nut, Harwer-Ra,
and all the deities of Egypt and the islands of the sea,
may they bestow your nose with life and power!
May they make you happy with their gifts!
May they give you eternity without end,
everlastingness without limit!
May fear of you permeate
all lands and hill-countries!
You have subdued everything encircled by the sun.
This is the plea of the humble servant to the Lord
who protects one from the West,
the Lord of knowledge who knows people,
(B, 215) and who, being the Majesty of the palace, knows
that which the humble servant was afraid to say.
It is like a thing too great to be repeated.
The great god, Ra's equal,
knows the prowess of the one
who served him willingly.
This humble servant is in the power of the one
who protects him, and under his command.
Your majesty is like the conquering Horus;
your arms subdue all lands.
May Your Majesty command
that there be brought to you Meki of Qedem,
(B, 220) the inhabitants of Front Kashu,
and Manus, from the lands of the Phenekhu.
They are rulers, witnesses,
whose names came to existence through the love of you.
I do not mention Retjenu which belongs to you like your hounds.

This flight which the servant made,
I did not plan it,
it was not in my heart,
I did not think about it,
I do not know what brought me to this place.
(B, 225) It is like a dream,
as if an inhabitant of Delta found himself in Elephantine,
a man from the marshes in the land of the Nubians.
I was not afraid, no one pursued me,
I heard no reproach,

nor was my name heard from the mouth of the herald.
Still, there were goose-pimples on my body,
my legs drove me.
my heart led me.
(B, 230) The god, who had ordained this flight, dragged me away.
I was no longer self-confident.
Feared is the man who is acknowledged by his land.
Ra made the fear of you permeate the land,
and brought the terror of you to all foreign countries.
Whether I am in the residence or in this place,
it is you who covers the horizon.
The sun rises through the love of you,
the water in the river is drunk when you wish,
the air of heaven is breathed at your order.

(B, 235) Your humble servant will pass his affairs on to his young offspring,
whom your humble servant begot in this place.
A journey was undertaken for your humble servant!
May Your Majesty act according to his will!
One lives by the air which you give.
Ra, Horus and Hathor love these, your noble nostrils!
May Montu, Lord of Thebes, wish that they live eternally!'

I was allowed to spend one day in the land of Yaa,
passing my affairs onto my children.
My eldest son became the head of my tribe,
(B, 240) my entire tribe and all my possessions became his,
my servants, all my cattle,
my fruit as well as all my fruit trees.
This humble servant undertook a journey to the south,
stopping only on the Ways of Horus.
The captain who commanded the frontier garrison
sent a messenger to the residence to inform them.

Then His Majesty sent the excellent overseer of the peasants of the royal estate
(B, 245) with ships laden with royal gifts
for the Asiatics who were in my suite,
and who had come to the Ways of Horus with me.
I called every one of them by his name.
The heart of each of them was performing his duty.
I set out to sail,
while everything around me mixed and boiled,
and I reached the port of Itj-tawy.
When it dawned very, very early,

Fig. 1.4 Depiction of a typical Asiatic (Tell el-Yehudieh, Palace of Ramesses II, Nineteenth Dynasty)

they came to summon me.
Ten men came and ten men left,
bringing me to the palace.
I touched the ground with my forehead,
(B, 250) the royal children who stood in the gate came to meet me.
The noble courtiers who usher guests to the reception hall
showed me the way to the council hall.
I found His Majesty on the great throne
in a niche of electrum.
I threw myself on the ground in front of him,
I did not recognise myself in his presence.
This god addressed me amiably.
I was like a man seized by darkness.
(B, 255) My soul disappeared,
my body grew feeble,
my heart was not in my body,
I could not tell life from death.

Then His Majesty said to one of these courtiers:
'Lift him up and let him speak to me!'
And His Majesty said:
'Look, you have come back after having roamed foreign lands,
after having been seized by flight.

You are weak, you have reached old age.
Your burial is no negligible affair,
you shall not be buried by barbarians.
Do not act against yourself, do not act against yourself!
(B, 260) You have not spoken when your name has been called out,
do you fear punishment?'
I answered the answer of one in fear:
'What was said to me by My Lord,
so that I could answer?
I do not act in disrespect to the god.
Terror is within my body, like that which had caused the fateful flight.
Look, I am in front of you, to you belongs life,
Your Majesty acts according to his wish!'

Then the royal children were brought in,
and His Majesty said to the King's wife:
(B, 265) 'Look, Sinuhe returned as an Asiatic,
like one fashioned by the barbarians!'
She gave a very loud cry,
and the royal children shrieked as one.
Then they said to His Majesty:
'Is it really he, O sovereign, our lord?'
And His Majesty said:
'It is really he.'
Then they brought their menat necklaces,
their rattles and their sistra,
and they gave them to His Majesty.
(B, 270) 'May your hands be on this beauty, merciful king!
These jewels of the Mistress of Heaven!
May the Golden One give life to your nostrils,
may the Mistress of the Stars embrace you!
The crown of Upper Egypt is sailing northward,
the crown of Lower Egypt is floating southward,
united and alike
by the words of Your Majesty,
on whose forehead are the Two Goddesses!
You have divided evil from wrong,
so that Ra, Lord of the Two Lands, is satisfied with you.
Hail to you, Mistress of the Universe!
Untie your bow and lay down your arrow!
(B, 275) Give breath to him who is breathless!
Give us this beautiful gift on this beautiful day!
Give us this son of the northwind,
the barbarian born in Egypt!

He fled only for fear of you!
He fled the country for terror of you!
Now the face that sees your face need no longer become pale,
the eye that beheld you need no longer be afraid!'

And His Majesty said:
'He need not be afraid,
(B, 280) he need not fear horrors!
He shall become a friend among the officials,
he shall be placed in the ranks of the courtiers!
Go to the dressing room and wait for him!'

I left the audience hall,
the royal children giving me their hands,
(B, 285) and then we passed through the great gate.
I was placed in the house of the king's son,
with noble things in it.
There was a bathroom,
and divine cult images of the horizon.
There were riches from the Treasury,
clothes of royal linen, myrrh and choice royal oil,
(B, 290) and officials whom the king loves in every room,
and every servant did his duty.
Years were removed from my body,
when I was shaved and my hair done,
the burden was left to the foreign country,
and the clothes to the Bedouin.
I was dressed in fine linen,
I was anointed with choice oil,
I slept in a bed,
I gave the sand to those who live on it,
(B, 295) and the oil of the trees to those who anoint themselves with it.
I was given a house with a garden,
which used to belong to a friend (of the king).
Many craftsmen had built it,
all its trees were planted anew.
Meals were brought to me from the palace
three to four times a day,
apart from that which the royal children were giving me
(B, 300) incessantly.

They built for me a pyramid of stone among the pyramids.
The workers of the necropolis, who build pyramids,
measured out its foundations.

The overseer of draughtsmen drew it,
the overseer of sculptors sculpted in it,
and the overseer of the works in the necropolis himself worked on it.
(B, 305) The entire burial equipment, which was to be placed in the burial shaft,
the need of it was satisfied.
Mortuary priests were assigned to me,
a funerary estate was allotted to me.
There were fields in it and a garden in its place,
as it was done for a best friend.
My image (e.g. statue) was overlaid with gold and
its skirt with electrum.
It was His Majesty
who ordered this to be done.

There are no men of low birth for whom the like of this had been done.
(B, 310) I was endowed with royal gifts,
until the day of landing came.

It was written from beginning to end as it was found in the book.

Sinuhe's flight from Egypt

It has already been indicated above in the Introduction that Sinuhe's story as such was fictional. Actually, it is not even likely (or, at least, there is no evidence) that a courtier of this name and with a similar destiny ever existed. Sinuhe's story is nonetheless a valuable narrative that provides us with accurate and important information about the world that surrounded the ancient Egyptians at the beginning of the Middle Kingdom (20th century BC). The account relates the fate of a high official at the royal court, whose titles 'noble' and 'prince' suggest that Sinuhe was a member of an old, prestigious family, which could even have played an important role in Mentuhotep II's struggle for the unification of Egypt. Sinuhe himself further reports that he was the overseer of royal estates in Asia and also held a high rank at the court in service to the royal family.

The story begins as the army under the command of the crown prince, Senwosret, returns from a campaign against the Libyans in the Western Desert. This expedition was one of the frequent military campaigns that were carried out in order to pacify the rebellious nomadic tribes migrating across the Egyptian border. Just as the Nubians south of the First Cataract, or the Asiatics northeast of Egypt, these tribes represented incessant potential danger to the stability of Egypt. Sudden attacks on Egyptian settlements in the Nile Valley were not uncommon at various times throughout Egyptian history. The threat of raids of the immensely mobile Bedouin tribes could thus be effectively averted only by preventive campaigns.

The most likely course that the Egyptians took on their way back to the Nile valley, would have been the ancient road joining the Wadi Natrun Oasis with the Nile valley. This road, which began north of today's Giza, was later used by

Fig. 1.5 The landscape of Wadi Natrun as it appears today

Christian pilgrims, who called it Darb el-Hagg el-Mararbe (the road of the pilgrim Mararbe). Ahmed Fakhry's 1940 study shows that Amenemhat I was most probably the first king who started with a military protection of the area. The site of Qaret el-Dahr near Wadi Natrun shows clearly that there existed a fortress dated to this period. While the troops were on their way back from their latest campaign, Senwosret's father, King Amenemhat I, was assassinated in the capital. The Egyptian army met the royal messengers who had been sent from the residence (maybe waiting for the troops in the fortress built by Amenemhat I?) to inform the royal princes of the news during their return from the Libyan campaign. By accident, Sinuhe overhears their confidential report to the crown prince Senwosret and the royal children, concerning the violent death of their father. Worried about his own future and afraid of the possible repressive measures that the king's successor could use against him, Sinuhe decides to flee from the army. The reasons for his escape are unclear. Perhaps he was worried that, as a high-ranking court official, he could be accused of conspiracy against the successor to the throne Senwosret. It was probably not mere coincidence that Amenemhat I had been assassinated in the rooms of his own palace, at the time when his successor was absent. Sinuhe might also have feared for his life because of the possibility that a civil war might break out as a result of the strife between a potential usurper from the royal family and the legitimate successor, Senwosret.

The route taken by Sinuhe seems fairly clear: his account indicates that after he had reached the Nile Valley, he continued southward past Giza, the site of the gigantic constructions of the pyramids of the most famous Old Kingdom rulers,

Fig. 1.6 The Pyramid and Sphinx of Khafre in Giza

*Fig. 1.7 The Bent pyramid of Sneferu at Dahshur.
It was here that Sinuhe decided to cross the Nile*

Khufu, Khafre and Menkaure. Close to Giza, he passed by the sanctuary of the Lady of the Sycamore, Hathor. This may be either an echo of his own name, *Sinuhe*, which translates as 'son of the sycamore,' and/or an allusion to Sinuhe's place of birth.

The Egyptians had a very cordial relationship with trees, which they tried to grow even in the necropolis. Trees symbolized protection against the burning sun and a source of refreshment. Therefore, in the minds of the Egyptians, even the dead sought out trees in order to refresh themselves in their shade. The sycamore was one of the most highly praised trees where Egyptians were concerned. It was connected with the goddess Hathor or occasionally with Nut, both of whom were considered protector goddesses (see below). According to one of the religious concepts contained in the so-called Pyramid Texts (religious texts engraved on the walls of the inner apartments of the pyramids of the rulers from the end of the Fifth to the end of the Sixth Dynasty), the sun would rise each day in the east between two sycamores. Thus, this tree was also, to an extent, a symbol of rebirth. Scenes from numerous non-royal New Kingdom tombs depict the sycamore with Hathor hiding in its branches. The tomb owner rests in the shadow of the tree and the goddess refreshes him with cool water. This was one of the most typical concepts connected with the ancient Egyptian belief in existence in the hereafter.

After he passed Giza and undertook a half-day long journey, Sinuhe finally reached Dahshur, the place of two pyramids of King Sneferu, the founder of the

Fig. 1.8 Eastern Delta with remains of one of the later fortresses protecting Wadi Tumilat (Tell el-Yehudieh)

Fourth Dynasty and father of the builder of the greatest Egyptian pyramid, Khufu. Here, Sinuhe decided to ferry himself across the river in a boat to the eastern bank of the Nile. In the evening, for fear of being noticed, he searched out a cattle ford with a raft for the transport of cattle. This, however, had no oars. Sinuhe had to push the raft off the bank and rely on the help of the stream and of the west wind. The direction of the wind is very important for navigation in Egypt, since the west winds there blow only during the khamseen season, which lasts for fifty days, from the end of February until April. These winds that blow from the Western desert often cause sandstorms, which are even today greatly feared in Egypt. This fact allows us to form a better idea of the season at the time of Sinuhe's flight. The period between February and April was also very advantageous for military campaigns into the desert, since in these months the temperatures in the desert are still within bearable limits. The wind and stream carried Sinuhe very far north, all the way to the so-called Red Mountain, Gebel el-Akhmar, to the northeast of Cairo. Here Sinuhe turned north and reached Wadi Tumilat, Egypt's frontier zone with a line of fortresses. These fortresses had been constructed already before the Middle Kingdom. Sinuhe's account, as well as the Prophecy of Neferti, explicitly state that the Walls of the Ruler were built to prevent the influx of Asiatics into the Egyptian Delta and into Egypt:

'The Walls of the Sovereign, may he live, prosper and be healthy, will be built, so that the Asiatics can (no more) enter Egypt. They will ask for water as if they were begging, in order that their cattle might drink.'
(The prophecy of Neferti, XVa–XVd)

This part of the Prophecy of Neferti is concerned with the time of Amenemhat I, who, in all likelihood, built a line of smaller fortresses across the northern desert after he had successfully expelled the Asiatics from eastern Delta. The fortification line began perhaps at today's Tell el-Rataba, approximately 40 km west of Lake Timsakh, and extended to the northeast to protect Egypt's eastern frontier from the raids of the Asiatic nomads. The journey through the fertile valley, which led to Egypt's eastern border and is now called Wadi Tumilat, was the only possible route connecting the Egyptian inland with the eastern frontier. Having reached the Walls of the Ruler at the eastern end of this valley, Sinuhe spent the day crouched behind a bush so that he would not be noticed by the guards of the fortress. At night he continued his journey until he reached a place called Peten, from where he made his way across the river to the island of Kemwer. It is thus likely that Peten must have lain at the eastern end of Wadi Tumilat.

Kemwer, the 'Great Black', was the last place which Sinuhe had to pass before finally leaving the land of Egypt. It has not been successfully identified, but it is certain that it must refer to either the great Lake Timsah at the eastern end of Wadi Tumilat to the east of contemporary Ismailia, or to the Bitter Lakes that lay a little to the north. Since Sinuhe was able to cover the distance between the Walls of the Ruler and the lake in a night's walk, it is more likely that 'Kemwer' refers to Lake Timsakh. It is highly improbable that he would be able to cover more than 40 km within one night.

Fig. 1.9 The Ways of Horus, connecting Egypt with the Near East since prehistoric times

Sinuhe's arrival in Syria-Palestine

After Sinuhe crosses the border, a Bedouin sheikh, whom the text identifies as a 'foreign chief' who had been in Egypt, takes care of him. The fact that this man had known Sinuhe from a previous occasion is rather interesting and indicates that Sinuhe may even have been entrusted with foreign missions on a previous occasion. This is also corroborated by a passage in the beginning of the text, which states that Sinuhe had been in charge of royal estates in the land of the Asiatics. The fact that he decided to flee east, instead of west, when he was already so close to the Libyan border at the time he made his decision to run, also suggests that Sinuhe was familiar with the eastern terrain – or maybe even felt some affinity with the so-called 'Asiatics'.

Sinuhe spends the following year and a half travelling and trying to reach the city of Byblos. He does not get past the land of Qedem, which lay in the area of the cedar woods east of the city of Byblos, which in the third millenium BC belonged to the greatest trade centres of the area and had maintained close contact with Egypt since the Old Kingdom period. It is therefore logical that Sinuhe wanted to reach a place highly influenced by Egypt, one with an urban culture similar to that to which he was accustomed at home.

A year and a half later, Sinuhe is summoned by Amunenshi, the ruler of the land of Upper Retjenu. Based on later parallels, this place is often identified with the area around the river Bahr el-Litani (the largest river in Lebanon flowing into the sea north of Tyre) in today's Lebanon, where the Egyptian border was to lie several times in the future (for example during the reign of Thutmosis III after the battle of Megiddo in 1468 BC). In the very beginning of their conversation, Amunenshi points out that his people speak Egyptian – perhaps in order to persuade Sinuhe to stay with his tribe. He then questions Sinuhe about the reasons for his flight from Egypt and about the circumstances of the king's death. Amunenshi expresses true concern about the death of Amenemhat I, being perhaps quite uncertain about the future attitude of the new king Senwosret I to his Asiatic neighbours. Sinuhe proclaims his own innocence and loyalty to the ruler, and asserts that his flight from Egypt had been the will of god. He denies knowledge of any details whatsoever about the king's death. We also learn that Amunenshi had been well aware of Sinuhe's qualities and that the Egyptians themselves had eloquently reported about Sinuhe's virtues. All this indicates that Sinuhe must have been in a place often visited by Egyptians.

The text continues with the famous eulogy on Senwosret I. At its end, Sinuhe bids Amunenshi to remain loyal to the king of Egypt. Following this dialogue, Amunenshi invites Sinuhe to stay with his tribe, he gives him his daughter in marriage and allots to him a piece of territory, which he can either cultivate or in which he may wander with the tribe assigned to him. The reasons why Amunenshi decides to adopt Sinuhe into his own tribe are unknown, but the fact that Sinuhe had been a high-ranking official at the Egyptian court (and thus may have been Amunenshi's guarantee of favourable relations with Egypt) surely played a role.

Amunenshi's grant of land to Sinuhe is a typical feature of nomadic populations, as is testified among others by the epigraphic materials from Mari, which provide an unparalleled account of the lifestyle of tribal societies of that time. One of these documents describes patterns of land redistribution. In these communities, land could not be formally sold, but only given. In order to receive land from a tribe, the future owner had to become a member of the tribe or clan, since the land of a tribe had to remain in its possession and ownership could change only within that community.

The documents mention the Avi clan, which allots part of its land to Yarim-Addu, a high-ranking official from the palace of Mari. At first, the document refers to the 'sons' of the Avi clan, that is the individual families that constitute it. The text further implies that Yarim-Addu first had to formally become a member of the clan, so that he could subsequently be granted territory, entirely free of charge. Sinuhe undergoes exactly the same process of integration into the tribe and gaining the grant of land as Yarim-Addu had done: Amunenshi first gives Sinuhe his daughter in marriage, by which he becomes a member of the tribe. Subsequently, land is allotted to him, probably from the possession of Amunenshi's tribe.

Sinuhe describes his newly acquired territory as one rich in grain, gardens, olive groves, vineyards, sycamore trees, and honey. The area abounds in cattle, fowl, and milk, it offers good opportunities for hunting, etc. This theoretically suggests that it was inhabited by a sedentary population engaged in agriculture and animal husbandry. According to our present state of knowledge, however,

Fig. 1.10 Central Sinai: only Bedouins can survive in this hostile region

such a situation may be presumed for only a few coastal cities. Elsewhere, the population continued to lead a nomadic life, as Sinuhe himself suggests when he describes his possessions as consisting merely of cattle and fruit-bearing trees. Throughout his narration, Sinuhe never uses the terms for a village (or a city) and mentions only camps and tents. He refers to his people as *wekhayt*, a tribe. When describing his duel with the strong man, he declares his principal objective as being to seize his opponent's cattle, people and possessions, and to gain access to his wells, pastures and to his entire territory. In the report on his battles, Sinuhe declares: *'Every country against which I campaigned, I conquered them and drove them away from their pastures and wells. I seized their cattle, captured their inhabitants...'* Each detail in his story is in accord with the customs of nomadic populations. Sinuhe's account is the more interesting, in that it relates to the conditions of the time which is now believed to correspond approximately to the time of the arrival of the patriarchs headed by Abraham into Syria-Palestine. Sinuhe's account is therefore a valuable report on the way of life in the area, which was familiar to Abraham himself.

The fact that Sinuhe's story corresponds to a real situation, and that its author had been familiar with the contemporary situation of this area is also confirmed by recent works concerning modern Bedouin societies living in the Sinai peninsula and in the desert of the Negev. In the light of these studies, it is likely that the subsistence patterns of the Bedouin tribes have not changed in any significant way since the time of their ancestors, who had wandered the area a few thousand years ago. Moreover, archaeological evidence clearly indicates that at the turn of the third and second millennia BC (i.e. at the end of Early and at the beginning of Middle Bronze Age), most of the population of southern Syria-Palestine turned to a nomadic way of life due to lack of other subsistence possibilities (for details see Chapter 3).

Concerning these nomadic tribes, it is appropriate to explain first that this term does not mean just cattle-herding populations, who spend their life travelling the desert and depend solely on their herds. On the contrary, these groups are not so specialized and, besides herding, they also grow some staple, crops, and possess gardens and orchards in suitable places. They may even settle in one place for a longer time, and enrich their subsistence by hunting and gathering.

As a typical example of a contemporary nomadic tribe, we may consider the Khushmaan tribe, who live in the Egyptian Eastern Desert. Their subsistence patterns are based on the exploitation of various natural resources, and are, given our records, probably very similar to those in the end of the Early Bronze Age (about 2000 BC). The Khushmaan are nomads who practice sheep and goat herding. Sheep and goats are very resistant species, able to survive even in semiarid or totally arid areas. Sheep have an almost constant bodily temperature and both species can survive up to a 30% loss of body mass due to dehydration. Their average lifetime varies between 10 and 12 years. Surplus individuals are sold to the inhabitants of the Nile Valley. An average herd of goats amounts to fifty individuals and can, under favourable circumstances, yield up to 11 litres of

Fig. 1.11 Bedouin woman selling handicrafts, Central Sinai

milk per day. Milk is valued highly – even in present times, although now the type preferred is mostly camel milk. This is once again a trait typical for nomadic, but not for sedentary populations. It is appropriate to mention here that in his account of the riches of the country Yaa, Sinuhe stresses that dairy products were prepared for him.

The Khushmaan like to combine sheep and goats in one herd in order to decrease the danger of possible losses by hyenas and natural environment. Herding is the work of women and children, who leave the encampment with their herds in the morning and come back only late in the evening. They also breed camels, although mainly as transport animals – an average family possesses one to four camels. The camel was, however, domesticated late and in the beginning of the second millennium BC, it had surely not yet been used.

Today, one finds that the Khushmaan also own a limited number of donkeys, which are very effective transport animals, above all in rocky desert and in mountainous areas. In Sinuhe's times, the donkey was possibly the only animal used for transport, as is testified by numerous depictions preserved from ancient Egypt. The principal component of their subsistence economy is thus the breeding of

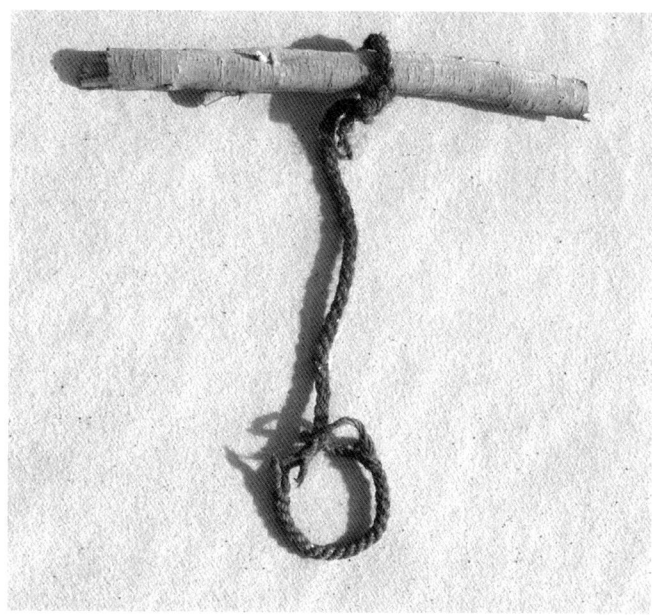

Fig. 1.12 One of the traps used by the Bedouins for millennia (El Hayez Oasis, Beer Shareef, Egypt)

sheep and goats. In times of drought, the Khushmaan search out acacia clusters, which can survive even under unfavourable circumstances and whose leaves serve as food for sheep, goats and camels.

Apart from animal husbandry, the Khushmaan collect wild grains and fruits and hunt gazelles and ibex to widen their diet. Today, the gazelle and ibex hunt is still performed the way it was in Neolithic times approximately 7000 years ago, as was recorded in numerous rock paintings from prehistoric times. The hunt is assisted by domesticated hounds and proceeds as follows: the dogs start the animal, and it tries to escape over a steep slope which the dogs cannot climb. When the dogs are unable to continue their pursuit, the animal stops and waits until they run away. The hunters use this occasion when the animal has been driven up the hill, surprise it from above and kill it with stones or arrows. This is surely the same method that Sinuhe's account indicates, when it mentions hunting with the assistance of dogs. The Bedouins, however, also use another hunting method, as ancient as the first one. They make a loop out of palm strings, about 15 cm in diameter, the inner side of which is skirted by tips of palm leaves or acacia thorns pointing inwards. Close to a water source or somewhere along the animals' path, the hunters dig out a shallow, 10 cm wide and 30 cm deep pit over which they place the loop, connected by a string with a stone or piece of a branch. The animal that steps into the trap, tries to get rid of the loop, which tightens and with its thorny interior, cuts the entrapped leg of the beast. While the animal is trying to escape, the stone or branch leaves an easily detectable trace in the soil for the trappers to follow and, simultaneously, causes constantly small injuries. The hunters catch up with the failing game in a short time. These facts strongly suggest that their lifestyle is an ancient one.

In favourable circumstances, i.e. when spring rains are sufficient, Khushmaan Bedouin grow various crops. The preparation of these fields is, however, subject to certain regulations. The fields must be fenced to protect the crops against wild animals, and they are created in the immediate vicinity of water sources, or at the end of wadis – the valleys which in spring months collect water flowing down from the neighbouring hills. Canals are dug to lead this water directly to the plants in the fields and gardens. It has been proven that one sufficiently strong spring rain can sustain substantial crops up until the autumn. The typical crops are barley, millet, corn, water melons, sweet melons, jute, cucumber, hibiscus, peas, Egyptian beans, lentils, kidney beans, trigonella, date palms, etc. It is also sometimes the case that old members of the tribe, who are no longer able to keep up with the physical strains of the nomadic way of life, settle in the vicinity of such fields and gardens, where they can relax and take care of the crops. They are also regularly visited by members of their tribe.

Even Bedouin customs related to tribal burials have a lot in common with the description of burial customs recorded in the account of Sinuhe: *'Do not let yourself be buried by the Asiatics! Do not let a sheepskin become your primitive grave!'* When death comes, the Bedouin proceed to bury the deceased as quickly as possible. The body is cleansed and wrapped in seven layers of cloth. A grave is hollowed out, two metres deep and two metres long, oriented in the east-western direction.

Fig. 1.13 Tyre, an ancient harbour town dominating the area of Upper Retjenu (Lebanon)

Fig. 1.14 King's Highway landscape, area of Kerak (Jordan)

A niche is cut into the northern wall at the bottom of the grave, and the body is buried within it, with the head to the west. In this way, no earth will fall on the body when the grave is refilled, for that would be a defilement for the Bedouin. These graves with a niche at the bottom of the pit resemble the shaft tombs which were discovered, for example, by Kathleen Kenyon in Jericho and were dated to the end of the Early Bronze Age (i.e, the late third millennium BC). These graves also had a niche at the bottom, which was blocked after the burial with a large stone.

The Bedouin mostly desire not to be buried alone. The body is in most cases transported to the tribal necropolis, despite the fact that it may take a long journey, lasting several days. These necropoleis are located near water sources, so that visitors can ritually purify themselves before entering the burial grounds. Water sources possess yet another advantage – they are the natural gathering places of tribe members, and thus allow them to regularly honour their ancestors and make sure that their grave mounds are properly covered with stones and remain in good order. During these visits, they place branches on the graves and fasten a piece of white cloth to the palm tree that grows next to it. The opportunity to compare ethnographic sources with the details of Sinuhe's account allow us to make a relatively precise picture relating to conditions in his time, even though Sinuhe's era is divided from our own by almost four millennia.

During his prolonged stay in Syria-Palestine, Sinuhe took an active part in the affairs that concerned his tribe. This was also connected with his prominent position at the head of one of the tribes. In connection with the Bedouin way of life, the passage between B 100 – 105 deserves mentioning. Sinuhe describes how he loyally served his saviour and lord, Amunenshi, as the commander of his troops. As such, he probably took part in the campaigns against the neighbouring tribes. When briefly describing his victories, he mentions the expulsion of his enemies from their pastures and from their wells and he claims that he seized their cattle. Unfortunately, he does not mention any particular military campaign in this context – with a single exception.

Sinuhe has purportedly taken part in the skirmishes between the Asiatic tribes and the rulers of the hill-countries, who had undoubtedly infiltrated the area of Syria-Palestine from the east. Sinuhe mentions these battles only briefly: *'When the Asiatics declared war, in order to attack the rulers of the hill-countries, I gave them advice concerning their conduct.'* This note is rather interesting, particularly if we take into consideration that Sinuhe's time may have been contemporary with that of Abraham's presence in the area. The Hebrew Bible records one episode of Abraham's life, which also describes battles with the tribes of the rulers of the hill-countries. This passage is the more significant as it is concerned with the Transjordan area (the area east of the River Jordan). North to south, this area was crossed by the ancient royal road (called King's Highway), which connected the southern areas, such as Egypt, the Sinai peninsula and Wadi Ariba with countries in the north, mainly Asia Minor. The road began in the south, close to today's Eilat on the Red Sea coast, and led all the way to Damascus in the

Fig. 1.15 The cave of Lot, overlooking the Dead Sea (Jordan)

north. Numerous caravans travelling south to north or making the return route had to pass along this road – unless they chose to travel on the sea or along the sea coast. It is, therefore, of some interest that when describing his stay in Syria-Palestine, Sinuhe mentions that every messenger, who travelled north or back to Egypt, paid a visit to him. We cannot exclude the possibility that the hypothetical stay of Sinuhe was intentionally situated in the vicinity of the King's Highway and that this was based on elements of a real political situation.

Let us now have a closer look at the passage from the Hebrew Bible, which describes Abraham's role in the wars south of the Dead Sea, in the area of Sodom and Gomorrah:

'At this time Amraphel, king of Shinar, Arioch, king of Ellasar, Kedorlaomer king of Elam and Tidal king of Goiim went to war against Bera king of Sodom, Birsha king of Gomorrah, Shinab king of Admah, Shemeber king of Zeboiim, and the king of Bela (that is, Zoar). All these latter kings joined forces in the Valley of Siddim (the Salt Sea). For twelve years they had been subject to Kedorlaomer, but in the thirteenth year they rebelled.

In the fourteenth year, Kedorlaomer and the kings allied with him went out and defeated the Rephaites in Ashteroth Karnaim, the Zuzites in Ham, the Emites in Saveh Kiriathaim and the Horites in the hill country of Seir, as far as El Paran near the desert. Then they turned back and went to En Mishpat (that is, Kadesh), and they conquered the whole territory of the Amalekites, as well as the Amorites who were living in Hazezon Tamar.

Then the king of Sodom, the king of Gomorrah, the king of Admah, the king of Zeboiim and the king of Bela (that is, Zoar) marched out and drew up their battle lines in the Valley of Siddim against Kedorlaomer king of Elam, Tidal, king of Goiim, Amraphel, king of Shinar and Arioch, king of Ellasar – four kings against five. Now the Valley of Siddim was full of tar pits, and when the kings of Sodom and Gomorrah fled, some of the men fell into them and the rest fled to the hills. The four kings seized all the goods of Sodom and Gomorrah and all their food; then they went away. They also carried off Abram's nephew, Lot and his possessions, since he was living in Sodom.

One who had escaped came and reported this to Abram the Hebrew. Now Abram was living near the great trees of Mamre the Amorite, a brother of Eshcol and Aner, all of whom were allied with Abram. When Abram heard that his relative had been taken captive, he called out the 318 trained men born in his household and went in pursuit as far as Dan. During the night Abram divided his men to attack them and he routed them, pursuing them as far as Hobah, north of Damascus. He recovered all the goods and brought back his relative Lot and his possessions, together with the women and other people.'

(Genesis 14, 1–16)

It is of course no longer possible to ascertain today if this description relates to the same event or not. Neither is it possible to decide with certainty whether the reports correspond to reality. Despite these problems, the account is of some interest even for contemporary readers, since it is closely connected with both Sinuhe and Abraham and records the dangers that both of these men had to face

Fig. 1.16 Lisan peninsula, the probable place of the five Biblical cities (Jordan)

in the area of Syria-Palestine. The objective of the punitive expedition of the coalition of four kings to the area of the Valley of Siddim was to guarantee safe passage to trade missions which passed the land from south to north. The names of the kings and their countries suggest that some of them came from the east (Elam and Akkad), while others were from the north (Northern Syria, Asia Minor). The local defensive coalition of five kings broke down in battle and the cities of these kings, which were left defenceless, became an easy prey to the victors. The triumphant kings then set off back to the north with their spoil. This is the moment when Abraham intervened, because his nephew Lot had been taken captive by these kings. Abraham finally saved Lot during a night attack, which was, as the account of Sinuhe indicates, a characteristic method of fighting for nomads. Abraham first besieged the enemy encampment at Tel Dan, the traditional northern outpost of ancient Israel, and then chased his foes all the way to the north of Damascus. This indicates that some of the allied kings who were defeated by Abraham must have come from somewhere in the area of today's northern Syria, location of the traditional centres, which were led by Damascus in their attempt to resist the power of the later ancient Israelite state and subsequently even against the states of Israel and Judaea.

The five Biblical cities mentioned here – Sodom, Gomorrah, Adma, Zeboiim and Zoar, are by no means entirely fictitious. In all likelihood, some of these cities have been discovered on the eastern bank of the Dead Sea and their fall was dated to the very end of the Early Bronze Age.

According to the archaeological evidence, we may claim that at least some of them were identified. They are concentrated east of the Lisan peninsula, close to

Fig. 1.17 Bab el-Dhra (Dead Sea area, Jordan)

the Cave of Lot, where, as the Biblical tradition has it, Lot was seduced by his daughters. One of the most important of them is Bab el-Dhra (Gate of the arm). The site was identified as early as in 1924 by a famous American archaeologist William F. Albright. The archaeological campaigns on the site, however, started some forty years later, in the 1960s and were led by Paul W. Lapp and later by Walter E. Rast and Thomas R. Schaub. The history of the city shows that it had already been founded by the end of the 4th millennium BC. At this period, the site was occupied by a semi-sedentary population grazing the herds in Wadi Kerak. The peak of prosperity was attained, however, only several centuries later, during the Early Bronze Age III (2700 – 2300 BC). During this time, the city was fortified by a 7 metres wide enclosure wall of stone and mudbrick protecting an area of about 10 acres. There were huge settlement areas also outside the city proper. The principal approach to the city was from the Dead Sea, i. e. from the west where the cultivation areas were situated. We may also suppose that from here one could gain effective control of the communications associated with the so-called 'King's Highway', an important merchant road leading north-south alongside the city to the modern city of Kerak and further north. Around 2200 BC the city was destroyed either deliberately or during an earthquake. The burnt human bones found in most of the charnel-houses in the city's cemeteries seem to favour the first hypothesis. Moreover, the new inhabitants decided not only to burn the charnel-houses but also to set up their houses next to the preceding ones and thus discontinue the settlement tradition of several centuries. Some other sites were identified close by: El-Safi, Feifeh or Numeira, a city that was probably established to diminish the demographic pressure of Bab el-Dhra. What was the raison d'être of these cities, no doubt important and vital local centres of power and crafts? Beyond any doubt one of the major stimulating factors was control of the important caravan roads securing steady and significant economical potential. But was this really all?

The answer may lie not so far away in Wadi Faynan, a district situated some 50 km southeast of the Dead Sea in Jordan. Here an American team from the University of California led by Thomas E. Levy has been excavating since the 1990s. Wadi Faynan has been traditionally known as an area rich in copper ore. Only recently Levy's team discovered the largest preserved Early Bronze Age metal factory in the Near East. The factory consists of a complex of over seventy rooms, courtyards, alleys and other architectural units linked to the production of copper metal. It is situated at Khirbat Hamra Ifdan and has been preserved almost intact due to an earthquake that affected the whole area around 2200 BC. In the early Bronze Age III (Stratum III) layers there were excavated about 500 tons of slag indicating that the whole copper ore production during the period under discussion might have amounted to some several hundred tons of copper. Such a vast specialised project must have needed an appropriate economic basis. Were the cities such as Bab el-Dhra responsible for the sustaining, organisation, backing and, last but not least, marketing of this extremely complicated and demanding enterprise and its outputs? There is no reason to reject such a hypothesis.

Fig. 1.18 Wadi Faynan, general view (Jordan)

Fig. 1.19 Wadi Faynan, site of Khirbet Hamra Ifdan, courtyard for the copper casting (Jordan)

Sinuhe's duel

The most famous passage from Sinuhe's narrative is probably that which reports his duel with a foreign chief. This chief comes to Sinuhe's encampment and challenges him to fight because he desires to seize his property and take hold of his tribe. This part of the narrative of Sinuhe's account is often compared to the Old Testament account of David's fight against Goliath. The description of the duel in Sinuhe's story may be divided into the following stages:

– Sinuhe is challenged to fight against the strong man of Retjenu (B 109–113),
– Sinuhe takes counsel with his friend, the ruler Amunenshi (B 114–127),
– Sinuhe prepares his weapons and trains with them (B 128–129),
– Verbal clash before the duel, and the duel proper (B 129–140),
– Sinuhe's victory (B 140–143),
– Sinuhe's triumph and seizure of the possessions of his opponent (B 143–147).

The night before the duel, when Sinuhe is preparing his weapons, is also very interesting. Since it is he who was challenged, he has the right to choose the weapons (as we learn from the ensuing description of the duel). He takes advantage of this right, and chooses the bow and the dagger. In his account, he says he has spent this night stretching the cord of his bow and sharpening his dagger. Both these weapons are typical for an Egyptian, and he must have possessed considerable skill in handling them.

Fig. 1.20 Tel Azeka, the probable location of the duel of David and Goliath (Israel)

At the beginning of the duel, Sinuhe's opponent lays aside the weapons that had not been chosen for the fight – his shield, axe, and lance – and the fight begins by firing arrows at each other. While the strongman misses, one of Sinuhe's arrows pierces the throat of his opponent. His precise shot enables Sinuhe to gain victory over the challenger and seize his possessions.

The corresponding passage in the Bible begins with a conversation between Saul and David, the only man in the army of Israel who has the courage to fight Goliath. Finally, David receives permission to accept the challenge. The ensuing duel between David and Goliah is reported as follows:

'Then he took his staff in his hand, chose five smooth stones from the stream, put them in the pouch of his shepherd's bag and, with his sling in his hand, approached the Philistine.

Meanwhile, the Philistine, with his shield-bearer in front of him, kept coming closer to David. He looked David over and saw that he was only a boy, ruddy and handsome, and he despised him. He said to David, 'Am I a dog, that you come at me with sticks?' And the Philistine cursed David by his gods. 'Come here,' he said, 'and I'll give your flesh to the birds of the air and the beasts of the field!'

David said to the Philistine, 'You come against me with sword and spear and javelin, but I come to you in the name of the Lord Almighty, the God of the armies of Israel, whom you have defied. This day the Lord will hand you over to me, and I'll strike you down and cut off your head. Today I will give the carcasses of the Philistine army to the birds of the air and the beasts of the earth, and the whole world will know that there is a God in Israel. All those gathered here will know that it is not by sword or spear that the Lord saves; for the battle is the Lord's, and he will give all of you into our hands.'

As the Philistine moved closer to attack him, David ran quickly towards the battle line to meet him. Reaching to his bag and taking out a stone, he slung it and struck the Philistine on the forehead. The stone sank into his forehead, and he fell face down on the ground.

So David triumphed over the Philistine with a sling and a stone; without a sword in his hand he struck down the Philistine and killed him.

David ran and stood over him. He took hold of the Philistine's sword and drew it from the scabbard. After he killed him, he cut off his head with the sword.

When the Philistines saw that their hero was dead, they turned and ran.'
(1st Samuel, 17, 40–51)

Only some aspects of Sinuhe's duel can be found in the Hebrew Bible account. A certain relationship between the two narratives is suggested by their conclusions: both the strongman of Retjenu and Goliath are defeated by their own weapons. Another interesting parallel is that both future victors rely on divine assistance. In the case of Sinuhe, this fact is mentioned only after the termination of the duel: 'I gave praise to Montu, while his men were mourning him.' David, on the other hand, appeals to God in the very beginning, and relies on His help. We may also see a strong parallel in the parable: while David defeats the Philistine in the name of God, Sinuhe, an Egyptian assisted by an Egyptian

Fig. 1.21 Ankhtify as depicted in his tomb at Moʻalla near Luxor

god, triumphs over a traditional enemy of Egypt – the Asiatic nomad. There is, therefore, an element of symbolism in Sinuhe's victory: Sinuhe, who is in the service of the Egyptian gods and of the king, defeats the representative of the traditional enemies of Egypt, the Asiatics. There is, of course, the significant difference that while David's Lord is the only God of his nation, Sinuhe turns to one of the many deities of the Egyptian pantheon.

There are other significant differences between the two compositions. The most important one is the time of their creation, since Sinuhe's account is almost a thousand years older than the Biblical version. Another problematic fact is that Sinuhe's report of the duel does not at first sight seem to have a parallel in

Egyptian literature and it could seem likely that it belongs to the tradition of the area of Syria-Palestine. There is, however, a possible solution that allows us to conclude that Sinuhe's account of his duel with the strongman of Retjenu is based on the situation in the area of Syria-Palestine in the beginning of the Twelfth Dynasty. A typical Egyptian dignitary included in his biographical inscription only the feats which he did in the service of the king. All his activities may thus be explained as a service to the Egyptian king and state. Every official could thus in his own way take part in the maintenance of the universal order, which the Egyptians called *Maat* and which was personified by a goddess of the same name. We know of virtually no texts from the time of the Old and Middle Kingdoms that would report the achievements of a single official in a way similar to the account of Sinuhe.

Reports like that of Sinuhe are known mainly from the autobiographical inscriptions of the First Intermediate Period, the time of a substantial weakening of royal power, when local government was in the hands of local princes. As an example, we could take the account of Ankhtify from Mo'alla, which is discussed in Chapter 2 of the present book. Ankhtify relates details of his military expeditions against Thebes, and he loses no opportunity to emphasize his own importance and credits: *'The noble, commander of the army of Hierakonpolis, the victorious Ankhtify, says: ... I sailed north, and I disembarked at the western bank of the Theban nome, ... But no one came out for their fear. A brave man, that's me, one who has no equal.'*

When we are considering the correspondence of Sinuhe's account to reality, it may appear to be rather dissimilar from what we know from contemporary Egyptian literature. We must, however, bear in mind that after his flight from Egypt, Sinuhe finds himself in an absolutely unprecedented position. He is no more a royal servant of the Egyptian king but, on the contrary, he becomes a member of one of the nomadic tribes on the territory of Syria-Palestine. The Egyptian king can no longer warrant him success, which must now be achieved by his own activities. Moreover, tribal societies abide by a totally different scale of values, one that could perhaps be compared to the conditions in Egypt at the time of the unification struggles, when the individual kings had to defend their position in everyday clashes with their opponents, who were striving to gain power over as much territory as possible and thus to frustrate the possible unification of Egypt. Sinuhe can therefore no longer maintain the leadership of his tribe by merely being loyal to his benefactor, who gave him his daughter in marriage and with whom he also takes counsel the night before the fight. He has to fight for his position. And because Sinuhe's story is one of a successful Egyptian, who despite his indubitable success abroad finally returns to Egypt to be a loyal servant of his ruler, the author of the narrative allows him to win the duel even against great odds. It is remarkable, that Sinuhe believes he owes his victory to the Egyptian god of war and fighting, Montu. This implies that Sinuhe felt aware of the fact that Egyptian, and not local deities could guarantee him success.

Fig. 1.22 Façade of the tomb of Harkhuf in Assuan, with his biographical inscription

It can therefore be stated that the description of the duel in Sinuhe's account is based on the environment of tribal societies, where only the man who was distinguished by his abilities and deeds could become the leader of a tribe. In the case of Sinuhe, the details of the account should emphasize the exceptionality of Sinuhe's victory – the fact, that it is Sinuhe who is protected by the Egyptian gods headed by Montu, and whose victory these gods guarantee. Even the choice of weapons with which Sinuhe fights corresponds to the typical equipment of an Egyptian warrior: the bow *pḏt* and the dagger *bȝgsw*.

A similar, and essentially contemporary, 'heroic' account can be found in the inscription from Abisko in Nubia (approximately 28 km south of Assuan, Graffito I). The Nubian soldier Tjehemau reports how he alone boldly faced his enemy, even though his allies succumbed to panic and fled. The background of this story is the same as that of the account of Sinuhe. Although Tjehemau was an Egyptian mercenary, he was also a Nubian, brought up in a tribal society which acknowledged the same value system as the tribes described in the account of Sinuhe. His short report runs as follows:

'The inscription, which Tjehemau made in the year of the defeat of the southern foreign countries. I started to fight as a soldier in the time of the reign of Nebhepetre, when he sailed downstream to Ben, I went to the ruler together with my son. He occupied the whole land and he planned to conquer the Asiatics from Djati. The Thebans were on the run, but the Nubian (i.e. Tjehemau, author's note) *faced the enemy. I defeated the Djati. He* (i.e. the king) *unfurled the sail in order to sail upstream.'*

Tjehemau joined the army during the reign of Nebhepetre Mentuhotep II, in the time of his campaign to Nubia against the Ben tribe. Further he describes the unification of Egypt in the time of this ruler and the subsequent campaign against the *Djati* tribe, with all probability somewhere close to southern Syria-Palestine. In the battle against this tribe the Egyptian army turned back and fled, and it was Tjehemau who did not flee and on his own, by means of his personal courage, saved the day.

It is very interesting to note that, in the description of his stay in Asia, Sinuhe uses phrases which are typical of autobiographical inscriptions of ancient Egyptian dignitaries. This is another indirect confirmation that Sinuhe's account is in many aspects derived exactly from this genre. The following passages from Sinuhe's story illustrate this point:

'I gave water to the thirsty, I showed the way to the one who went astray, I saved the robbed one … This ruler of the country let me spend many years as the commander of his troops.'

A similar passage forms a ubiquitous component of ancient Egyptian autobiographical inscriptions. Its more developed parallels in Egyptian tombs may run along lines in the fashion as follows:

'I came from my city,
I descended from my nome,
I built a house and erected its door,

I hollowed a pond and planted sycamores.
The ruler held me in his favour.
My father made his testament to my advantage.
I was honoured,
beloved of my father,
praised by my mother,
one, whom all his brothers loved.
I gave bread to the hungry,
clothes to the naked,
I ferried the boatless to the other bank.'
(The autobiography of Harkhuf, Assuan, Sixth Dynasty)

or:
'It was King Kheperkare, who placed me among his companions, because His Majesty valued me... I travelled north and south of the capital knowing that I would do more than was ordered for me.
I committed no crime against people –
nothing that the god would detest.
I buried the old ones of my city,
I fed the hungry.
I am the one who is silent among the ones who speak,
one of whom it is said: "Wait until he comes",
one whose heart performs his duties,
one who is dispatched on errands, because he is esteemed.'
(The autobiography of Wepwawetaa from Abydos, Twelfth Dynasty)

These inscriptions served a dual purpose: to express the loyalty of the given official, and to persuade the reader that he was a righteous man, who acted in accord with the will of the king and of the gods. Such inscriptions were commonly placed on the tomb façade, so that everyone could easily note them. Their aim was to proclaim that the tomb owners acted according to their authority, and above all to persuade their contemporaries that they did not abuse their positions, but rather enhanced the prosperity of their cities. In return, the tomb owners expected to receive offerings in their funerary chapels and hoped that their funerary cult would thus be sustained long enough to guarantee them an undisturbed existence in the afterlife.

The story of the duel of Sinuhe with the strong man of Retjenu may indeed have been composed in Egypt, following an Egyptian tradition of the time and the heritage of the First Intermediate Period. We can also mention the frequent analyses presuming that knowledge of the account of the duel may have reached the area of Syria-Palestine in connection with the expulsion of the Hyksos from Egypt to south Palestine in the end of the 16th century BC. According to this hypothesis, the tradition was carried and transmitted by the Hyksos, Semitic tribes from western Asia, who from Middle Kingdom times gradually penetrated the Egyptian Delta. Finally, in the middle of the 17th century BC, they founded their own independent Fifteenth Dynasty, centred in Avaris in the eastern Delta.

The city was probably chosen quite deliberately for two main reasons: it lay close to the centre of maritime trade, and it was the starting point of two important trade routes to the east, one to the Sinai and the other to Syria-Palestine. It is remarkable that these Asiatic rulers adopted the Egyptian culture, including the royal titulary of Egyptian kings. Besides the Asiatic deities Anat and Astarte, they also worshipped Egyptian gods, above all Seth. The Hyksos era ended in the middle of the 16th century BC, when they were expelled from Egypt by King Ahmose. Josephus mentions that there was agreed a treaty which allowed them to leave unhindered, and the archaeology of Avaris suggests that this was indeed the likely circumstance of their departure. After their escape from Egypt, most of the Hyksos set up quarters in the Sharuhen fortress in eastern Palestine, which Ahmose besieged and after three years finally conquered. This point marks the end of the Hyksos era, and their subsequent fate remains a mystery.

Sinuhe's return to Egypt

After his victorious duel, Sinuhe receives a letter from the ruler, who invites him to return to the country of his birth. Together with his letter, Senwosret also sends royal gifts as a sign of his favour and respect for Sinuhe. The king also stresses the fact the flight from Egypt had been Sinuhe's own decision, which in no way shattered his good name. Sinuhe's answer expresses his respect and gratitude to the king and lists the individual deities who should protect him: Montu, Lord of Waset, Amun, Lord of the thrones of the Two Lands, Sebek-Ra, Horus, Hathor, Atum with his divine Ennead, Sopdu with his epithets Neferbau-Sesher and Eastern Horus, Lady of Imhet, Horus-Min, Wereret, Lady of Punt, Nut and Harwer-Ra. These deities allow us to draw a very precise picture of the character of Sinuhe's religious faith. This typically Egyptian religious concept was based on the idea that the individual deities were connected with various, and – for the Egyptians – very important, aspects and phenomena which surrounded them and affected their lives. The choice of deities made by Sinuhe best documents some aspects of his faith based on the character of the Egyptian religion at the beginning of the Twelfth Dynasty.

In the first place, Sinuhe mentions Montu, the god of war, whose cultic centre lay in the Theban area, the place of origin of the Eleventh and Twelfth Dynasty kings. This god, who was usually depicted with the head of a falcon, became

Fig. 1.23 A Thirteenth Dynasty King Sebekhotep venerating the Theban god Montu (Luxor, Open Air Museum)

the chief deity of Egyptian rulers in the time before the reunification of Egypt at the beginning of the Middle Kingdom. He probably attained his privileged position due to his military character in connection with the political situation in Egypt during the struggles for unification. It is not by chance that the last rulers of the Eleventh Dynasty – the Mentuhotep kings – had their names construed precisely with the name of this god. Their name means 'Montu is satisfied'. And also Sinuhe, having defeated his enemy, directs his gratitude to Montu. Gradually, however, this god was superseded by Amun, another deity worshipped in the Theban area.

Although he is first mentioned already in the third millennium BC, Amun's popularity began to grow, slowly but steadily, only in the course of the Middle Kingdom. Gradually, he became the king of gods, creator of the world and divine father of the king, so that Egyptian rulers began to include in their titularies the epithet 'beloved by Amun'. The fact that Amun became even the father of the gods resulted in his identification with the sun god Ra, hence the version of his name Amun-Ra, which was popular during the New Kingdom period. Amun was the head of the divine triad worshipped in Thebes. Beside him were two other divinities: his divine wife Mut (whose name means 'mother'), who was worshipped as a lion-headed female goddess in her own temple south of Karnak, and their son, the moon god Khons. Amun's epithet 'king of gods' first appears in the time of Senwosret I, in the so-called White Chapel, one of the earliest examples of building activities in Karnak at the beginning of the Middle

Fig. 1.24 Karnak, religious centre of Egypt from the Middle Kingdom onwards

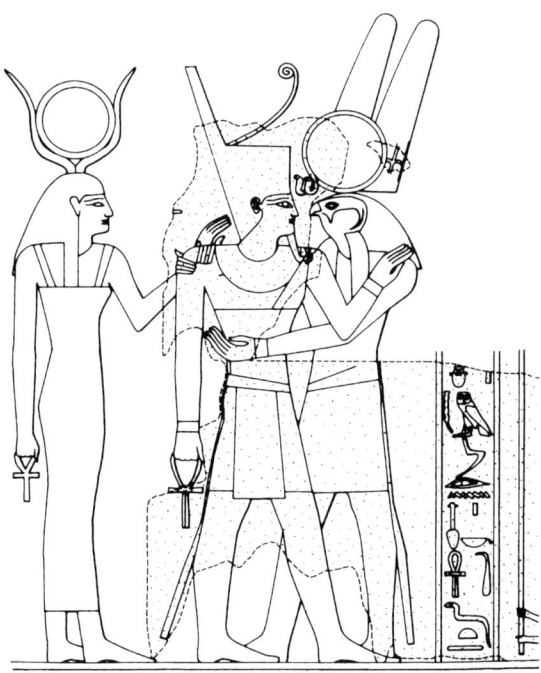

Fig. 1.25 Montu embracing Mentuhotep II in his temple at Deir el-Bahri (Western Thebes, Luxor)

Kingdom. Present-day Karnak became the cultic centre of Amun from the time when two Middle Kingdom temples were built there – Karnak and Luxor. On these sites, and mainly in Karnak, temples, kiosks and statues dedicated by the individual Egyptian rulers were erected in the course of over two millennia to serve the cult of Amun. Thus grew the largest temple complex on Egyptian territory. Somewhat later, probably the largest hypostyle hall in the world was built at Karnak – the so-called 'Great Hypostyle' between the second and third pylons (tower-like gateways, in whose façade an entrance was placed). This hall covers an area of 6 000 sq. m. and includes 134 gigantic columns. Built in the reign of Sethi I and finished by his son Ramesses II, the hall is decorated with an astounding area of reliefs with the names and titles of these rules and scenes depicting the worship of Amun in the prime of his cult. It is not by chance that we possess evidence that in this time, 160 cities in Egypt and nine in Asia belonged to the Amun priesthood.

Amun's sacred animal was the ram, hence the numerous ram-headed sphinxes that flank the entrance colonnade to the Karnak temple, for example. Amun was probably the most remarkable Egyptian deity, whose significance is heralded by his name, which translates as 'the hidden one'. Numerous aspects of his cult can be considered henotheistic (worship and emphasis of one god against the background of the cult of other deities), although the character of his cult itself is to be sought in the polytheistic concept of ancient Egyptian religion.

The other god whose assistance Sinuhe invokes is Sebek-Ra, worshipped in the form of a crocodile. The prime of his cult belongs to the time of the Middle Kingdom, and was probably connected with the transfer of the activities of the Egyptian rulers to the Fayyum area, as well as with the large-scale irrigation projects executed here.

The falcon deity Horus (the name means 'distant' or 'high') is one of the most ancient in the Egyptian pantheon. He appears already in the end of the fourth and beginning of the third millennia BC, and right from the beginning he is considered the guardian and patron deity of the Egyptian king. The Upper Egyptian rulers from pre-unification times called themselves the 'followers of Horus'. In this time, Horus was often depicted as the personification of the Egyptian ruler, destroying enemy cities. His importance is emphasized by the fact that one of the five official names of the Egyptian kings included his name. Horus was therefore often regarded to be a personification of the Egyptian ruler as such, and it is exactly this aspect of his cult that Sinuhe may have had in mind, since Horus was considered the ancestor of ancient Egyptian kings. He, however, had to fight first for his heritage against his uncle Seth, who had cunningly murdered his own brother, Osiris, in order to seize kingship over the world (after his death, Osiris became the ruler of the Netherworld). Brought up by his mother Isis in

1.26 The cow goddess Hathor, Mistress of foreign lands. Temple of Hathor in Memphis (Nineteenth Dynasty)

Fig. 1.27 Sopdu, the protective god of the Eastern Desert, escorting foreign captives (pyramid complex of Sahure, Abusir)

the Egyptian marshes of the Nile Delta, Horus deprived Seth of his power over the earth and became the mythical ruler of Egypt and the prototype of later Egyptian kings.

The cult of the goddess Hathor had various different aspects, two of the most important of which will be mentioned here. Hathor was the mother of the king and the Mistress of foreign lands. These two aspects were often intertwined, since as king's mother, Hathor could easily endow her son with power over foreign enemy countries, the conquest of which was considered a sign of the will and favour of gods. According to tradition, the Egyptian ruler was the son of Ra, the sun god who had created Egypt and the surrounding countries, which he placed under the protection of his son. The sacred animal of this goddess was the cow, and consequently the most frequent way of depicting her was either as a cow-headed woman, or simply as a cow. As the Mistress of foreign countries, she was commonly worshipped in her aspect of the Lady of mineral resources (for example on the Sinai as the Lady of Turquoise, *Nbt mfk3t*), her cult was widespread in Nubia, Syria-Palestine (especially at Byblos), as well as on the Sinai Peninsula.

The god Atum was regarded as a sun god and a demiurge. He stood at the head of the so-called Divine Ennead. Out of himself, he created Shu and Tefnut (the personifications of air and moisture), who in turn conceived Geb and Nut (earth and sky), who finally gave birth to the four deities connected with the Osiris cycle – Osiris, Isis, Seth and Nephthys. Atum was thus a very similar deity to Amun, but his cultic centre was at Heliopolis in the north of the country. According to the religious text called the Shabaka stone, Heliopolitan priests considered Atum the true demiurge – the creator of the world, of the basic natural powers, of the people, as well as of the culture and cities as such.

Sopdu, on the other hand, (with his epithets Neferbau Semsher and Eastern Horus – another god mentioned by Sinuhe) – was a very specialized deity. He was the patron of the Eastern Desert and the Sinai, and he protected the Egyptian ruler on his campaigns against the eastern nations. The 'Lady of Imet' was also a guardian deity of the king; the phrase is an epithet of Wadjet, the personification of Lower Egypt, who was often depicted as a cobra fastened to the crown of the king. Her cult was centred in Buto, the sacred city in the eastern Delta. Another deity with a similar connection to the eastern countries can be found in Horus-Min, a god who appeared at the time when Sinuhe was first recorded. This was a combination of two, originally independent deities – Min as the Lord of the Eastern Desert, and Horus as the protector of the ancient trade route which connected the Egyptian eastern Delta with southern Syria-Palestine. The goddess Wereret, connected with the royal uraeus (the rising cobra on the crown of the ruler), was also a guardian of the king.

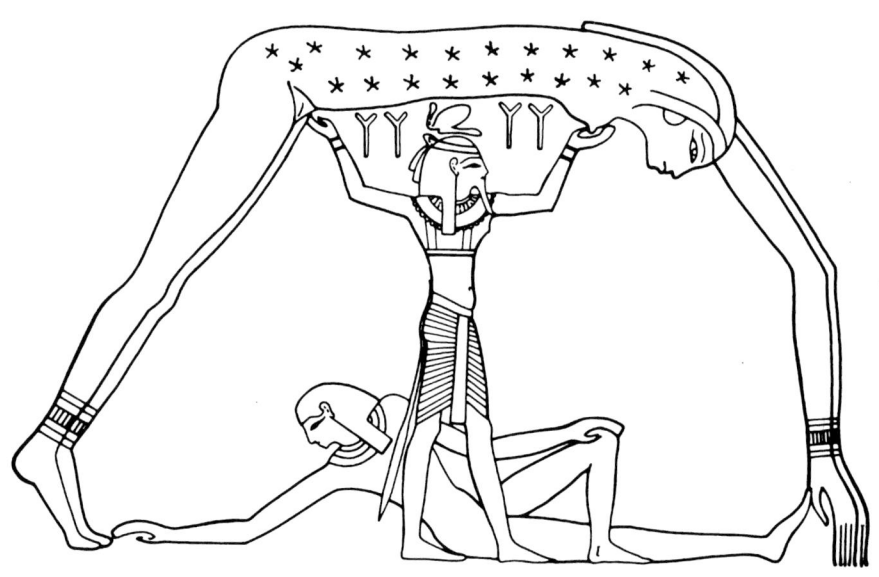

Fig. 1.28 The sky goddess Nut, the earth god Geb, and the air god Shu supporting the sky

Fig. 1.29 The city of Qedem as attested on a Luxor monument (Open Air Museum, Luxor)

The list of gods ends with Nut and Harwer. Nut was the goddess of the sky; she was often depicted as a female figure resting with her feet and hands on the ground. According to Egyptian concepts, her body stretched from east to west. Each day, the sun god Ra was born in her womb, only to be swallowed by her in the evening, when his daytime journey across the sky came to an end. The following day, this cycle was repeated again. Nut was also depicted on coffins and sarcophagi, where she symbolized the night sky. The god Harwer was considered a war and protector god. He was the adult Horus, who defeated his uncle Seth, took hold of his heritage and became the legal ruler on earth. Harwer was therefore only one specific aspect of Horus.

The characteristics of the individual deities allow us to conclude that Sinuhe's religious piety was directed towards both the universal gods, such as Amun, Atum and Hathor, and to the deities whom he chose in connection with his position in a foreign country in the east, asking mainly for the protection of the warrior deities such as Montu, Horus, Sebek-Ra, Sopdu, Wadjet, Horus-Min, Wereret, and Harwer.

In the context of the Egyptian pantheon we can explain the allusion in passage B 45: '...*the fear of whom (i.e. Amenemhat I) pervaded the foreign lands like Sekhmet in the year of the pestilence.*' This is a reference to the myth of human rebellion against the sun god Ra. When Ra was king on earth, the people turned against him in rebellion. Ra summoned the gods and decided to follow their counsel and send the goddess of war Sekhmet against the humans (sometimes, the texts mention Hathor instead; this is because Hathor was considered, in a truly Egyptian way of thinking, to be Sekhmet in her peaceful mode). She began a ferocious slaughter against humanity and within the first day notably reduced their numbers. At night, she crept out in secret to combat the humans again. Ra was worried that humans might become extinct altogether, and he ordered red paint to be brought from Elephantine. He also had many thousands jars of barley beer prepared, mixed it with red colour and had it poured over the earth to resemble human blood. When, on the next morning, Sekhmet once again set out to fight, she saw 'human blood,' the beer, and she got drunk instead of continung her murderous campaign. Thus, humanity was saved from extinction, but Ra was so disgusted by the people and their rebellion that he gave up his kingship on earth and departed to heaven.

In his answer to the king, Sinuhe does not forget to enumerate his merits in order to emphasize his loyalty. He lists the chiefs of the areas that remained loyal to the Egyptian ruler: the subjects of the chieftain Meki of Qedem, the area of the cedar woods to the east of Byblos – while the true home of the subjects of

Fig. 1.30 The cedars of Lebanon, one of the most important commodities in the Ancient Near East

Meki was probably the Bikah valley; the subjects of the chieftain of Front Kashu probably dwelt in the area of the Biblical city of Geshur in today's Syria; the inhabitants subject to the chieftain Manus from the land of Phenekhu may have been the ancestors of later Phoenicians who lived on the coast of today's Lebanon. The reason why Sinuhe explicitly lists his neighbours by name is probably to add credibility in his appeal to the king. These individual tribes could prove that Sinuhe, in voluntary exile from his country, still acted in favour of his ruler Senwosret I and of Egypt. It is of some interest that Sinuhe refers to the inhabtants of foreign countries in the same way that appears in the oldest so-called execration texts from the beginning of the Twelfth Dynasty. The enumeration of the countries – obviously Sinuhe's neighbours – also indicates that, for quite comprehensible reasons, Sinuhe was trying to stay in the vicinity of the city of Byblos, which pursued an active relationship with Egypt. From here he could thus, albeit tenuously, stay in contact with his home. That he might indeed have maintained at least some form of contact with Egypt is indicated by the fact that king Senwosret I knew where he was and even addressed a letter to him asking him to return to his home country.

Within one day, Sinuhe hands over all his affairs and possessions to his eldest son and immediately starts his journey home. On his way to Egypt, he describes his arrival to the place known as the Ways of Horus, which formed the border between Asia and Egypt. A deputy of the king already awaits him here, and Sinuhe is officially greeted. Both he and the Asiatics in his suite receive gifts. Sinuhe parts with his companions, giving them numerous presents, and joins a festive suite *en route* to the capital and to the royal court.

The name 'Ways of Horus' denoted the northern road leading through the Qantara projection and around the border fortress of Sila, continuing over Tell Abu Seipha, Tell Hebua and Tell Heir along the regular chain of wells all the way to Rafah in southern Palestine. According to the English Egyptologist Sir Alan H. Gardiner, this name of the road originates from prehistoric and early historical times, when the Egyptian ruler, who was often referred to as Horus, used it for his campaigns to Syria-Palestine. The Ways of Horus was a very important trade route, above all in the Early Dynastic period, before the growth of importance of maritime trade. Even in the Early Dynastic period, this road was probably of extreme importance, as a land route between Egypt and Palestine. It was with all probability along this road that the Palestinian imports of pottery with wine were transported to the Upper Egyptian site of Abydos, the place of the tombs of Early Dynastic rulers. In the course of Egyptian history the road increased in importance, since it became the gateway for the migrating population of Syria-Palestine to the Nile Delta, as well as the starting point for Egyptian military campaigns to the Near East. This important land juncture is attested even in a drawing in the Karnak temple from the time of Sethi I (Nineteenth Dynasty). We also know that in the last regnal year of his father, Ramesses I, Sethi I undertook a military campaign to Palestine. It is therefore likely that Sethi I knew this road from first-hand experience. After his succession

Fig. 1.31 A well on the Ways of Horus. As in the past settlements concentrate today only in these areas, usually separated by a one-day march (the coastal region of Egypt)

to the throne, right in the first year of his reign, he also encountered the Bedouin in a battle on the Ways of Horus near Gaza, in order to secure the road for trade caravans.

The Karnak scene shows Sethi I on his Palestinian campaign and during his triumphal return to Egypt. Sethi I is depicted in a sequence of three scenes. In the middle of this composition, he is depicted in a military chariot. Egypt and the desert of the Sinai are divided by a canal which swarms with crocodiles. Its banks are flanked with reeds. The accompanying inscription labels this canal as *t3 dmjt*, which translates literally as 'the canal'. The canal is joined at right angles by another water source, which is full of fish. This may be the Mediterranean Sea. The canal with crocodiles has only recently been identified with the fresh water juncture between Pelusium and Qantara. This waterway served for traffic, as an important source of potable water for the area of the eastern Delta, and, last but not least, as Egypt's eastern border, protecting the eastern Delta against the Bedouin.

Of the toponyms found on the Karnak relief, only Gaza and Rafah may today be identified with certainty, and perhaps also Sila and Migdol on the eastern border of Egypt. These sources document the fortresses which were built on this road in the immediate vicinity of wells, in order to protect them from potential attackers from Palestine and to guarantee their security during Egyptian campaigns.

In the time of the Twelfth Dynasty, the term 'the Ways of Horus' denoted also the fortress of Sileh, which stood at the beginning of this road and was connected with Itj-tawy by water. This view is supported by Sinuhe's account. Since Sinuhe reports about having used a waterway from the frontier fortress to the capital, it is likely that it was Sila where he had been waiting for the messengers from the residence, who then accompanied him ceremonially all the way to the royal court.

The Karnak scene contains altogether eleven sites and nine water sources, which are mentioned as the major points on the Ways of Horus. The credibility of this scene was confirmed between 1972 – 1982, when the area of the presumed Ways of Horus was excavated and explored by the expedition of the Beer-Sheva Ben Gurion University led by an Israeli archaeologist, Eliezer D. Oren. In the course of this project, over eighty New Kingdom sites were explored in the area between the Suez Canal and Gaza. This large-scale exploration enabled us to draw a detailed picture about the character of this region and about the settlements, which were set up in connection with this road.

Apart from the fortress built by Amenemhat I in Wadi Natrun, there is so far no contemporary evidence of a Middle Kingdom fortress in this area. The fortress excavated by Ahmed Fakhri was almost completely destroyed by the local Salt and Soda Company in 1933. All what has remained was an outer mudbrick wall (groundplan of 50 × 60 m) and granite threshold, jambs and a lintel with the name of Amenemhat I. To get an idea what might the fortresses look like during the period under discussion we have to turn to the contemporary evidence from Nubia. A whole chain of fortresses was built in Lower Nubia and in the Second

Fig. 1.32 Palestinian scene of Sethi I at Karnak (Nineteenth Dynasty)

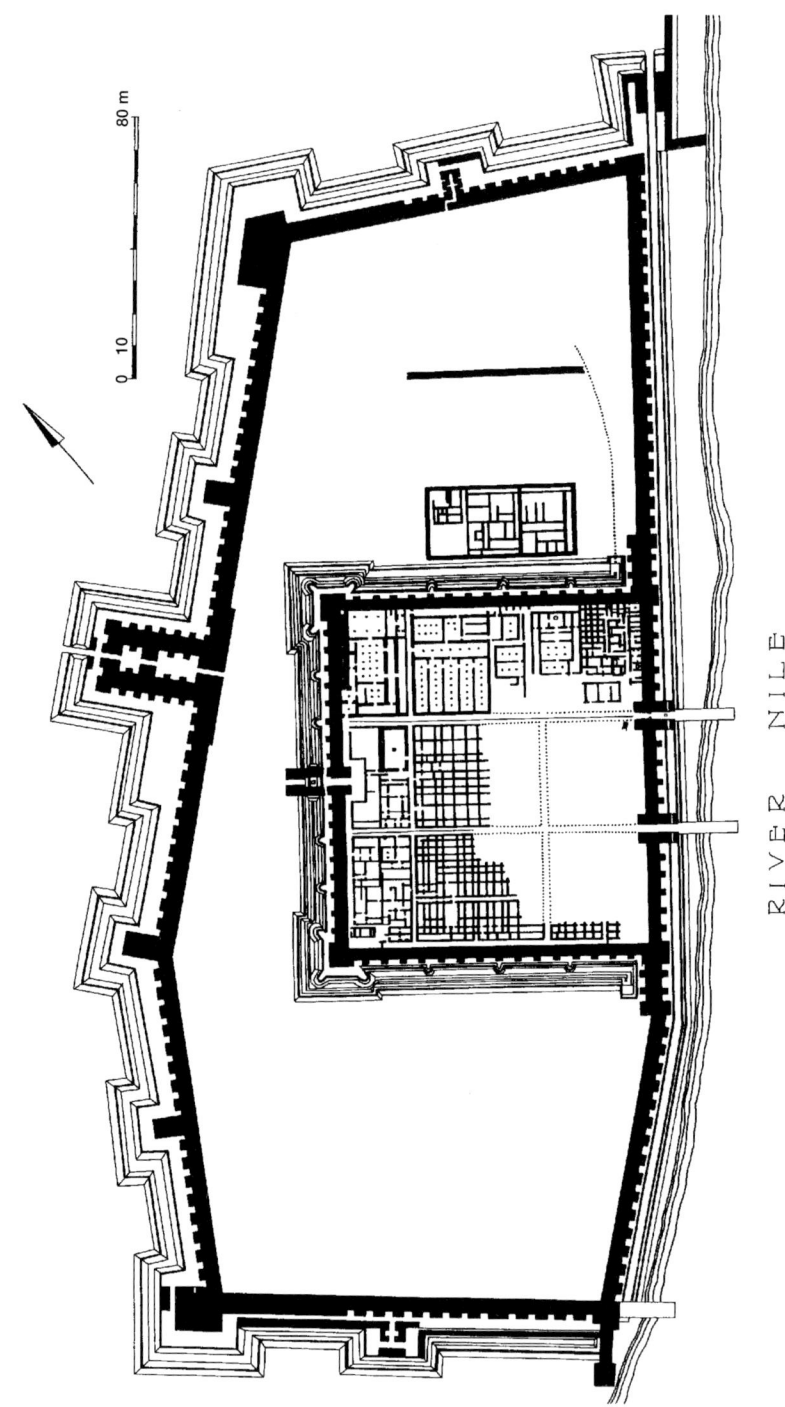

Fig. 1.34 Ground plan of the fortress of Buhen (after W. B. Emery, H. S. Smith, A. Millard, The Fortress of Buhen. The Archaeological Report, London 1979, pl. 3)

Fig. 1.35 Reconstruction of the entrance fortification of Buhen (after W. B. Emery, H. S. Smith, A. Millard, The Fortress of Buhen. The Archaeological Report, London 1979, pl. 11)

Cataract area. They were set up here to control the southern border of Egypt and to protect the African caravan routes. During this period at least fourteen fortresses were built in this area, most of them being submerged in the 1960s by the Assuan High Dam waters (Nasser Lake). The most imposing defending structures developed, for instance, in Buhen (fortress with a groundplan 215 × 460 m), Khor (250 × 600 m), Mirgissa (190 × 295 m), Semna (135 × 135 m) and Dabenarti (60 × 230 m).

One of the most impressive structures of the time was the fortress in Buhen, built by Senwosret I. This monument was protected by an outer perimeter wall more than 700 m long which was 4 m wide and strengthened with several bastions. The fortress itself measured 150 × 170 m, the perimeter walls being 5 m wide and 11 m high, protected with 32 semicircular bastions and strong towers in the corners. The fortress disposed of two shallow gates opening to the river and one monumental fortified gate opening to the northwest. Inside the fortress there were settlement units for the garrison, stables, house of the military commandant, store-rooms and a temple outside the enclosure wall.

Such is our contemporary evidence for Middle Kingdom fortresses, mainly preserved in Lower Nubia, south of the Assuan First Cataract. From the area of the Ways of Horus the evidence is much later in date, starting in the New Kingdom. Nevertheless, the fortress of Amenemhat I in Wadi Natrun allows us to presume that the Middle Kingdom situation here was quite similar as far as the formal appearance of the fortresses is concerned, since the frontier system with an identical function must have already existed.

The greatest concentration of settlements along the Ways of Horus was traced to the east of the Delta and to the south of Lake Bardavil. They are mostly New Kingdom sites, which lay in the inland and therefore had no connection to the Mediterranean Sea or to the trade that was going on there. The settlement in these areas was concentrated around the fortresses, which were surrounded by smaller camps of the caravans and expeditions that were passing by. There were also seasonal camps of the indigenous population (probably nomadic), who lived in tents and simple light dwellings and depended on the local Egyptian centres for potable water. In return, this nomadic element was possibly responsible for supporting the permanent garrisons by providing them with some foodstuffs. At least ten fortified sites were recorded between Rafah and the Suez canal. The best explored among them are Bir el-'Abd and two sites in the immediate vicinity of Harubah. They also illustrate the character of the activities of the fortresses along the Ways of Horus, that is its military, administrative and production aspects.

The site of Bir al-'Abd consisted of the central area designated BEA-10, which was surrounded by about thirty small campsites covering the area of 3–4 km. These encampments, which were usually located in small valleys between dunes, were archaeologically very poor. Among the most common discoveries were fireplaces, waste pits, milling stones for grain, a large amount of pottery, mostly of Egyptian origin, and a few metal objects. The area BEA-10, the centre of this settlement, encompassed around 25 hectares, although buildings covered only

Fig. 1.32a Palestinian scene of Sethi I at Karnak (Nineteenth Dynasty) – detail, King Sethi I on his chariot

about a tenth of the total area. A quite massive fortification of the original mud brick fortress was discovered in the centre of the settlement. This structure covered approximately 1 600 sq. m. Inside was a large open court with brick appliances and ovens for baking, cooking, and the storage of provisions, as well as fireplaces and waste pits. The waste layers contained numerous animal and fish bones. To the south of the fortress was a complex of four silos for grain storage, which was adjacent to a large complex of storerooms. Only the ground plan of the silos was preserved, attesting that they were 4 metres in diameter. They were built of mud bricks, and each could contain around 11 000 litres (10 tonnes) of grain. Approximately 200 m to the south of the fortress was a pit for the collection of rainwater, 10 × 15 m large. Its bottom and walls were covered with several layers of clay, in order to prevent water from leaking into the sandy subsoil.

The Harubah area was excavated between 1979–1982. Gradually, over twenty New Kingdom sites were recorded and documented here. These sites were concentrated in the area of under 5 sq. km in an irregular sandy terrain, which was dominated by a military fortress designated A-28 and A-345, the administrative and economic centre of the site. On site A-345, numerous pottery sherds were found, some with the name of Sethi I in a cartouche, thus proving a considerable Egyptian presence on the edge of the Sinai. Egyptian influence in the area probably increased in connection with the modification of the Ways of Horus during his reign. The Karnak depiction of this road also comes from the time of his reign. The fortress of Harubah was built of mud bricks and extended over approximately 2500 sq. m. Its boundary wall was 4 metres thick, and it was preserved to the height of 1 m. The fortress was dominated by a large open court, which was surrounded by magazines, kitchen appliances and dwellings. A large area within the fortress was left free and served as horse stalls. The entrance to the fortress was protected by massive walls. The entire fortified entrance covered an area of 12 × 13 m. The entrance itself was almost 4 m wide and 16 m long, large enough to enable the cavalry to pass through to the interior.

Perhaps the most striking discoveries come from the final stage of the existence of the fortress (Stage II). In different places within the fortress area, men, women and children, who were probably somehow connected with it, had been buried. Anthropological analysis of their skeletal remains showed that all of them had Canaanite features. The Egyptian administrative apparatus thus made full use of the service of the indigenous population of the northern Sinai, whom the New Kingdom sources call the Shasu Bedouin.

Owing primarily to the discoveries from the Harubah fortress, we are now able to reconstruct the appearance of the fortresses that in the time of the New Kingdom stood along the Ways of Horus and which were – given their favourable topography – probably constructed on the sites of their Middle Kingdom predecessors. There is also no doubt that functionally they were similar with defensive structures that must have hypothetically existed there during the Middle Kingdom. Some of them were very strong, with corners fortified by towers. The larger ones could even contain another, smaller fortress within them.

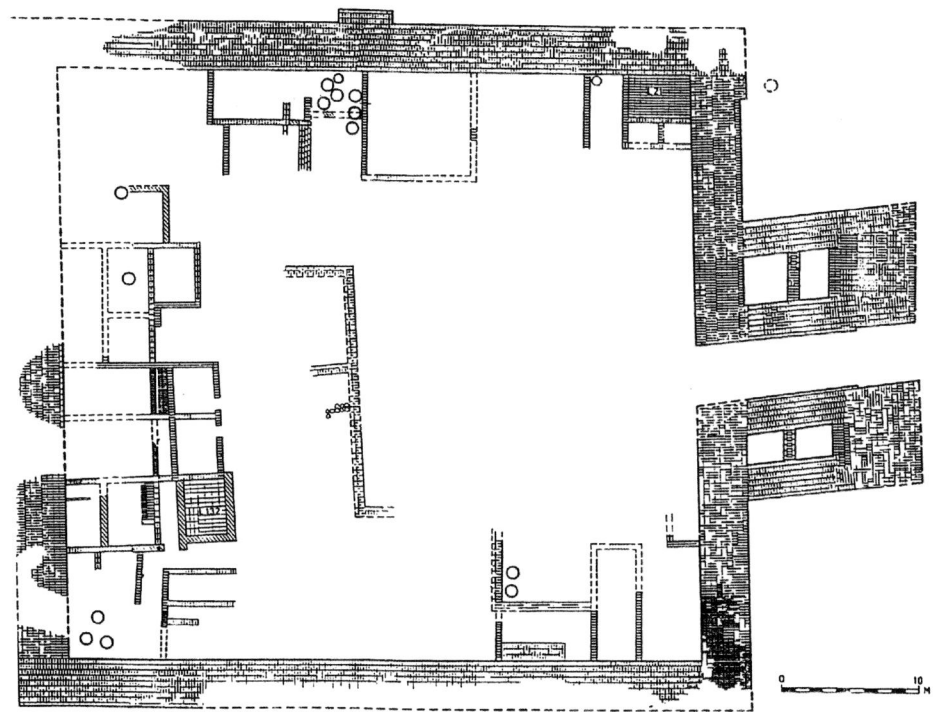

Fig. 1.36 Ground plan of the fortress at Haruba (after E. D. Oren, 'The "Ways of Horus" in North Sinai,' in Rainey, A. F., Egypt, Israel, Sinai. Archaeological and Historical relationship in the Biblical Period, Tel Aviv 1987, p. 88, fig. 6)

Small settlements, magazines and workshops were often constructed outside. Their chief function was to ensure the operation of the fortress and to provide for the needs of the Egyptian expeditions passing through the area. They were not only military outposts; the bigger ones were also administrative centres which in all likelihood supervised the trade in the area of northern Sinai and southern Palestine. Some of them even served as production centres, supplying their products (mostly pottery) not just to the fortress itself, but also to its surrounding areas.

Sinuhe returns to the Palace

In the morning after his return to the capital, Sinuhe is summoned to present himself in the audience hall, where the king sits in splendour. At the entrance to the palace he meets the royal children, and then, frightened, he proceeds to enter into the presence of the king. The king greets him amicably and has the royal children brought in. The children are, however, alarmed by Sinuhe's appearance, for he still looks like an Asiatic, and they want to know whether or not this strange person is really he. Their reaction allows us to conclude that they had known Sinuhe from before, probably from the time of his stay at the royal court. The children intercede for Sinuhe, and the king places him among the high court officials again. He is also provided for, just as any royal official who has all his life loyally served his king. Thus, he may spend a peaceful old age at the court. He is given a luxurious house with a garden, all his material needs are satisfied, and above all, his afterlife existence is secured, for the king builds for him a tomb in the necropolis. The tomb was an indispensable provision for the afterlife of any Egyptian. The fact that the king himself takes an interest in the construction of Sinuhe's tomb may be considered as a unique expression of his favour.

This final passage gives us a detailed picture of the religious conceptions of the Egyptians of this time, which were connected to ideas of an existence in afterlife. So complex and important was this collection of concepts, that we will dedicate to it the closing chapter of this book.

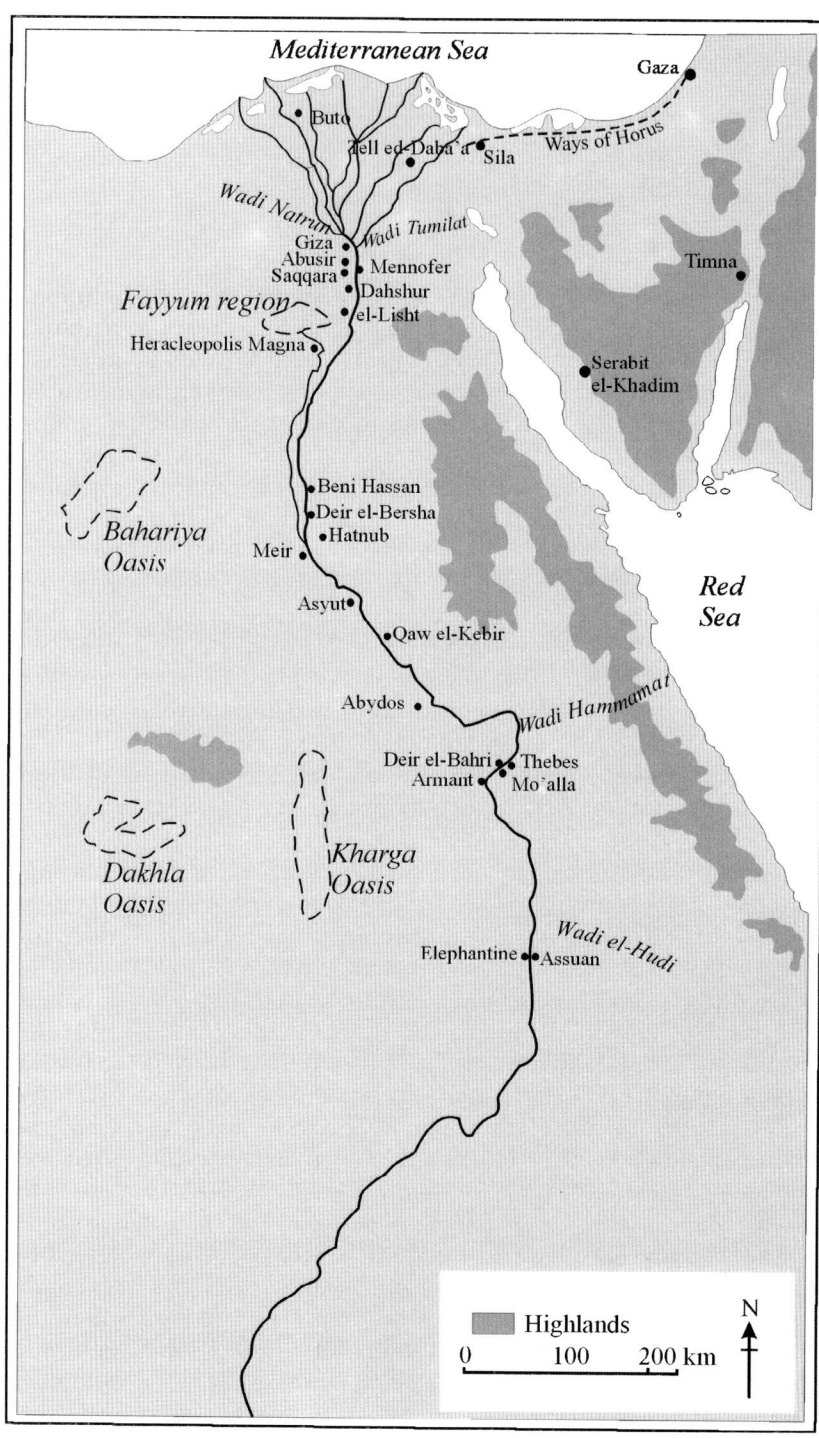

Egypt in the Time of Sinuhe's Flight

The time of Sinuhe's flight from Egypt corresponds to the beginning of the Twelfth Dynasty, almost four thousand years ago. When reading Sinuhe's story, we must bear in mind that by this time, Egypt had experienced many years of unification struggles. This period provides us with many interesting insights into contemporary life in Egypt, and also allows us to make a picture of Sinuhe's surroundings and background – a time that can be sketched for the reader mainly through texts and archaeological finds. The period of ancient Egyptian history that will interest us is of necessity a little longer than the actual time of Sinuhe's flight and forced sojourn in Syria and Palestine. In order to understand this literary creation, we need to get a glimpse of the main events that happened immediately before Sinuhe's lifetime, as well as of those that followed it. We will therefore consider the period between the 21st and 19th centuries BC; thus surveying three centuries of ancient Egypt's history, from the so-called First Intermediate Period which followed the era of the pyramid builders until the end of the Middle Kingdom proper, the reign of Amenemhat III.

When the era of the creators of the monumental projects of the Old Kingdom who have left behind them numerous pyramids on the sites of Dahshur, Saqqara, Giza, Abusir, etc., gradually faded away, a somewhat indistinct period began in c. 2150 BC. It was characterized by rapid changes of rulers on the Egyptian throne, and by a gradual decline of the centralized power of the king and his administration. This epoch is called the First Intermediate Period and it is commonly defined as the period from the end of the Sixth Dynasty to the reign of King Mentuhotep II, at the end of the Eleventh Dynasty. It can be formally divided into two parts, the time of the Seventh and Eighth Dynasties (2150–2134 BC), and that of the Ninth and Tenth Dynasties (2134–2040 BC). During the Seventh and Eighth Dynasties, the Egyptian throne was in a state of flux, and over fifty kings appeared on the throne during this time, willing to formally base their power on the tradition of the Old Kingdom kings. These rulers had either no or very little authority and only a slight chance of taking part in the management of the gradually disintegrating state. In the course of the entire First Intermediate Period, the Egyptian state was divided into several independent areas governed by local princes who were concerned only with their personal profit. Military conflicts for power and sphere of influence were thus very frequent. The situation in the state was undoubtedly very dangerous and difficult. The account known as the Admonitions of Ipuwer, with its precise report about Egypt's condition in the time after the end of the Old Kingdom, clearly illustrates this point:

Fig. 2.1 The Teti pyramid temple at Saqqara. In its vicinity lay one of Egypt's centres after the collapse of the Old Kingdom

'Slaves have become slave-owners.

Indeed, (the scribes) were killed and their scrolls were stolen! Woe to me due to misfortune in this time!

Indeed, the local scribes, their records were destroyed, and the grain of Egypt is a common possession!

Indeed, the laws of the courtroom were cast out,
people are even trampling over them
in public places, and wretches are tearing them (apart) in the streets!

... Behold! Things are being done which have not been done since eternity! The king has been deposed by wretches!

Look, he who was buried as a falcon (has no) bier, and that which the pyramid hid is empty!

Look, the land has been deprived of royal power by a few people (who are) ignorant of laws!

...Look, ... He who could not have a coffin made for himself owns a tomb!

Look, tomb-owners are cast out into the hills,
while he who could not have a grave dug for himself
owns a treasure!

....Look, he who had no grain (now) owns
granaries and he who had to borrow grain is (now) distributing it!

Look, he who had no subordinates owns
slaves and he who was an (official is now) acting under his own command!'

(after B. Vachala, The Wisdom of Ancient Egypt, 50–52)

In the time following the Seventh and Eighth Dynasties, which still held on to the tradition by residing in Memphis, Egypt was dominated by two realms, one centred in southern Egypt and the other in the north. They were the kingdoms of Thebes and of Herakleopolis, the main actors in the crucial events of this time, which finally resulted in the reunification of Egypt.

In the north of the country reigned the Ninth and Tenth Dynasties of kings who resided in the vicinity of today's Fayyum Oasis at Herakleopolis, the contemporary Ehnasya el-Medina. This Dynasty was founded in 2134 BC by King Meribre Kheti I who is known to have ruled Egypt down to the first Nile cataract, and said to have 'behaved more cruelly than his ancestors' and to have 'done evil to all people of Egypt' (Manetho). The Herakleopolitan rulers traced their lineage down to the last kings of the Old Kingdom and probably succeeded the weak Eighth Dynasty rulers who resided in the Old Kingdom capital of Memphis. In accord with this politically motivated policy, the Herakleopolitans had themselves buried in the Saqqara necropolis of the Fifth and Sixth Dynasty rulers.

The reign of the eighteen kings of the Ninth and Tenth Dynasties lasted approximately 100 years. According to a legend, one of the most famous rulers of this period, Merikare, was buried in the vicinity of the pyramid of Teti (perhaps to the east of it). Another Herakleopolitan ruler, Neferkare VII, first found a strong ally against Thebes in Ankhtify, the mayor of Hierakonpolis and *de facto* ruler of three nomes to the south of Thebes. Together, they formed a coalition

Fig. 2.2 Birket Karun and the Fayyum oasis

Fig. 2.3 Tomb of Ankhtify at Mo'alla near Thebes

and fought against their common enemy who resided in Thebes by attempting to cut the city off from the surrounding nomes. Commander Ankhtify distinguished himself in these battles, which are also documented in the autobiographical inscription in his tomb cut in the rock in the vicinity of Thebes. This autobiography includes a vivid description of his campaign against Edfu, the ancient cultic centre of the god Horus, the guardian deity of ancient Egyptian kings, who was prominent in the region of Thebes and its surrounds. According to his own account, Ankhtify marched at the head of his troops to Edfu and conquered it. When the ruler of Armant, whom the Theban troops had besieged in his fortress, asked him to come to his aid, Ankhtify arrived to help him and the Theban troops ran away before him without even starting a fight. He reports these events as follows:

'The noble, commander of the army of Hierakonpolis,
the victorious Ankhtify says:
I sailed north,
with my loyal and courageous troops.
I disembarked on the western bank of the Theban nome,
the front of the fleet was at the Sekhemsen hill,
the rear of the fleet was in the region of Tjemi.
My loyal troops searched (for) a victorious battle

in the area of western Thebes.
But no one came out because of their fear.
I sailed north,
and disembarked on the western bank of the Theban nome;
the front of the fleet was at the tomb of Imbi,
the rear of the fleet at the city of Sega.
Its walls were besieged
until it has opened its bars before them.
These courageous and loyal troops,
these loyal troops,
became a powerful guard,
and searched (for) a victorious battle
on the eastern bank of the Theban nome.
But no one came out because of their fear.
I am a courageous man,
one who has no equal.'
(The tomb of Anhktify at Mo'alla, inscription no. 7)

This inscription indicates that the Thebans, being probably outnumbered by the approaching Ankhtify's army, decided to retreat into the city and postpone the encounter until a more favourable time. Ankhtify became the ruler of the nomes of Hierakonpolis, Edfu, Ombos and Elephantine. This area was, however, immediately retaken by the Thebans (Inyotef I). The last great Herakleopolitan ruler, Kheti III, a contemporary of Mentuhotep II, also achieved several partial victories against his Theban adversaries – for example, he conquered and ransacked the city of Thinis. But, above all, he consolidated his rule in the north by expelling the Asiatics and the Bedouin out of the Egyptian Delta. His reign also witnessed renewed contacts and commerce with the area of Syria-Palestine, as well as the resumption of the import of cedar wood from Byblos. His successor Merikare, who also happened to be a contemporary of Mentuhotep II, was the last ruler of the Tenth Dynasty. Among other things, it is known that he undertook a journey to Asyut with his court, to install the local mayor, Kheti II, in his office:

'The north wind was blowing and papyrus stems were bending towards the water,
(when) he landed at Herakleopolis.
The city arrived to rejoice over its Lord,
the son of their Lord.
Women together with men,
the old and the young.
The king's son, he reached his city,
he entered the house of his father...
...the lord of the Two Lands,
King of Upper and Lower Egypt, Merikare,

monuments will be built for Wepwawet,
god, great of might,
who was given millions of years,
in order to repeat his jubilee ceremonies,
under the command of the royal confidant,
Kheti, son of Tefib,
the great nomarch of Upper Egypt.
See, your name will last for all eternity
in the temple of Wepwawet.'
(Asyut, tomb no. IV, 16–17, 22–23)

The composition known as 'The Instructions for King Merikare' was written prior to the reunification of Egypt, but certainly after the death of Kheti III. This work describes the situation in the Egyptian state in the time of the unification battles between the North and the South. The instructions are spoken by Kheti. In the form of short maxims; he gives Merikare advice on how to manage the affairs of the state during his reign:

'Build yourself a lasting monument with your popularity.
Enrich the peasants and support the cities.
Respect the nobles and make your people prosper,

Fig. 2.4 Armant, one of the Egyptian local power centres during the First Intermediate Period (ca 2100 BC)

strengthen the borders and the areas around them,
for it is right to act for the future...
Endow your notables with wealth so that they act according to your laws.
He who is wealthy in his house is also impartial,
for he who is rich has no need...
Do justice while you are on earth:
See to the weeping ones, do not oppress the widow,
do not deprive the son of the wealth of his father,
do not depose officials from their posts.
Beware of unjust punishment
and do not kill, for it shall bring no profit to you.'
(after B. Vachala, The Wisdom of Ancient Egypt, 71–84)

Unlike the Herakleopolitan rulers, the princes of the Eleventh Dynasty resided in Thebes. Thebes was the capital of the fourth Upper Egyptian nome with the cultic centre of the warrior god, Montu. Besides this deity, the god Amun was also worshipped here, but his cult did not reach its prime until well into the Middle Kingdom. The Eleventh Dynasty was founded by Mentuhotep I (called 'the Ancestor'), the son of Inyotef. He was not a king. He was succeeded by Inyotef I, who probably formed a coalition with the rulers of Coptos to fight Ankhtify.

Inyotef I first concentrated his military activities on regaining influence in the immediate surroundings of Thebes. Most of the battles must have taken place around the fortress of Armant, where the warrior god Montu was also worshipped. The Armant fortress, which had long formed one of the barriers against Theban expansion, finally fell. Inyotef I reigned for approximately 12 years and it is probable that after the defeat of Ankhtify he extended Theban territory southward to Elephantine, which was of immense strategic importance as a buffer city and border fortress protecting Egypt against Lower Nubia.

The recent discoveries of American Egyptologists John and Deborah Darnell of the Chicago Oriental Institute shed some new light on the early history of this war. The inscriptions they discovered along the desert 'Alamat Tal Road show that the expansion of the Theban rulers was made possible by opening this road starting on the western bank of Thebes, traversing the Qena Bend of the Nile and leading northwards up to Hu and Abydos. Inyotef I, who gained control over this road, was able to outflank the hostile ruler residing in Coptos and to attack the strategically important territory around Abydos. In this manner the Coptos ruler was cut off from the military support of the Herakleopolitans and besieged some time later. Moreover, the supremacy in the desert provided the Thebans with a direct access to the oases of Kharga and Dakhla and with control over the desert roads leading into the African interior.

Inyotef I was succeeded by his brother Inyotef II, the most famous of the Inyotef line, whose reign has been estimated to have lasted for 50 years. He finally managed to affirm his hold over the entire southern part of Egypt, as is indicated by the discovery of two sandstone cultic statues of this ruler on the island

Fig. 2.5 The octagonal pillar mentioning the construction of a monument for Amun by King Inyotef II (Open Air Museum, now in Luxor Museum)

of Elephantine. One of them shows the king seated, dressed in the cloak of the thirtieth regnal year jubilee festival. In the course of the ceremonies of the jubilee, called the Sed Festival, the king had to ritually demonstrate his ability to govern the Egyptian people. The statue proves that Inyotef II celebrated his regnal jubilee after having accomplished thirty years on the Egyptian throne. None of the other Inyotef kings managed to repeat this achievement.

In the north, Inyotef probably defeated the nomes of Abydos and Thinis. The conquest of these two ancient centres was presumably of great importance, since both Abydos with the tombs of the first rulers of unified Egypt in the early third millennium BC, and Thinis, the Egyptian capital of the First and Second Dynasties, were very prestigious and religiously important sites. This double conquest may have been interpreted as proof of the favour of the gods and may thus have legitimised the conquest and reunification of the whole of Egypt.

At the end of Inyotef's reign the border of his realm was extended to the Tenth nome of Upper Egypt, to Qaw el-Kebir (later city of Antaeopolis). Inyotef II also built at Karnak (as the discovery of an octagonal pillar with his inscription indicates), where he was the first to begin construction work for the god Amun, in addition to works for Montu, the most important deity of the Theban area. We also know the location of Inyotef's tomb, which was built, just as those of his ancestor and successor Inyotef I and III, at the site of El Tarif north of Deir el-Bahri.

Fig. 2.6 The Osirid statue of Mentuhotep II (Egyptian Museum, Cairo)

Inyotef II was succeeded by Inyotef III who ruled for approximately eight years. Only very little is known of his reign. One of his few monuments is the building inscription on Elephantine concerning the reestablishment of the cult of Hekaib, a beatified official from this province.

The struggle between the north and the south culminated under Mentuhotep II (2061–2010 BC), who, after prolonged battles, finally united Egypt. Mentuhotep II was the son of the Theban prince Inyotef III and his wife Iah. In the beginning of his reign in Upper Egypt he bore the name of 'He who causes the heart of the two lands to live' (the two lands are to be understood as Upper and Lower Egypt). At the moment of his ascent to the throne his realm extended from the first cataract in the south (Elephantine) to the tenth nome of Upper Egypt. Precisely at this time the Herakleopolitan rulers reached the conclusion that it would be necessary to achieve peace with the Theban rulers to avoid a debacle. The armistice was broken in the 14th year of Mentuhotep II who at first suffered a severe defeat. The Herakleopolitan ruler Kheti III, supported by the nomarch Tefib, conquered Thinis and burnt the tombs of the First and Second Dynasty rulers at Abydos. This deed, an act of desecration of the tombs of the first kings of the united pharaonic Egypt, is even mentioned in the Instructions for Merikare where it is interpreted as one of the reasons for the final fall of the Herakleopolitan rulers, whose sacrilegious act made the gods displeased with them. This deed is phrased as a warning for his successor:

Fig. 2.7 The cemetery of the powerful nomarchs at Beni Hassan

*'One regiment robs another,
as the ancestors have foretold.
Egypt fights even in the necropolis:
Don't destroy tombs, do not destroy them!
I have done so, and the same happened (to me):
thus God treats him who commits such a thing.
Do not be evil to the Southern land –
for you know the prophecy of the residence.
As it had happened, so will it happen.
They did not make offence by what they said.
I advanced to Thinis, all the way to its southern border in the valley,
I raced as a flood...'*
(after B. Vachala, The Wisdom of Ancient Egypt, 79)

In the course of further unification conflicts, Mentuhotep found a powerful ally in Baket III, the ruler of the 16th (Oryx) nome. The centre of this nome must have been located somewhere in the vicinity of the contemporary city of Minya and thus all that has come down to us are the rock tombs of these rulers in Beni Hassan. After the conquest of Asyut and the Fifteenth nome of Upper Egypt which actually signalled the defeat of the Herakleopolitan Dynasty, he assumed the Horus name 'He with the divine white crown' in order to demonstrate his Upper Egyptian origin. Owing to the loyalty of the nomarchs of the Oryx and Hare nomes he also managed to consolidate his power in the north of the country. During his campaign in the north against the Herakleopolitan rulers, his army marched through the Hare nome. The conditions that Egypt was in at that time are illustrated in the graffito of the nomarch Kai found in the alabaster mines at Hatnub:

'Year five of the prince, keeper of the two thrones,
the overseer of the priests, nomarch of the Hare nome,
overseer of the (residential) city, the vizier,
overseer of Upper Egypt,
first of the princes in the royal house
Kai (son of) Djehutinakht (son of) Neheri
may he live for ever...
I had trained a guard of youths,
and set out at the side of my city.
It was I who constructed its ... wells and inundated areas.
There was no one with me,
besides my guides,
the Medjai, men of Wawat, Nubians and Asiatics,
Upper and Lower Egypt allied against me.
I returned successfully,
my entire city with me,
without having suffered any losses.
It was I,
who protected the poor against the strong.
I made my house a gate
for everyone who feared the day of the eruption of civil war.
I was a nurse ... and a child's caretaker
for everyone who came injured without having recovered.
I gave clothes to everyone who came naked,
I was the bread of the hungry,
beer for him who came in thirst...'
(Graffito Hatnub no. 16)

Fig. 2.8 Tomb of Baket III at Beni Hassan, fortress siege (after P. E. Newberry, Beni Hassan II, London 1894, pl. 5)

The above account of the situation in Egypt during the struggle for power between Thebes and Herakleopolis indicates that it was the common population who suffered most, being literally decimated by the rival armies. Kai himself blatantly states that instead of fighting, he was mainly concerned with his nome and with the inhabitants of his city of Khemenu (Greek Hermopolis, today's Ashmunein), the centre of the cult of Thoth, the god of wisdom. We do have evidence, though, that he finally joined the victorious rulers from Thebes. An account of the unification fights can also be found in the famous rock tombs of Beni Hassan. One of these tombs, that of Baket III (tomb no. 15), which is often dated to the end of the Eleventh Dynasty, has preserved a scene of the siege of a fortress by Egyptian and Nubian soldiers. Since the fortress itself is also defended by Egyptian troops, this scene probably represents a record of the fierce internal strife during which, aside from the devastation of the countryside (see the text of Kai), some Egyptian cities were besieged and even destroyed. Last but not least, one document of the unrest in the time of the reign of Mentuhotep II can be found in a representation of this king. The scene comes from Gebelein and shows Mentuhotep II in a victorious position slaying an Egyptian adversary – according to his attributes, undoubtedly a noble nomarch – and together with him there are three other traditional enemies of Egypt – a Nubian, an Asiatic and a Libyan, who were perhaps allied with the Herakleopolitan army. The ac-

Fig. 2.9 Egyptian army, end of the Eleventh Dynasty (tomb of Mesekhti, Egyptian Museum, Cairo)

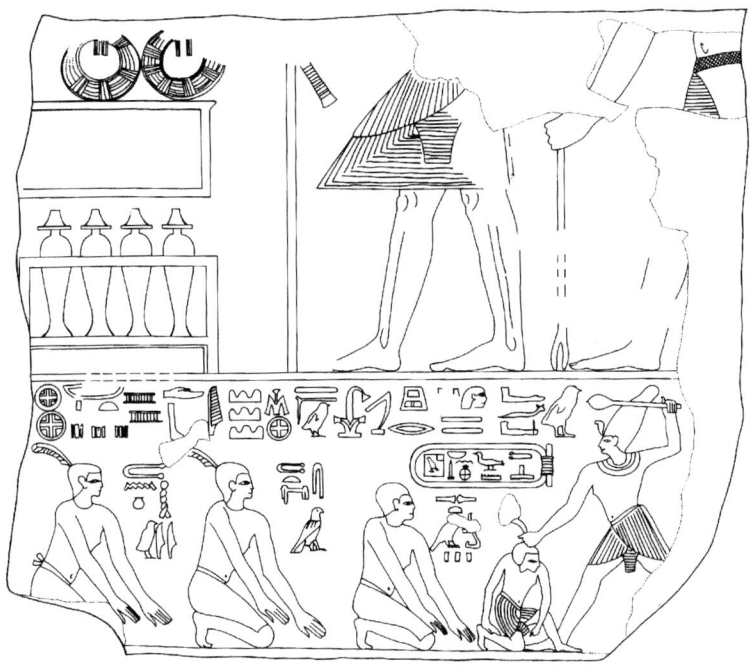

Fig. 2.10 Mentuhotep slaying his enemies, Gebelein, near Thebes (after L. Habachi, 'King Nebhepetre Mentuhotp: Place in History, Deification and Unusual Representations in the Form of Gods', in MDAIK 19, 1963, p. 39, fig. 17)

companying inscription explains that the scene depicts 'the subjugation of the chiefs of the Two Lands, the conquest of Upper and Lower Egypt, of foreign countries, of the two banks, of enemy nations and of the two cities.'

Seminal studies by Egyptian and German scholars Labib Habachi and Dorothea Arnold, regarding Mentuhotep's time and his journey to success, have shown that it was undoubtedly full of fierce encounters and severe losses. Some evidence of these uneasy times came to light with the discovery of a tomb from his time in Deir el-Bahri, which contained bodies of over sixty brave soldiers from his army. This tomb was discovered in 1923 by H. E. Winlock, of the Metropolitan Museum of Art in New York. It was cut into the cliff of the valley where Mentuhotep II also built his own tomb, to be joined much later by the Eighteenth Dynasty Queen Hatshepsut. In front of the tomb entrance was a small court hollowed in the rock, which gave access to an underground labyrinth of corridors penetrating the rock massif. Several side passages branched off the main corridor which ran through the entire tomb, each of them being terminated by a burial chamber. In these corridors and chambers, wrapped in linen, lay the bodies of approximately sixty soldiers who sacrificed their lives for their sovereign and commander. Undoubtedly they were physically very able men, almost

Fig. 2.11 Wadi Shatt el-Righal

170 centimetres tall and very robust in stature. All of them died quite young, in their thirties. Their bodies bore traces of severe war injuries and even of having remained lying on the battlefield for several days afterward, left at the mercy of birds of prey. Many soldiers still have arrowheads lodged in their bodies. A significant proportion of them bore, according to Winlock, typical skull and shoulder injuries induced by heavy stones falling from above. This fact brought Winlock to conclude that these soldiers lost their lives during the siege of some city, at the time of a frontal assault of its fortifications by means of ladders. The surviving soldiers were caught and their skulls were mercilessly crushed with war mallets. With their courage and loyalty, these soldiers probably deserved a corporate burial in a tomb close to the final resting place of their lord.

We possess clear evidence that some parts of the country did not acknowledge the rule of Mentuhotep II. For example, the Dakhleh Oasis became the stronghold of the opponents of his regime at this time. This is documented on a stela belonging to the official Kai, who was the commander of desert guards involved in the capture of enemies of the regime who were fleeing to the Dakhleh Oasis. He brought them back to the Nile Valley, where they undoubtedly had to face punishment.:

'... *I am an honourable man (who is) at the head of the army on an unfavourable day, one whom his lord praises for the execution of his mission. I had reached the territory of the Western Oasis and I searched all its roads. I brought back the fugitive whom I found there. (My) army remained in order...*'

(Stele Berlin Museum, Inv. no. 22 820)

Mentuhotep II also consolidated the administration of the country, re-introduced the office of the vizier (we know of three viziers from his time – Dagi, Bebi and Ipi,) and began to build Egypt's capital in Thebes. At this time, around the 39th year of his reign, he changed his Horus name to 'One who Unites the Two Lands'. During this period, he followed up on the policy of the Old Kingdom rulers in dispatching punitive campaigns against the Bedouin in the western, Libyan desert (the Tjemehu and the Tjehenu) and to the Sinai. He also sent his chancellor Kheti at the head of an expedition to the Qurqur Oasis and conquered it. Direct evidence of this event comes from the 39th year of his reign, preserved in Wadi Shatt el-Righal, the starting point of expeditions to this oasis, which lay approximately 40 km to the south of Edfu. Mentuhotep II is depicted here together with his father, Inyotef III, and his mother Iah, receiving Kheti after his return from the Qurqur Oasis. The conquest of this oasis was of utmost importance, since it lay on an vital caravan route. However, Mentuhotep II did not quite manage to retake Lower Nubia, the territory to the south of the First Cataract on Elephantine. Nonetheless, his role in the unification of the country is best attested by the fact that king lists mention him at the side of Menes, the founder of the Old Kingdom, and Ahmose, the founder of the New Kingdom, as the founder of the Middle Kingdom.

Mentuhotep II did not build his mortuary temple following the tradition of his ancestors (Inyotef I–III) in el-Tarif, but in nearby Deir el-Bahri. This tomb is a turning point in the history of Egyptian architecture, a new form in royal tomb construction, based on the Upper Egyptian tradition. Its place was probably ori-

Fig. 2.12 Mentuhotep II with Inyotef III and Iah, his parents, receiving the chancellor Kheti (Wadi Shatt el-Righal)

Fig. 2.13 Deir el-Bahri, the final resting place of Mentuhotep II (on the right)

ginally occupied by a chapel dedicated to the goddess Hathor, the mythical mother and guardian of Egyptian kings. Mentuhotep II initialized the construction of his tomb already in the course of his liberation war. This is the main reason why his tomb corresponded exactly to those of his ancestors, Inyotef I – III. The rock-cut tomb was approached by a 1200 m long and 46 m wide ascending causeway leading from the valley temple in the east (which lies under the contemporary village of Kom el-Fessad, still waiting for its excavator). Along its entire course, the causeway was flanked by statues of the king identified with Osiris. It was terminated by two tower-like structures, pylons, which formed the entrance to the tomb complex itself. Behind the pylons was a large rectangular open court. In the centre of the court was a huge entrance, now called 'Bab el-Hosan' (the Gateway of the Horse), which opened into a 150 m long rock cut corridor leading to the burial chamber.

The chamber contained an empty wooden sarcophagus and a black sandstone Osirid statue of the king. The black colour of the statue probably symbolized the idea of the resurrection of the king as Osiris, which it was thought he would experience after his death and after his body had been interred in the black Egyptian soil. In the floor of the burial chamber was the mouth of a 30 m deep shaft, the bottom of which concealed wooden models of boats that were considered indispensable for the king's afterlife.

Fig. 2.14 Detail of the decoration of the Princess Kawit sarcophagus (Egyptian Museum, Cairo)

Some distance from Bab el-Hosan was the main superstructure, in which six other shafts led to the burial chambers of six female members of the royal family – they belonged to minor queens of Mentuhotep II. These women died very early and very likely at the same time: the oldest Ashayit at age of twenty-two whereas the youngest Mayt was only five. The leading expert on the complex, German archaeologist Dieter Arnold considers them to be priestesses of Hathor, patronage goddess of the western Thebes. According to a more complex elucidation provided by an Australian Egyptologist Vivianne G. Callender, the women represent a token of the diplomatic marriages of the king by which he attempted to diminish the independence of local nomarchs and to unify the country. Two more and much more important wives of Mentuhotep II were buried in two different locations within the complex. These were king's wiwes, queens Neferu and Tem. Some decorated sarcophagi of these queens are among the masterpieces displayed in the Egyptian Museum in Cairo.

The second phase, constructed approximately at a time shortly after the reunification of Egypt, witnessed a great enlargement of the eastern part of the complex to make this final resting place worthy of holding the burial of the king of the Two Lands. This phase is also marked by a divergence from the Eleventh Dynasty architectural tradition of *saff* tombs. The ritual interment of a royal statue changed the burial chamber under the Bab el-Hosan into a symbolic Osirid grave which was subsequently sealed. The entire courtyard was rebuilt and the complex was divided into two parts, east and west. The easternmost part, located immediately behind the entrance, was formed by a large open courtyard

Fig. 2.15 The central part of the tomb complex of Mentuhotep II at Deir el-Bahri

with a great stone ramp flanked by tamarisks and sycamores. The ramp ascended to an artificially constructed terrace on which the funerary temple itself stood. Its façade, decorated with pillars, was divided by the aforementioned ramp leading to the southern and northern parts.

The temple consisted of a large stone construction – a platform which led into an open court with an offering altar and a columned court with a rock-cut sanctuary attached to it from the west. On its northern, southern and eastern sides, the large rectangular platform was flanked by a double row of pillars and by three rows of octagonal columns; there were only two rows in the west. Atop of this platform there are the remains of another structure, but their nature is enigmatic: a pyramid could have stood in this place, symbolizing the power of the king, in accord with the tradition of the Old Kingdom pyramid builders. Other theories suggest that the top was formed in the shape of a primaeval hill where, according to ancient Egyptian mythology, new life was born after the floodwaters had receded in the time of the creation of the world. According to the most recent theory, a small hill was heaped on the top and planted with trees. This would be in accord with the tradition of the burial of Osiris. This view is, moreover, supported by the fact that immediately below this platform lay the above-mentioned older 'Osirid' tomb with the black statue of the king. The eastern part of the complex was, as the foundation deposits (objects ritually buried within the foundations of a building) indicate, dedicated to Montu-Ra.

The westernmost part of the complex contained the rock-cut cult chapel of the king. Its longer sides were each flanked by four octagonal columns. In the

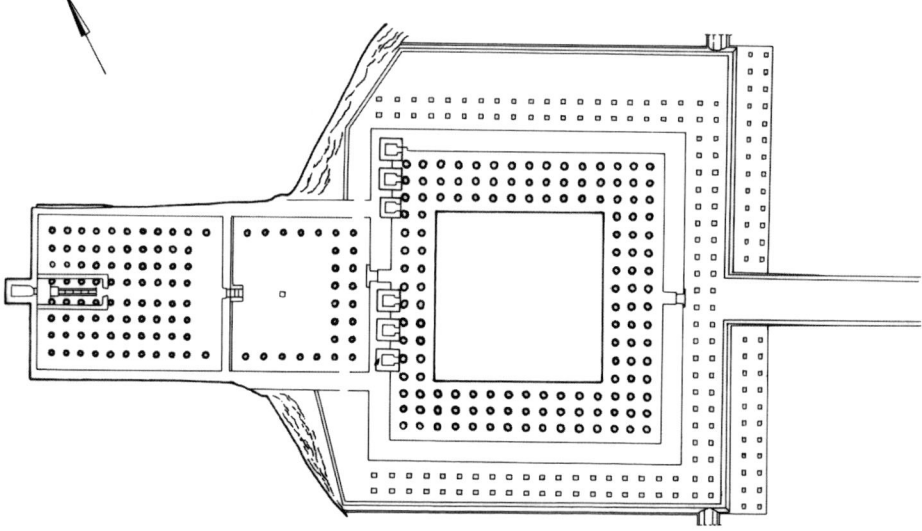

Fig. 2.16 *The simplified plan of the complex of Mentuhotep II at Deir el-Bahri (after Di. Arnold, Der Tempel des Königs Mentuhotep von Deir el-Bahari. Band I. Architektur und Deutung, Mainz 1974, pl. 27)*

middle of the chapel was an ascending ramp, divided into five steps, which led to the offering altar. The western wall of the chapel probably contained a niche with the so-called false door (this door, usually made of stone, imitated a true door in shape and symbolized a bridge between the world of the living and that of the dead, a gate through which the soul of the deceased king could return to this world). The false door enabled the soul of the deceased king to enter the chapel during the rites performed in his honour. A new entrance to the burial chamber was placed in an open court in front of the rock-cut chapel and, after 150 m, this corridor opened into the burial chamber. Just like the burial chamber itself, this corridor was panelled with granite blocks. Inside the burial chamber stood an alabaster sanctuary with the sarcophagus prepared for the burial of the king.

The complex of Mentuhotep II is the first to reflect a conceptual shift in the meaning of royal burial. Unlike circumstances in the Old Kingdom, when the ruler had been considered a god equal to the other deities of the Egyptian pantheon and when the cult in the royal pyramid complex had been directed exclusively toward the king, from now on certain Egyptian deities were worshipped in his temple together with him. In Deir el-Bahri they were mainly Montu and Amun-Ra, whose cultic images were annually taken from the Karnak temple and transported by the Egyptian priests to the western bank to visit the temples of kings. It is also worth mentioning that Middle Kingdom rulers are regularly depicted as subordinates to the gods. It is the gods who lend the rulers their power and their divine nature. In this way, the king's dependence on the will of

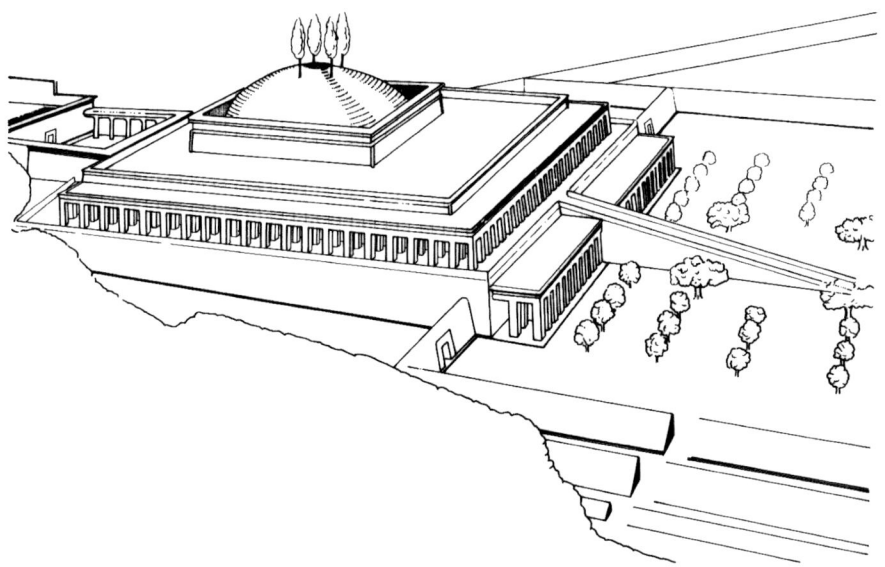

Fig. 2.17 One of several possible reconstructions of the Deir el-Bahri complex of Mentuhotep II (after R. Stadelmann, Die ägyptischen Pyramiden. Vom Ziegelbau zum Weltwunder, Mainz 1991, p. 232, fig. 74)

Fig. 2.18 Valley south of Deir el-Bahri, burial place of Mentuhotep III

the gods is emphasized, and his funerary complex becomes a meeting place of gods, whom the king merely represents on earth.

The successor of Mentuhotep II, Mentuhotep III Sankhkare, ruled for about 12 years and continued his father's policy. We have evidence of his expedition to Lebanon for cedar wood, which the Egyptians valued as their favourite material for the construction of boats and different architectural elements of buildings. In the eighth year of his reign, one of his officials, Henenu, undertook a long journey on behalf of the king: at the head of 3000 men, he crossed Wadi Gasus to the Red Sea coast and continued further to the south to Eritrea, the site of the land of Punt, which no Egyptian expedition reached since the Sixth Dynasty. Travelling through the long wadi, the expedition hollowed out 15 wells, each a one day's march (ca. 20 km) from the other, thus enabling regular traffic to move easily between the city of Coptos in the Nile Valley and the Red Sea coast. Henenu's men received regular rations in the form of 20 pieces of bread and two jugs of water a day. When they reached the Red Sea coast, Henenu ordered boats to be built. The boats, which were of the type used for expeditions to Syria-Palestine, were fully loaded and dispatched to Punt on a trading mission. After their arrival there, the Egyptians loaded on board a cargo of precious myrrh, and then set out on their return to Egypt. On his way home Henenu made a stop in Wadi Hammamat, where he supervised the extraction of several blocks of *bekhen* stone (grey-green schist) for the king's statues, and where he also left a long inscription which informs us of his expedition:

'(My lord) sent (me) to lead seafaring vessels to Punt, so that myrrh be brought to him from the chieftains ruling the Red land, out of the fear of him in the foreign lands. I set out from Coptos immediately, for the journey on which His Majesty had dispatched me and the Upper Egyptian army of the wabw military quarters of the Theban nome, from Imiotru to Sabet. All royal officials were gathered and followed me. Four police squads cleared the road in front of me, conquering everyone who revolted against the king. Hunters, the indigenous desert dwellers, were hired as guards and all royal counsellors were placed under my command to report the arrival of messengers to me, the sole commander whom millions obey.

When I set out with an army of 3000 men I made the road a river and the desert a field boundary, since I gave daily to each of them water skins and a haversack of bread with two djes-measures of water and twenty loaves of bread. Donkeys were laden with sandals, (so that) when a foot became naked, another (sandal) was ready.

I also hollowed twelve wells at the bottom of the valley and two in Idahet, one of which measured ten cubits and the other one thirty. I dug another well in Yaheteb, one that measured 10 x 10 cubits at all water levels. Then I reached the sea and built this fleet. When I had made for it a great sacrifice of cattle and goats, I loaded it with all things.

When I returned from the sea having fulfilled all that I had been commissioned to do by His Majesty, I brought to him all kinds of gifts that I had collected on the coast of the land of god. I came down from Wagu and Rahenu, bringing him precious blocks of stone for temple statues.'

(Wadi Hammamat, Inscription no. 114)

Fig. 2.19 Wadi Hammamat, one of the large stone quarries in the Eastern Desert of Egypt

Fig. 2.20 Assuan, possibly the place of origin of Amenemhat I

High above the western bank of Thebes, on a place known as Thoth's hill, Mentuhotep III built a temple dedicated to Montu-Ra. He began building his tomb a little to the south of the final resting place of his father. Recent research also indicates that he was buried in a rock tomb close by.

During his reign, he also made an effort to consolidate the situation in the eastern Delta and began to construct forts (the Walls of the Ruler) along its eastern border in order to protect it against Asiatic assaults. It is exactly this border that Sinuhe crossed during his hurried flight from Egypt to Syria-Palestine. Later tradition ascribed the initiation of the construction of this frontier fortification line to Kheti III, who was together with Mentuhotep III worshipped in the Delta city of Khatana (Qantir).

Mentuhotep IV was the sixth and last ruler of the Eleventh Dynasty. He is attested only through rock inscriptions in Wadi el-Hudi and Wadi Hammamat. We also know that in the second year of his reign, the vizier Amenemhat (in all probability, the later king, Amenemhat I) led 1000 men in an expedition to Wadi Hammamat, among other things, to fetch a sarcophagus for his lord. The reign of Mentuhotep IV marks the end of the Eleventh Dynasty. It was succeeded by the Twelfth, to the beginning of which Sinuhe's story has been dated.

Amenemhat I (1991–1962) was the founder of the Twelfth Dynasty, which lasted for 208 years. The fact that we are now faced with an entirely new tradition is evident already in his royal Horus name: 'he who repeats births'. Two literary accounts of the origin of Amenemhat I and of his ascent to the Egyptian throne have come down to us: the Prophecy of Neferti and the Instructions of King Amenemhat I. Both works were composed in order to justify his claim to the Egyptian throne. According to the Prophecy of Neferti, which calls him by his nickname Ameni, he came from the south and his mother was Nofret of Elephantine, his father the priest Senwosret. The Prophecy of Neferti is antedated to the time of king Sneferu. Neferti, who has been summoned to the royal court where he foretells the rise of the Twelfth Dynasty, describes Amenemhat's ascent to the Egyptian throne as follows:

'He will be a king who comes from the south,
Imeni, justified, will be his name.
The son of a woman from Ta-seti, born in the residence of Nekhen,
He will take the White crown,
He will seize the Red crown,
He will unite the Two Mighty ones,
He will reconcile Horus and Seth
With that which they desire.'
(The Prophecy of Neferti XIII a-e)

In the above passage, the white crown symbolizes Upper Egypt and the red crown symbolizes Lower Egypt. The unification of the Two Mighty ones – i.e. of the goddesses Nekhbet and Wadjet, who were the guardian deities of the Two

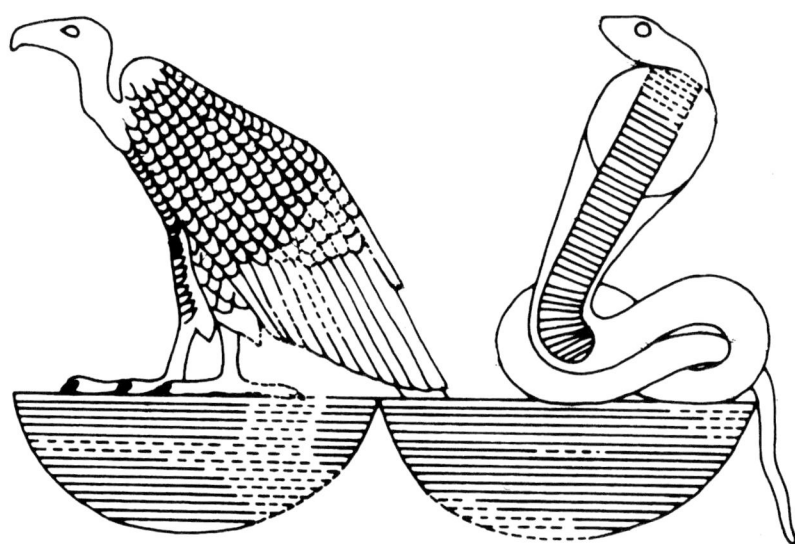

Fig. 2.21 The cobra goddess Wadjet and the vulture goddess Nekhbet, protective goddesses of Lower and Upper Egypt

Fig. 2.22 The rock inscription of Inyotefiker from the Czech concession in Lower Nubia

Lands – symbolizes the unification of Egypt. The same is true about the reconciliation of Horus and Seth. Amenemhat I was probably the very official who in the second year of the reign of Mentuhotep IV led the expedition to Wadi Hammamat. His ascent to the throne was not without complications, since he had to deal with other two claimants to the throne: a man named Inyotef and the Nubian, Segerseni. Shortly after his ascent to the throne, Amenemhat dispatched a military expedition against the latter. The expedition was led by the nomarch Khumhotep I of Beni Hassan. At this time Amenemhat I also undertook a punitive expedition to the eastern Delta, whence he expelled the nomads of Syria-Palestine, who had been using the Delta's rich pastures and water to sustain their herds. In the twenty-third and then again in the twenty-ninth year of his reign he turned his attention to the area south of the First Cataract, to Nubia. He extended his sphere of influence all the way south to the region of Korosko and the Second Cataract, where he built the Semna fortress. The name of Amenemhat I has also been recorded at Gerf Hussein and Toshka at Abu Simbel, in the mines which were founded by one of the most important rulers of the Old Kingdom and builder of the greatest pyramid on Egyptian territory, Khufu.

Undoubtedly, the campaigns against the Nubians were severe as shows one of the inscriptions found and documented by the Czech (then Czechoslovak) expedition led by Zbyněk Žába in El-Girgawi in Lower Nubia in the 1960s. The inscription probably dates to the 29th regnal year of Amenemhat I and attests to the fact that the expedition against the Nubians was led by his famous vizier Inyotefiker. From the inscription we know that Amenemhat I built a fortress nearby and subsequently ordered a preventive attack against the dangerous Nubians that might threaten the Egyptian garrison. The inscription reads as follows:

'Enyotefoqer [whose nickname is] Gem, said: I am a valiant man of vigour, a pleasant man from [the city called] She-in-front-of-her-Lord, [a scribe] excellent with [his] fingers, a humble one, yet great in affection of [His] Majesty, [distributing] clothes among his troops. I speak well in the midst of people and am a man enjoying respect among his friends.

One has been engaged in building this stronghold. Then the Nubians of the entire remaining part of Wowet were slaughtered. Thereupon I sailed victoriously upstream, slaughtering the Nubian on his river-bank(s) and then I sailed downstream plucking corn and cutting down their remaining trees. I (?) put fire into their houses, as one has to act against him who rebelled against the King (of Upper Egypt). Never did I hear (about) any other military man who accomplished the like (thereof).

Renoqer said: I have made (i.e. written) this when I have been with the hereditary noble, the prince, the overseer of the (pyramid) city, the Chief Justice, the Prime Minister, the overseer of the Six Great Mansions, Enyotefoqer, in the (ship called) Great Oar, which the King of Upper and Lower Egypt Shetepyebre – may he forever live for the benefit of the City! – brought (here).

The scribe Renoqer, born to Heqet, justified.'

(after Zb. Žába, The Rock Inscriptions of Lower Nubia. Czechoslovak concession, Prague 1974, pp. 99–100).

Fig. 2.23 The courtyard in front of the temple of Thutmosis III at Karnak, location of the ruined Middle Kingdom temple of Amun

Amenemhat I is also famous for having built all over the country (Khatana/Qantir, Bubastis, Heliopolis, Memphis, Abydos, Dendera, Tod, Thebes, Armant), as well as in the Sinai. As a man with traditionally Upper Egyptian roots, Amenemhat I was a great worshipper of the Theban god Amun, whose cult reached one of its peaks in popularity in the time of the Middle Kingdom. The greatest cultic centre of Amun was the Karnak temple. Despite this allegiance to Thebes, however, one of the most important decisions of Amenemhat I was the transfer of Egypt's capital back to the north of the country. This – as yet undiscovered – capital was called 'Amenemhat seized the Two Lands' and was founded on virgin soil at the Fayyum oasis, close to the site of Lisht. Amenemhat's decision to build a new city was stimulated mainly by the fact that from Thebes it was impossible to effectively manage the country which lay 800 km further to the north and whose relations with the Near East and above all with Syria-Palestine were of crucial importance.

It was in Lisht, too, that he built his pyramid complex, just like his son. Among his most important deeds of interior politics belongs the erection of stone stelae delimiting the borders of the individual nomes of the country. Amenemhat I also fought the Asiatic Bedouin with great vigour. The stele of the general Nesmontu from the twenty-fourth year of his reign provides us with valuable information about the fighting of Amenemhat I with these traditional enemies of Egypt (stele Louvre C1). Nesmontu's stele contains the following account:

1. 'Year [2]4, fourth month of the harvest season,
2. under the reign of His Majesty, the living Horus of repeated births, the Two Ladies: one of repeated births, the King of Upper and Lower Egypt, Sehetepibre,
3. son of Ra: Amenemhat, living forever like Ra, Horus, the living birth, the Two Ladies: Living birth, the King of Upper and Lower Egypt, Kheperkare, son of Ra:
4. Senwosret, living forever like Ra, his true servant, one loving their praise, doing all that they praise every day, one well provided, lord of provision.
5. King's confidant, noble and prince, chancellor of the King of Lower Egypt, commander of the army, Nesmontu, the commander, the eldest of the entrance portal, he who approaches the throne, the confidant of the royal palace,
6. whose counsel was important in the royal office, to whom the great ones came bowing and in front of whom princes prostrated themselves on their bellies. I was the only one (whom one called)
7. 'the Bull of Montu', one whom his lord praises every day. He subjugated the great ones of the royal palace to me in my presence for that which he had done to me and he let me accede to this office, because of my counsel
8. I was excellent in his heart. I was informed about the announcement concerning the laws of this country, since I was sharp in the heart of my lord. I was one strong of steps, excellent of counsel, one whose steps his lord praises.
9. The Theban troops loved me. I have never acted cruelly. The Great ones praised me, the Great ones bowed,

Fig. 2.24 Stele of general Nesmontu (Louvre, Paris)

10. the lowly came in a reverent posture. I was the pillar of the old, a wet-nurse of the child, an advocate of the poor,

11. [I provided] warm shelter for him who was cold in Thebes. [I was] a refuge of the hunted one. There is none equal to him in Upper Egypt,

12. the ruler of the Nine Bows. I was the only one (whom they called) 'The strongman of this land'. He whose arms are quick and whose legs stride, an excellent man

13 at arms. My troops were loyal to me when I was entrapped. In the morning the village gathered around me, I stood at the head of the squad and I conducted

14. the battle of the Two lands, which I won. My arms performed putting to ground, I destroyed the enemies, I killed the enemies of my Lord. I have no equal who could say (the same).

15. An offering which the king gives, and Osiris, lord of Busiris, and Khontamenti, great god, Lord of Abydos. The presented offering: bread and beer, cattle and fowl, a thousand of alabaster vessels, a thousand pieces of cloth, a thousand offerings, supplies...

16. from which the god lives, as part of the (income) of the wab-priest in the presence of Osiris, for the soul of the well-provided, the army commander, Nesmontu, justified, son of (the mother) Khemut, justified.

17. As for the inscription on this stela, it testifies to that

18. which has happened through my action. That which happened is what I have indeed done.

19. Nothing is boasting or lies.

20. I destroyed the tents of the Montji tribe who live

21. on the sand. I destroyed their tents.

22. I approached them as one approaches

23. the edge of the desert. I set out and travelled

24. its banks, no one equalled me in this,

25. following the command of Montu the victorious...'

Nesmontu's stele is a doubly valuable testimony. Firstly, it provides us with a typical picture of a high official's loyalty – loyalty which the ruler required from all his subjects. His account first describes how he was installed in his office in front of all other officials of the country and how they subsequently paid him due homage. At the same time he relates that he acted rightly and justly, supported the poor and helped those in need. The text also twice mentions that he fought the Bedouin, pulled down their tents and killed many of them. Although these allusions are quite brief in comparison with other texts, they do indicate that even the time of Amenemhat I witnessed major military expeditions against the Bedouin, and that they were so important that Nesmontu considered it necessary to include them in his biography. The final passages of this stela include Nesmontu's prayer to the major deities, Osiris and Khontamenti, to grant him an undisturbed afterlife existence. There is also an allusion to Nesmontu's precautions to perpetuate his funerary cult; namely that he hired one *wab*-priest for this purpose (*wab* means 'pure' in ancient Egyptian, and it signified the ritual purity of the priest, who could thus present offerings to the soul of the deceased).

Fig. 2.25 Serabit el-Khadim, temple of Hathor in Sinai

The reign of Amenemhat I witnessed a further expansion of the Egyptian sphere of influence in the Sinai. It is in the reign of this king that the small semi-rock-cut temple in Serabit el-Khadim, where the Egyptians mined turquoise, was founded. The temple was dedicated to Hathor, Lady of Turquoise, and to Sopdu, Lord of the Highlands. It appears that this expansion was, judging by the concomitant circumstances, peaceful. This is also supported by Sinuhe's account, which does not mention any Egyptian military activity in the area of Syria–Palestine. Further, and this is also very important and noteworthy, we know of no traditional depiction from the Sinai of the King crushing the heads of his enemies with a mace that would date from the time of the Twelfth Dynasty. This very same scene, however, was very frequent in preceding times, i.e. in the Old Kingdom and in the Eleventh Dynasty.

According to the story of Sinuhe, Amenemhat I was assassinated. This event is the central theme for the *Instructions of Amenemhat I to his son*. After the king had dined and rested for an hour, he lay down to sleep. When he was later awakened by noise, he saw his guards fighting amongst themselves. He tried to take up his own weapons, only to become the helpless victim of his assailants. Thus, he died before he even had the chance to install his son Senwosret I to the throne:

'It was after supper, when night came,
I spent a pleasant hour,
I was lying on my bed,
I was tired.

My heart began to take the course of sleep,
and the weapons [of my guards] begun to go round to protect me.
I was like a desert snake.
I awoke in order to fight.
I stirred, and found that the elite guards were in combat.
Had I really taken up my arms,
I would have chased the coward back to his hole.
But there is no courage at night, one does not fight.
There is no victory without aides, and I was left alone.
Look, this assassination happened while I was without you.
The courtiers had not heard that I would hand over (the reign) to you,
before I was seated on the throne with you.'
(The Instructions of Amenemhat I to his son, VIa–VIIIc)

After his violent death, Amenemhat I was succeeded by his son Senwosret I (1971 – 1926), who ruled for almost 45 years. He devoted most of his power to the consolidation of state administration, and his foreign expeditions were few. Sinuhe's account relates that at the time of his father's violent death, Senwosret I was on a military campaign against the Libyan Bedouin Tjemehu and Tjehenu from the Western desert. In the first year of his reign he probably waged a campaign in Nubia and three years later, another one to Palestine. Envoys of the Egyptian ruler streamed into the entire region to the northwest of Egypt, while numerous trade caravans were headed mostly for the Mediterranean coast. A necklace from Ugarit bearing the name of Senwosret I also testifies to his rather

Fig. 2.26 The Osirid statue of Senwosret I from Lisht (Egyptian Museum, Cairo)

Fig. 2.27 The White Chapel of Senwosret I at Karnak (Open Air Museum, Luxor)

peaceful relations with this area. The king devoted much more of his effort to mining expeditions, since he needed quality building stone for his numerous construction projects throughout the country; he dispatched three expeditions to Wadi Hammamat for the *bekhen* stone, six to the amethyst mines in Wadi el-Hudi, two to the alabaster mines at Hatnub, still other ones to the Sinai – (Serabit el-Khadim), etc. In the thirty-eighth year of his reign he dispatched an expedition of 17 000 men to the mines in Wadi Hammamat to fetch stone for 60 sphinxes and 150 statues.

Senwosret I is renowned for his numerous construction projects. One of his most significant buildings is the temple of Ra-Atum in the famous city of Heliopolis, a place where legend says the Holy Family much later dwelt during their flight to Egypt. During the reign of Ptolemy VI (after 168 BC) the High Priest of the temple of Jerusalem, Onias, also lived here. Senwosret I had this temple built in the third year of his reign. In his thirtieth year, on the occasion of the first *sed* Festival (during which he had to ritually prove that he still possessed enough physical strength to rule his people), he set up two obelisks in front of the temple's pylon; one of these obelisks may still be seen on the site, though all traces of other buildings in this place have vanished. He also erected a huge pillar in Abgig in the Fayyum, thus proving the growing interest of the Twelfth Dynasty rulers in this fertile area. Undoubtedly the most beautiful architectural achievements of his reign were built in Karnak, the place of worship of the god Amun-Ra. One of the most important of these is the so-called White Chapel built in the 30th year of his reign at the occasion of his *sed* Festival.

Fig. 2.28 Senwosret I venerating the god Amun, White Chapel (Open Air Museum, Luxor, detail)

Its walls were decorated with figures of Amun and inscriptions describing the individual nomes (counties) of Upper and Lower Egypt. The chapel was accessed from two sides via low ramps leading to a stone base which originally held the sacred barque of Amun. This boat contained the cultic image of Amun and during festivals was carried by priests in a festive procession. Just like his father, Senwosret I built his funerary complex in Lisht.

The pyramids of these two rulers are located approximately 40 km south of Saqqara, one of the main cemeteries of the kings of the Old Kingdom and First Intermediate Period. Amenemhat I chose the northern part of the cemetery as his final resting place. His pyramid complex was built in the tradition of the Old Kingdom pyramid builders, although it also incorporated several Upper Egyptian traits, such as the open ascending causeway and the vertical shaft hidden within the pyramid, which led to the burial chamber. Moreover, to the west of the pyramid, his complex included tombs of the members of his family, just as in the case of the tomb of Mentuhotep II in Deir el-Bahri. He constructed his pyramid complex on two terraces, the temple to the east on a lower level and the pyramid to the west at a higher level. The base of the pyramid was relatively small, corresponding approximately to Sixth Dynasty pyramids (side length 80 m), and the pyramid itself was constructed mainly out of re-used material from older buildings, such as the valley temples and ascending causeways of the Saqqara and Giza pyramid complexes. It is interesting to note that a large proportion of the blocks came from the pyramid complex of Khufu, of which now only the base platform remains. Its destruction must have begun at least in the beginning of the Middle Kingdom. On the northern side of the pyramid, the cultic north chapel was preserved, while only the sad ruins of the temple, which was reconstructed in the time of Senwosret I, remain on its eastern side. Even the tiny remains of relief decoration indicate that its authors copied the achievements of their Old Kingdom predecessors with great precision. In the western part of the temple, at the foot of the pyramid, they placed the limestone false door though which the ruler's soul entered the chapel to take part in religious ceremonies. In front of it was an altar of red granite. The burial chamber was approached by a descending corridor leading from the north, from the level of the base of the pyramid. The corridor was panelled with red granite and opened into the vestibule, in the floor of which was a shaft leading into the burial chamber. The burial chamber lies exactly in the centre of the mass of the pyramid and is now flooded by ground water. In the southeastern corner of the complex stood the mastaba of vizier Inyotefiker and in the west there are the shaft tombs of the princesses and queens of the king's court.

The pyramid of Senwosret I, located to the south of the first pyramid, was constructed on a slightly larger scale (side length 100 m), and constitutes an even more accurate copy of the Old Kingdom complexes. The ascending causeway, which connected the valley temple with the funerary temple, was roofed. The pyramid temple had two parts, outer and inner. The latter was dominated

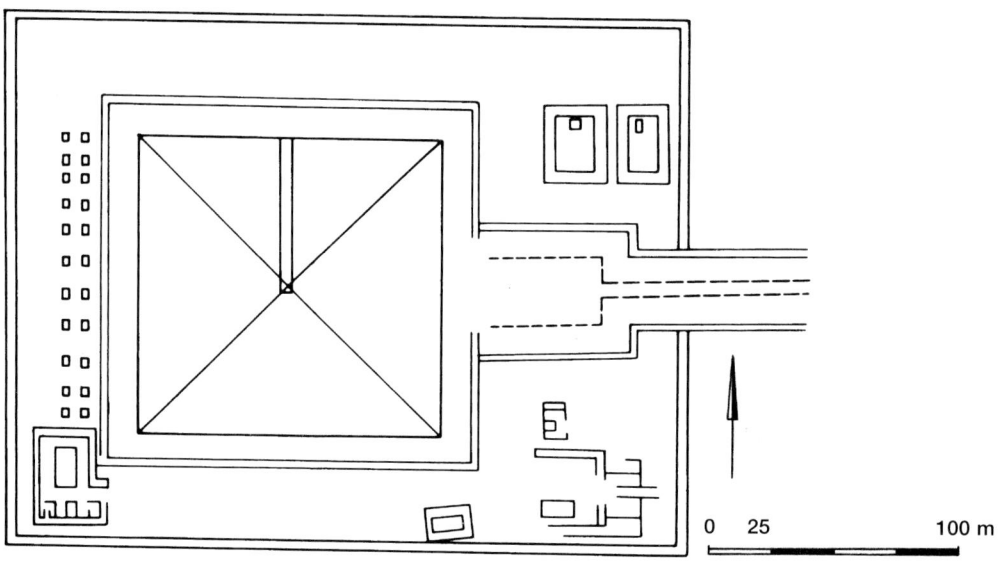

Fig. 2.29 Groundplan of the pyramid complex of Amenemhat I at Lisht (after R. Stadelmann, Die ägyptischen Pyramiden. Vom Ziegelbau zum Weltwunder, Mainz 1991, p. 233, fig. 75)

Fig. 2.30 Mortuary temple of Senwosret I at Lisht

by a great pillared court with an offering altar and a group of ten seated statues of the king. These statues were not found *in situ*, but in a drainage shaft in the northern part of the complex, and are now kept in the Egyptian Museum in Cairo. The eastern and western sections of the temple were separated from one another by the transverse corridor which the Egyptian sources call *areret*. A small flight of steps led further west, to the room with five niches – a room that with all probability contained royal statues. This room gave way to a vestibule with its roof supported by one column with a papyriform capital. The cultic chapel itself contained the false door in its western wall. In front of the false door was an altar of red granite. The ceiling of the chapel was vaulted. To the north and south of this room were two groups of rooms, which served as storerooms of cultic equipment, stone and metal vessels, pottery and other commodities intended as offerings for the spirit of the deceased ruler. To the north of the pyramid was the north chapel. In the floor of the court of this building was the entrance of the descending corridor which led into the king's burial chamber.

The entire pyramid complex was enclosed within two boundary walls, the outer and the inner one. Between them stood altogether nine small pyramid complexes of the queens and princesses of Senwosret I's family. Until now, only two were ascribed to historical personalities: the queens Nofret and Itakaiet. Nofret was a daughter of Amenemhat I and the wife of Senwosret I. From the east and northeast, the pyramid complex was flanked by several mastabas of the officials of his court – Imhotep, Sesenebenef, Nakht and above all

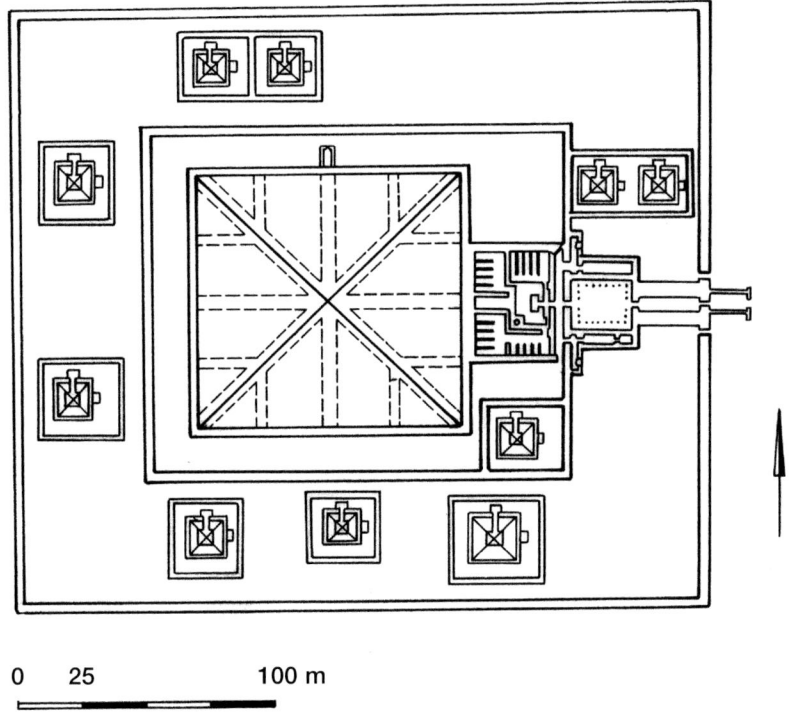

Fig. 2.31 Ground plan of the pyramid complex of Senwosret I at Lisht (after R. Stadelmann, Die ägyptischen Pyramiden. Vom Ziegelbau zum Weltwunder, Mainz 1991, p. 235, fig. 76)

Senwosretankh, whose tomb was decorated with passages from the Old Kingdom Pyramid Texts. If Sinuhe were a historical personality, his tomb would have been located somewhere in this area.

After his death, Senwosret I was succeeded by his son Amenemhat II (1929–1892), who had been his co-regent in the last three years of his reign. Just like his successor Senwosret II, Amenemhat II conducted only sporadic military campaigns outside Egyptian territory and directed his effort mainly to the consolidation of his realm. For example in Nubia where, in addition to gold, turquoise was also mined, he rebuilt and refortified the Aniba fort. Numerous traces of evidence for the presence of Amenemhat II or his contemporaries were discovered throughout Syria-Palestine. For example, a statue of his daughter and of an official named Senwosretankh were found in Ugarit. Furthermore, an unique discovery comes from Upper Egypt – the treasure from the temple of Tod (a religious centre close to Thebes). It contained gold, silver and coarse-grained lapis lazuli (10 ingots of gold and 13 of silver, lumps of lapis lazuli), as well as various objects: 150 metal beakers and 25 metal chains, amulets, beads and over 50 stone cylinder seals). Most of the beakers were crumpled and deformed by hammer blows; the cylinder seals, some of which bore cuneiform inscriptions,

Fig. 2.32a, b The site and the treasure of Tod (Louvre, Paris)

were mostly broken. Most of these objects were valuable and were included in the treasure because of the material from which they were fashioned. The beakers and silver pendants were either of Cretan origin, or perhaps were imitations of Cretan models, made in Syria-Palestine.

A unique historical inscription was written in the beginning of the independent reign of Amenemhat II. It was published only recently, and gives us detailed information about the expedition to the area of Syria-Palestine during his reign. The inscription is a part of the annals of Amenemhat II, and it was discovered in the temple of Ptah in Memphis, on the territory of the capital of Old Kingdom Egypt. The hieroglyphic text was carved on a block of red granite of which two parts, 188 × 250 cm and 125 × 137 cm large, have been preserved till the present. The extant text is written in vertical columns following one another from right to left. Its individual sections describe the foundations of Amenemhat II for his father Senwosret I, and include accounts of expeditions beyond the frontier of Egypt and of their returns, precise lists of commodities brought and their quantity, as well as a list of donations for different temples, chapels and festivals of gods throughout Egypt.

We will not be concerned with the entire text, but only with the passages that describe Egyptian expeditions to the area of Syria-Palestine and to the Sinai. The importance of the details they give lies mainly in the fact that they provide us with an answer to the question of what was imported from these regions and in which quantity. This data then shed fundamental light on the question of Egyptian interests in Syria-Palestine. The following excerpts are based on the publication of the German and Egyptian Egyptologists Hartwig Altenmüller and Mohammad Moussa. The letter C denotes a new column in the original text of the annals.

Excerpt 1 – The expedition to Lebanon and Asia
C7 – *'Dispatching an army to Lebanon'*
C8 – *'[Recruitment of troops...] from the cities with the exception of all places under labour duty involving the taxes for the king and which are recorded (in the archives) of the pyramid city "Amenemhet is mighty".'*
C8 – *'Dispatching of troops with the overseer of the combat unit of the army to crush Asia (štt) and the foreign country Jw^c.'*

The first excerpt illustrates mainly the mechanism of assembling an expedition to be dispatched abroad. Although such expeditions were called *mš^c*, army, troops formed only their part, albeit an important one. The expedition also included artisans, who worked on tasks such as stone-mining, wood-cutting, etc., scribes, who kept detailed lists of booty and work activities; priests, who took care that the expedition was looked upon with favour by the Egyptian deities. The dispatching of an expedition to Lebanon is mentioned again in C18 – C21, lines which record the return of the expedition and provide us with a detailed account of the booty it brought back. The return of the expedition is described in columns C16–18 and the other relevant columns, C25–26, describe the rewarding of its participants.

Excerpt 2 – Bringing tribute from Asia
C12 – *'Coming of the children of the princes of Asia, their heads bowed. They are bringing:*
silver: 220 deben
gold: ...'
C13 – *'Bovine and ovine cattle, total: 56 units of cattle,*
Asiatics (captives): 1002
lead: 6 deben,
white lead: 55 deben.'
(*Note: 1 deben = 13.6 g)

This type of text is uncommon, since it describes the voluntary tribute of the princes of Syria-Palestine. Egyptian political thought often mentioned the transfer of princes with the purpose of educating these royal children at the court of the king, and thus to guarantee the loyalty of the princes governing the subdued territories. It may also be the case that the princes were sending their children instead of themselves, in order to avoid their own forced stay in Egypt. It is in this regard that we have to consider the quantity of the commodities sent to the king by these princes: less than 3 kg of silver, a certain amount of gold, cattle, over a thousand captives who were probably taken from the Bedouin, and

Fig. 2.33 The Annals of Amenemhat II at Memphis – large stone next to the statue base

a small amount of lead and white lead. H. Altenmüller and M. Moussa correctly stress that the quantity of the commodities brought as tribute to the Egyptian court is rather symbolic and that it ought to express the loyalty of the subdued princes. Only the relatively high number of captives given to the king is somewhat striking.

Excerpt 3: The return of the expedition from the Sinai
C13 – *'The return of the army which had been dispatched to the Terrace of Turquoise, bringing:*
turquoise: 14 + 13/32 hekat and 1 part,
the ḫt-ʿw3 mineral: 8700 deben
the bj3-kjs mineral: 5570 deben,'
C14 – *'the ... mineral: 6 hekat,*
a special kind of alum: 26 + 13/16 hekat,
natron: 10 + 9/16 hekat.
starfish: 8,
aromatic substance sš3jt: 41 sacks,
silver: 9 + 3/4 deben,
cattle: 10,
young ibex: 3,
cheetah skin.'
(*Note: 1 hekat = 4.8 l; 1 sack = 48 l)

There was only one reason for the Egyptian expedition to the Sinai: stone mining for the needs of the king and of the Egyptian state. The term 'Terrace of Turquoise' which occurs in the text denotes Serabit el-Khadim, where mainly turquoise was mined, but also the ore called *ḫt-ʿw3*, probably copper ore, and the *bj3-kjs* ore. Besides these items, small quantities of other products were brought, which may have entered the expedition's possessions merely by chance or by a non-systematic search, such as the starfish from the sea or the ibex, the typical inhabitants of the mountainous regions of the Sinai and the Eastern desert.

Excerpt 4: The return of the army from Asia
C16 – *'[The return of the army and of the] combat squad which were dispatched to destroy the fortress Jw3j and to damage the fortress J3sjj. The number of captives who were brought from these two foreign lands:*
Asiatics: 1554,
bronze and wood:
axes: 10,
sickles: 33,
daggers: 12,
saws: 4 and 1/4,
knives: 79,

wedge: 1,
razors: 4,
C17 – ...
spears: 2,
swords (?): 45,
spears: 6,
w3g – bowls: 3,
six – wheels: 60
pieces of copper: 646 deben,
new copper: 125 deben,
bronze and wood: spear blades with triangular point: 30,
spear blades with elliptical point: 26,
blade: 1,
bracelets: 3,
head and ear jewellery: 38,
wood and silver: staff with a decorated handle: 8'
C18 – *'amethyst: 58 deben,*
ḥsbḏ: 1 and 1/4 deben,
malachite: 1734 deben,
ivory tablets: 4,
wood: home equipment of the Asiatics: 54 pieces,
litter: 1,
combs: 13,
chariot axes: 8,
lead: 375 deben.'

This passage, which comes from a military expedition against two cities, represents one of the most detailed contemporary lists of war booty. It was undoubtedly a straightforward military action with a definite military objective. Its results include, apart from the destruction of both cities, the capturing of 1554 Asiatics who were subsequently in part deployed to work on the numerous construction projects of Amenemhat II and in part given out as slaves to various officials and dignitaries as reward. Since the context indicates that the expedition could not have lasted more than four months, it is most likely that both cities must have been situated somewhere north of the Egyptian frontier, perhaps in the area of Southern Palestine, where the Egyptians traditionally directed their interest. Apart from captives, the booty also included bronze and wooden weapons and various household items from the two cities, and even parts of chariots.

Excerpt 5: List of the commodities brought by the expedition to Lebanon
C18 – *'The return of the army which has been dispatched to Lebanon in two ships. It is bringing:*
silver: 1676 and 1/2 deben,
C19 – *bronze: 48 882 deben,*

copper: 15 961 deben,
white lead: 1410 deben,
marble: 13 blocks,
abrasive sand: 16 588 deben,
polishing sand: 39 556 deben ... '

C21 – '...*Asiatics – men and women: 65...*'

This passage, too, describes the return of an expedition, this time from Lebanon. Its most interesting part is the detailed list of the obtained raw materials (not all of which are mentioned in this translation), mostly stone, oils of various kinds of trees, wood, gold and silver. It finally also lists captives taken probably from the nomadic tribes of the area. Captives were a favourite booty in the military expeditions to Asia. Once brought to Egypt (apart from military expeditions, slaves were also acquired by trade), they could become either the property of the king or they became private property, which could even be inherited. According to papyrus Brooklyn 35.1446, the household of one higher official owned 95 slaves. The nationality of 68 of them could be determined – 33 were Egyptians and 45 Asiatics. The Asiatics were mostly women, who often worked as cloth-weavers. Asiatics were also employed as workforce in breweries and as cooks. Some of them also worked in the funerary complexes of the Twelfth Dynasty kings. On the other hand, the typically Egyptian jobs – agriculture, horticulture, sandal making, hairdressing and barbering were reserved to Egyptian serfs. It is also likely that Asiatics were employed as mercenaries in the army.

Excerpt 6: Rewarding of soldiers and officials for their services (during the military expedition to Asia)
C25 – '*Distributing rewards (consisting) of servants, fields, gold, clothes and all very beautiful things to:*
– the overseer of the combat squad,
– the commander of troops,
– troops,
who returned after they had trampled down the fortresses of Jw3j and J3sjj and who supplied (the workforce) of captives for the pyramid city 'Amenemhat is mighty';
C26 – *from the cities of these two foreign countries, and who had eaten Asiatic food of the captives:*
– for the royal children,
– for the noble royal officials
– for the commander of the palace and of the fowlers of the king.'

This passage completes the above-mentioned excerpt concerning the expedition of the Egyptian army against two fortified cities in Syria-Palestine. It tells us that the ruler himself rewarded almost all members of the expedition, including the members of his family, nobles, and even the commander of the royal palace. It is highly likely that this took the form of distributing shares from the booty of the expedition, the most important part of which was Asiatic captives.

Amenemhat II was a great organizer. Although he did not gain fame in military expeditions, he tried to consolidate the provinces occupied by his ancestors. He did not concentrate his activity only in the area of Syria-Palestine, his interests were also directed to the desert oases west of Egypt. In those days, the oases were probably managed from the 19th nome of Upper Egypt, which was called 'the (cult) place of the god Igai'. The interest of Amenemhat II was directed to the legendary African land of Punt, which must have been located somewhere in the area of today's Eritrea. Two stelae from the 28th year of Amenemhat II, describing the return of expeditions form the land of Punt, were preserved and found in the ancient Egyptian port of Savu, today's Wadi Gawasis, on the eastern coast of the Red Sea.

Amenemhat II was buried at Dahshur, in the so-called 'White pyramid'. This pyramid owes its name mainly to the disintegrated blocks of white limestone in the region, that are today the only evidence that once such an important building stood here. It now requires some effort on the part of visitors to find the place where it once stood. Even on the very site of the pyramid, it is difficult to believe that it was here that a king from the royal annals of Memphis and the organizer of so many expeditions lived his eternal life, so badly has the monument been destroyed.

The entrance to the pyramid was in the north, through a descending corridor leading to the centre. The last, horizontal, part of this corridor opened into the

Fig. 2.34 The White Pyramid of Amenemhat II at Dahshur

east-west oriented burial chamber. Along the western wall of the burial chamber stood the north-south oriented granite sarcophagus. The burial equipment that must once have filled the chamber was long lost to ancient tomb robbers: such also was the destiny of the king's funerary temple, which adjoins the eastern side of the pyramid.

The historically most interesting archaeological discoveries were made to the west of the pyramid. This part of the pyramid complex contained the tombs of the royal family of Amenemhat II – of Prince Amenemhat and of the princesses It, Khnumit, Itaweret and Sithathoriunet. Apart from the common funerary equipment, such as the wooden coffin, the alabaster ointment vessels, and canopic jars (containers of the mummified viscera of the deceased) etc., the tombs of It and Khnumit contained beautiful jewellery which even today is one of the highlights of the Egyptian Museum in Cairo.

Senwosret II (1897–1878) was probably the first ruler to direct his attention strongly to the area of the Fayyum Oasis. He reigned for about fourteen years, but during the last five years of his father Amenemhat II, he took part in the management of the country as a co-regent. No expeditions that could be regarded as military campaigns are attested from his reign. His work was concentrated rather on organizing expeditions for the mining of mineral resources in the areas belonging to the sphere of Egyptian influence. During his reign, expeditions were undertaken to the mines in Wadi Gawasis, to Wadi Hudi, to the Sinai, to Wadi Hammamat and to the diorite mines in Toshka. The king's prime interest in guaranteeing security at the junctions of these roads is attested, among other things, by the fact that he built a fortress at Mirgissa as well as a protective wall along the boat journey leading through the First Cataract, south of today's Assuan. Among the most important activities in his internal policy were waste irrigation works carried out in the area of Fayyum. The central point of this oasis was the lake which was later called Moeris, although today it is known as *Birket Karun* among the local inhabitants. This lake was fed by the Nile canal called the Bahr Yussuf, 'Joseph's River'. By lowering the inflow of water into the lake through minor canals, Senwosret II gained many thousands hectares of new arable land. In order to separate it from the lake, he built a great embankment, which was designed to protect the land from floods. With the help of this new irrigation scheme more arable land could be irrigated and cultivated.

This was probably one of the decisive factors that detemined the location of his pyramid in the Fayyum Oasis, which later increasingly became the focus of interest for the Middle Kingdom rulers. It was built close to the contemporary village of Illahun. The excavation of this pyramid was originally hampered by the fact that Senwosret II decided to enhance the security of his final resting place by completely changing the layout of its infrastructure. This was supposed to hinder the access of robbers into the pyramid's underground rooms. Thus, the entrance to the pyramid was located not at its northern side, as had hitherto been the habit, but to the south, some distance from the southern temenos wall. The pyramid core itself was built around a protrusion of a rocky massif that jutted up from

Fig. 2.35 Drawing of the original appearance of the burial chamber of princess It in Dahshur as discovered by Jacques de Morgan. Together with the wooden coffin containing the burial, numerous items of burial equipment were discovered here (after Jacques de Morgan, Fouilles à Dahchour en 1894, p. 46, fig. 105)

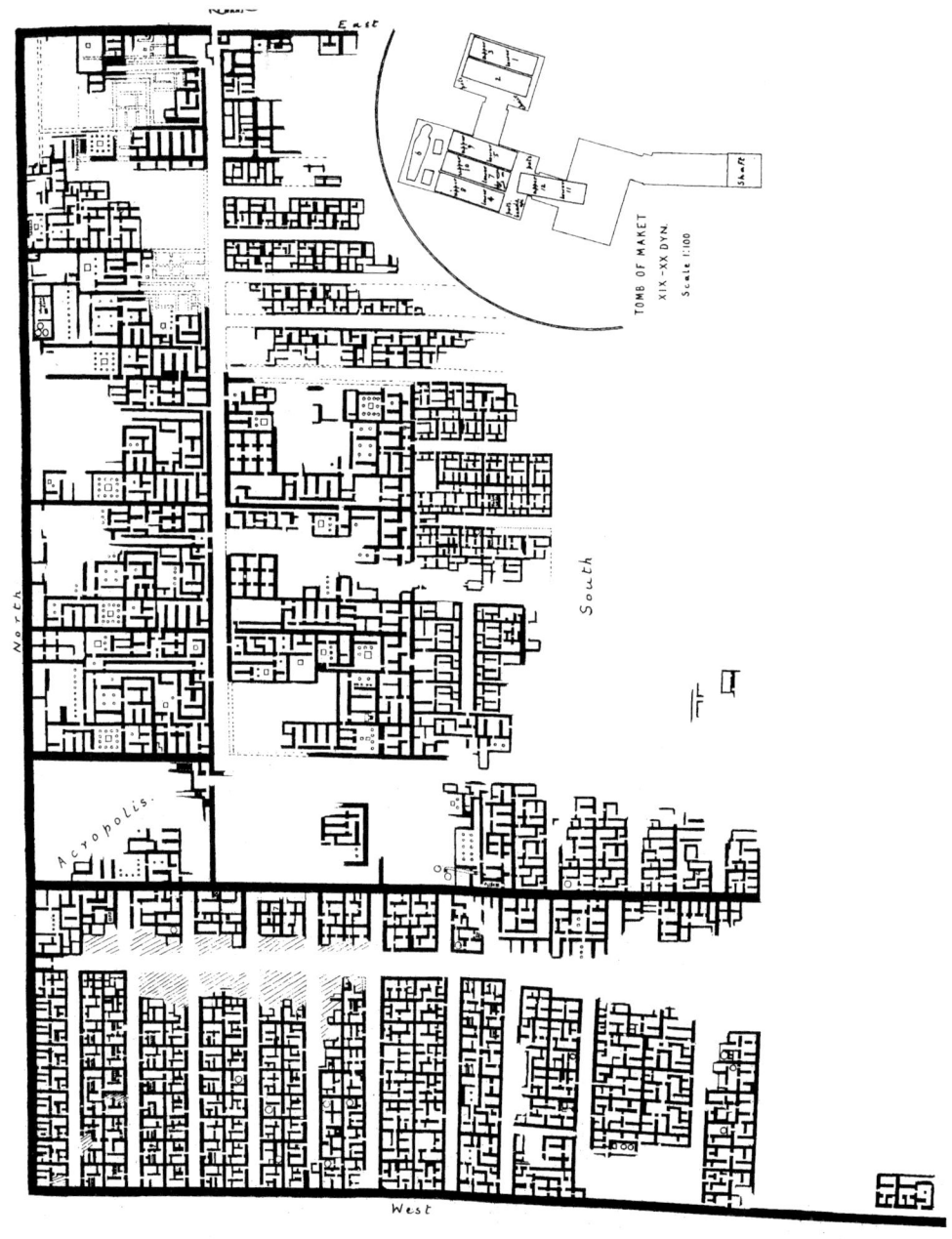

Fig. 2.36 The town of Kahun as excavated by W. M. F. Petrie (after W. M. F. Petrie, Illahun, Kahun and Gurob, London 1891, pl. 14)

the desert floor. It was further reinforced by limestone buttress walls that radiated out from the centre. The spaces that were thus created between these limestone walls were then filled in with mud bricks. To further enhance the monument's stability, a ditch was dug around its four sides and filled with sand. This ditch formed a drainage system which would draw the destructive rainwater away from the walls of the pyramid. Rainwater was considered one of the manifestations of Seth, the god of chaos and evil forces, and this had to be neutralized in the royal complex.

As was already indicated above, the entrance to the substructure lay outside the pyramid at its southern wall. The substructure was entered through a shaft, which, after leading 16 metres under the ground, gave way to a horizontal passage opening to a vaulted hall. The corridor then passes another two rooms and finally turns west to the burial chamber, which was not located exactly in the centre of the pyramid, but under its southwestern part. The entire burial chamber, including the sarcophagus, was constructed of red granite. To the south of the burial chamber remains of the funerary equipment (including a golden uraeus – a cobra, symbolic protectress of the king) were found by the eminent English archaeologist William Matthew Flinders Petrie. The burial chamber was encircled by a corridor, and so in itself symbolized the idea of the primeval hill entwined by the primeval waters of the demiurge god, Nun.

The entire pyramid complex was enclosed by a wall, and a small cultic chapel adjoined the eastern face of the pyramid. Mastaba cenotaphs (false tombs) associated with members of the royal family lay to the north of the pyramid. These

Fig. 2.37 *The pyramid of Senwosret II at Illahun*

Fig. 2.38 The pyramid of Senwosret II at Illahun, detail of the masonry construction

structures (they were eight in number) were modelled out of bedrock and cased with mud bricks. The small pyramid of the queen was built to the east. The greatest modern discovery was, however, made to the southeast of the pyramid, in the tomb of Princess Sithathoriunet, and consisted of objects from her burial equipment. Among them were golden necklaces and bracelets, rings and scarabs, a silver mirror, golden pectorals inlaid with semi-precious stones, stone canopic jars etc. Today, the 'Illahun Treasure' may be seen in the Egyptian Museum in Cairo.

The valley temple of the complex was situated relatively far to the east of the pyramid. To its northeast, a town was built for the craftsmen who worked on the royal pyramid complex. Later, the town was inhabited by the priests who were employed in the funerary cult of the king. This town was known as Lahun, but Petrie erroneously called it *Kahun*. Originally, however, it was called 'Senwosret is satisfied'. It was built exclusively of mud bricks and enclosed within a massive wall. Inside, the individual houses were built according to a unified plan, and a wall divided the area into two unequal parts. The larger, easternmost part, contained great houses and palaces of the high officials who lived in this town, while crammed into the western, substantially smaller section, were the crowded dwellings of unimportant officials and common workers. It may be estimated that several hundred houses could accommodate up to five thousand inhabitants at a time. The importance of this town was enhanced by the discovery of a papyrus archive, which yielded not only extremely valuable information about the life in this town and the royal cult, but also contained numerous literary, astronomical, medical and religious texts.

Senwosret II was succeeded by Senwosret III (1878–1841), probably one of the most famous Middle Kingdom rulers, who is even mentioned in Herodotus' account. The length of his reign is uncertain, but most estimates hover around nineteen years. From the seventh year of his reign comes the first record concerning the rising of Sirius, which plays such an important role in establishing the absolute chronology of ancient Egypt.

In his foreign policy, Senwosret III concentrated primarily on the region of Nubia, which was, aside from other exotic goods, an important source of gold and valuable skins of wild animals. His interest in Nubia is indicated by at least four expeditions he made to this area, during which he reached the Second Cataract and consolidated Egyptian dominion in this region. This is also probably the reason why in New Kingdom times he was considered the patron of Nubia. An inscription preserved on the island of Sehel at Assuan mentions that this king had a canal dug through the First Cataract, with the aim of facilitating ship transport south to Nubia and back. This canal was purportedly 75 m long, 10 m wide and 7.5 m deep. A similar canal may have existed here already in the time of the Sixth Dynasty, built originally by the official Weni, who worked for King Merenre. It was supposedly constructed mainly in order to enable fast transport of troops south to Nubia, where the Egyptian stronghold around the Second Cataract was at times under threat. In order to avert this danger, Senwosret III undertook several campaigns to the south. He built – or, in some cases, rebuilt – altogether eight fortresses to protect Egyptian interests in Nubia, with the aim of maintaining his dominion in the area. Among the most impor-

Fig. 2.39 Sehel island at the First Nile Cataract

tant of these were the forts of Semna, Kumma and Uronarti. Just like his predecessor, Senwosret III gained fame as an organizer of expeditions to stone mines. We also possess evidence of his expeditions to Wadi el Hudi, Wadi Hammamat, Hatnub and to the Sinai.

One of the most important achievements of Senwosret III was his reform of the entire administrative apparatus of the country. The main change was his creation of a centralized administration of the country, so that all nomes were managed by the three offices of the residence. These offices were called *waret*, and the individual ones were: 'waret of the north', 'waret of the south', and 'waret of the head of the south'. Each was headed by the first and second governor, who was also chairman of the council of officials of every waret (the so-called *djadjat*). Scribes were at the disposal of the officials. The entire country was managed by the king's deputy, the vizier. The most important duties of these three departments included the surveillance of affairs in the provinces, the assessment of taxes (according to annual flood measurements) and their collection, the surveillance of royal construction projects, the organization of royal expeditions and the control of the workforce.

Another far-reaching change that happened during the reign of Senwosret III was the implementation of measures to redirect the power and position of strong provincial leaders, the nomarchs. The seminal study of a German Egyptologist

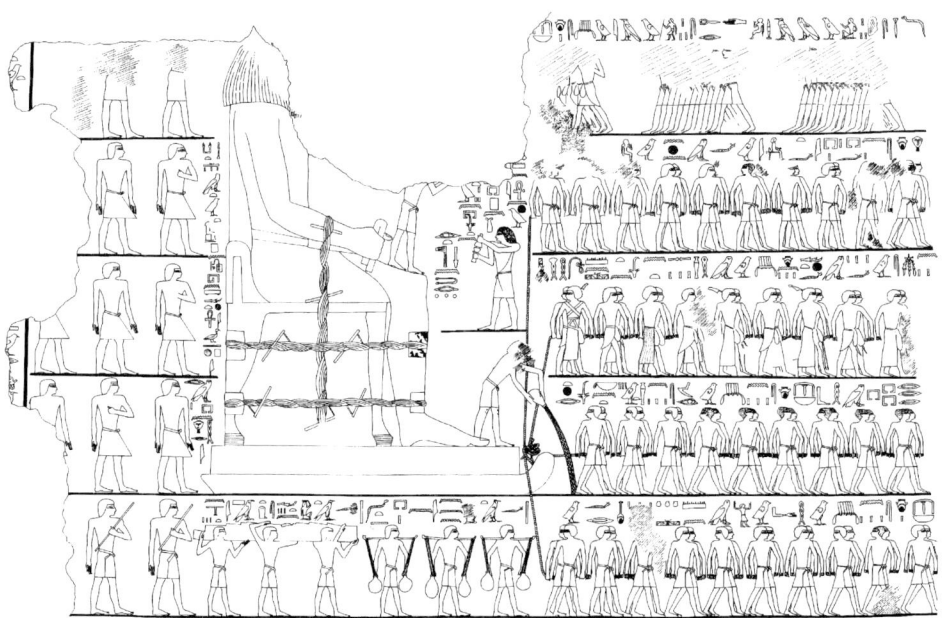

Fig. 2.40 Token of wealth and power – dragging a colossal statue of the nomarch Djehutihotep, from his tomb in el-Bersha (after P. E. Newberry, El Bersheh. Part I. The tomb of Tetuti Hetep, London, pl. 15)

Detlef Franke has shown that Senwosret III was the king who appointed high provincial officials with important state duties that they executed in the residence of the ruler. In fact, already his father took children of the nomarchs to grow up and to be schooled in the residence, thus having them under control and, equally importantly, winning their loyalty. The implementation of this policy caused provincial cemeteries with their rich tombs to come to an abrupt end. Primarily affected were the nomarchs of the Oryx and Hare nomes, who consolidated their positions during the reigns of his predecessors – mainly thanks to their contribution to the victory of the Theban rulers at the end of the Eleventh Dynasty. Their largely independent position and considerable wealth are indicated mainly by their splendid tombs in Beni Hassan and el-Bersha. The power of these nomarchs is also illustrated by the famous scene from the tomb of Djehutihotep from el-Bersha, which depicts the transport of his colossal alabaster statue from the Hatnub mines. We know of only a single military campaign to Asia from the time of Senwosret III, which is described in the bibliography of Khusebek. This inscription is engraved on a stele that was discovered in 1901 during excavations at Abydos. According to this account, the expedition of Senwosret III reached the city of Sekhem, before it turned back to Egypt. The text of the stele begins with a prayer which includes a wish for regular offerings to the spirit of the deceased:

'Offering which the king gives, and Osiris, Lord of Abydos: (namely) beer, meat, poultry, alabaster and cloth, incense and all the beautiful, good and pure things to the soul of the noble and prince, who said what was good and repeated what was loved by day, every day, the great city official of the waret, Khusobek called Djaa, son of It.'

The text continues with the description of the campaign to the area of Palestine:

'His Majesty sailed north in order to conquer the Menti tribe from Asia. His Majesty reached the foreign country called Sekmem. Then he set out (back) to the residence of life, prosperity and health. (But) he was attacked by Sekmem together with a cowardly country. I was the rear guard. Then the troops rallied in order to fight the Asiatics. I captured one of them and ordered two soldiers to hold him without even interrupting the fight. My face was satisfied. I did not turn around and run from (this) Asiatic. (I swear) by the life of Senwosret that I have spoken the truth! Then (His Majesty) gave me a staff of electrum, and a bow and dagger of electrum...'

This passage indicates that on his Palestinian campaign Senwosret penetrated all the way to the city of Sekhem. This city was of great significance for communication, since it lay on an important road which connected the Mediterranean Sea with the area of Jordan, its fords and the Transjordan areas. The text does not specify whether Senwosret actually conquered the city, although it seems more likely that he did not. After what was probably an unsuccessful siege, he

Fig. 2.41 The pyramid of Senwosret III at Dahshur

finally set out back home to Egypt. On the way, he was repeatedly attacked by the city garrison and by the neighbouring Retjenu tribe. Khusebek captured one Asiatic during one of these skirmishes, and the king rewarded him for this deed. Therefore, it appears that this campaign of Senwosret III was not overly successful, its only achievement – judging from the aforementioned account of the stele of Khusebek – being to ward off enemy troops on their way to Egypt.

As was already indicated, Senwosret III became one of the rulers whose reign was later described by Herodotus. While Herodotus' account of Senwosret's administrative activity is in accordance with reality, his views of the campaign to Asia are undoubtedly mistaken:

'Most of the memorial pillars which King Sesostris erected in the conquered countries have disappeared, but I have seen some myself in Palestine.

Once home again in Egypt, Sesostris... proceeded to employ his prisoners of war in various tasks. It was they who were forced to drag the enormous masses of stone which were brought during Sesostris' reign for the temple of Hephaestus, and to dig the dykes which one finds here to-day, thereby depriving Egypt – though it was far from their intention to do so – of the horses and carriages which were formerly in such common use throughout the country. All Egypt is flat; yet from that time onwards it has been unfit for horses or wheeled traffic because of innumerable dykes, running in all directions, which cut the country up.

The king's object was to supply water to the towns which lay inland at some distance from the river; for previously the people in these towns, when the level of the river fell, had to go short and to drink brackish water from wells.

Fig. 2.42 The enclosure wall of Senwosret III at Dahshur

It was this king, moreover, who divided the land into lots and gave everyone a square piece of equal size, from the produce of which he exacted an annual tax. Any man whose holding was damaged by the encroachment of the river would go and declare his loss before the king, who would send inspectors to measure the extent of the loss, in order that he might pay in future a fair proportion of the tax at which property had been assessed. Perhaps this was the way in which geometry was invented and passed afterwards into Greece.'
  (Herodotus, The Histories)

Senwosret decided to build his final resting place in Dahshur. This pyramid, the northernmost one on the site, was built of mudbricks arranged in steps. For reasons of economy, limestone blocks were used only for the outer casing. The real entrance to the pyramid lay, again somewhat unusually, at the northwestern corner of the pyramid, outside its western wall. A descending corridor led to the east, then turned south, and finally opened into the vestibule, to the west of which lay the burial chamber with the granite sarcophagus of the king. The circumstances of the discovery indicate that Senwosret III was never buried here, and consequently Abydos, the cultic centre of the god Osiris, is sometimes considered his real burial place.

The pyramid was enclosed within a boundary wall, which also included the small temple at the eastern side of the pyramid, the north chapel and the shafts of the queens of Senwosret III. We may assume that the north-south orientation of the complex was an attempt to imitate the appearance of the complex of Djoser from the Third Dynasty. During the second construction stage, the wall

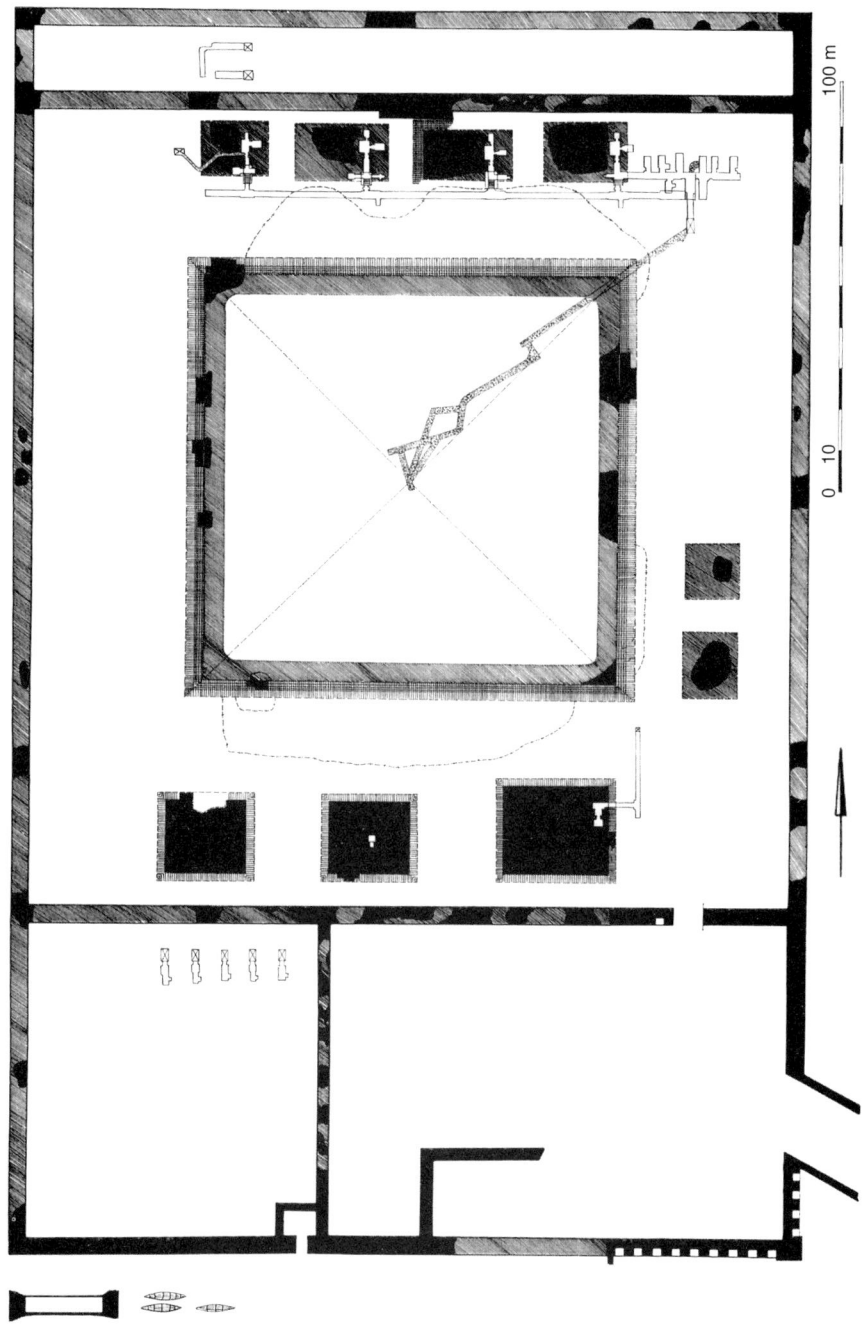

Fig. 2.43 Ground plan of the pyramid complex of Senwosret III at Dahshur (after Jacques de Morgan, Fouilles à Dahchour en 1894, fig. 105)

was extended to the south, where a significantly larger, but today entirely destroyed, pyramid temple was built. The wall was also extended to the north, so as to include the small pyramids of queens. These small pyramids stood not only on the north. On the southern side of the pyramid there are another three small pyramids. Queen Weret, the wife of Senwosret II and the mother of Senwosret III, was buried inside one of these southern pyramids. The northern pyramids had a common substructure, which consisted of two corridors with diversions to the burial chambers of the individual princesses and queens. The burial chambers were built of stone blocks and contained sarcophagi, canopic jars, and burial equipment. In two cases – the burials of princesses Sithathor and Meret – the burial equipment was discovered undisturbed and consisted, just as in the earlier cases, of many objects of gold, silver and semi-precious stones.

Senwosret's symbolic grave at Abydos is sometimes considered to be his final resting place. This tomb, built in the vicinity of the tombs of the First and Second Dynasty kings and at the same time on the place of the cult of Osiris, the lord of the ancient Egyptian Netherworld, included a large courtyard at the foot of a rock hill and a temple built on the edge of the fertile Nile valley. From the courtyard a corridor led into the rock massif. It gave way to several rooms, shafts, and blind sideways in order to confuse tomb robbers. Behind one of these rooms a chamber lay hidden, containing the granite sarcophagus and canopic chest to hold the viscera of the mummified ruler. These were the items that, together

Fig. 2.44 Burial chamber of one the queens of Senwosret III in Dahshur

with the complex system of corridors, rooms and traps, should have protected the burial chamber from unauthorised entrance. The complex protection system is one of the chief reasons for considering this tomb as the final resting place of the king. Several hundred metres to the east of the tomb stood the temple, the place of the cult of the king. Two large pylons flanked the entrance to the temple. The heart of this temple was a limestone chapel, surrounded on its sides by store rooms. In front of the building was a pillared court with an offering table and two large quartzite seated statues of Senwosret III. The cult of the king in this temple persisted for over two hundred years.

The time of the reign of the son of Senwosret III, Amenemhat III (1844–1797) is considered one of the peaks of the Egyptian history for the Middle Kingdom. Amenemhat III did not have to engage in the consolidation of the Egyptian strongholds in Nubia and Asia, for these had already been secured by his father. He could thus direct his attention to the further development of the Fayyum Oasis and to the exploitation of Egyptian stone mines. His reign was the time of the most frequent expeditions to the turquoise mines in the Sinai. At Serabit el-Khadim, 49 inscriptions were found that bear witness to his expeditions to this place. During his reign, temporary campsites were transformed into regular settlements with houses for expedition leaders and simpler dwellings

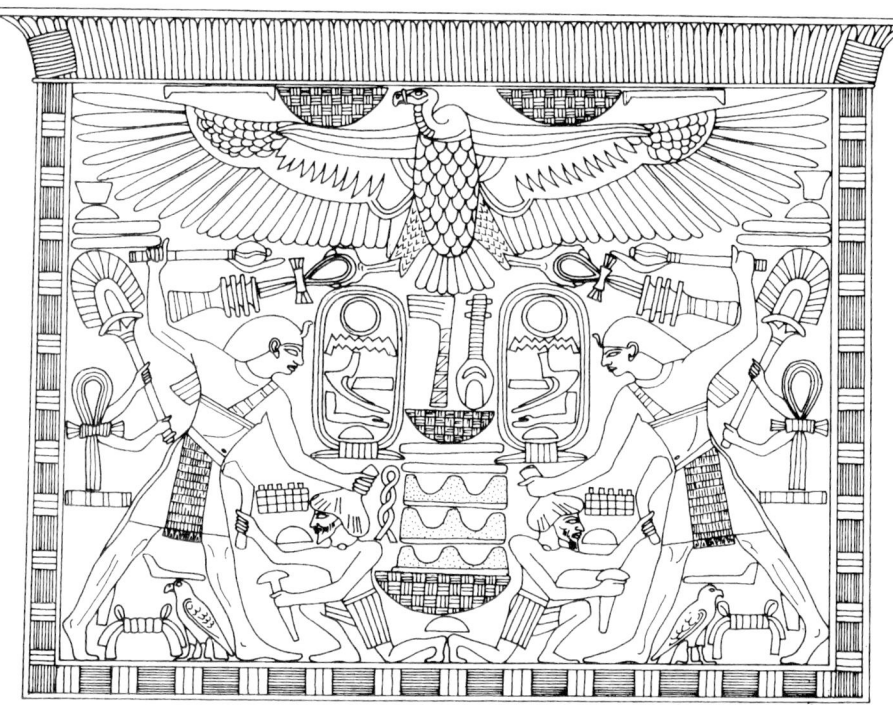

Fig. 2.45 The pectoral of Amenemhat III depicting the king smiting his Asiatic enemies

Fig. 2.46 Wadi Hammamat inscription of Amenemhat III referring to an expedition that took part during his second regnal year

for workers. Cisterns and wells were also constructed to store and provide fresh water, as well as fortifications against Bedouin raids, and even tombs for those who would no more return to Egypt. The necessity of the construction of fortifications at this time is indirectly proved by the pectoral from Dahshur, which depicts Amenemhat III defeating the Bedouin from the Sinai and from Palestine. Other evidence for stone-mining of Amenemhat III comes from the Tura mines, from Wadi Hammamat, Assuan and Toshka.

In the economic sphere, Amenemhat III concentrated on further acquisition of newly won, arable land in the Fayyum Oasis. His activities in the oasis were probably one of the reasons for his decision to build his final resting place in Hawara, where the Bahr Yussuf enters the Fayyum Oasis.

The sad ruins of the first pyramid of Amenemhat III can be seen in the southern tip of Dahshur, not far from the northern bank of the Lake of Dahshur. Today this pyramid, which was also built of mud bricks, reminds us only very remotely of the original magnificent monument. Due to its black mudbrick building material, the local population has dubbed it the 'Black Pyramid'. This pyramid was originally also cased with white limestone blocks, which were, however, in the course of history carted away to other construction sites. The substructure of the pyramid consisted of two systems of corridors, pits, rooms and blocking constructions, one reserved for the burial of the king and the second for the burials of his two queens. The entrance into the king's tomb was situated at the eastern wall of the pyramid, near its southeast corner. After several sharp turns the east-west oriented corridor opened into a burial chamber. At its west wall stood a pink granite sarcophagus with a vaulted lid and the motif of niching on the walls imitating the outer enclosure wall of Djoser's pyramid in Saqqara. The respective entrance into the underground associated with the king's two wives was situated at the south wall of the pyramid.

Fig. 2.47 The Black Pyramid of Amenemhat III at Dahshur

Due to the overly ambitious concept of the substructure of the pyramid, the walls and individual underground rooms gradually began showing considerable cracks, which threatened to hinder the safe burial of the king. Therefore, in the 15th year of his reign, Amenemhat III decided to construct a new funerary complex, this time, again following the example of his ancestors, in the Fayyum Oasis, on the site known as Hawara. His original pyramid thus held only the burials of two of his queens. It is interesting that both the pyramid and the valley temple with the ascending causeway were finished in this complex, but this is probably because the daily ritual for the king was performed during his own lifetime, as well as after death.

The pyramid at Hawara thus became the real final resting place of this ruler. In contrast to his first pyramid, the king decided not to employ the common east-west orientation to the entire complex, but he returned to the archaic north-south orientation which was inspired by the ancient pyramid complex of Djoser at Saqqara, that had influenced already his father Senwosret III. The pyramid was entered from the west, through a descending corridor which first headed north, then turned east and after two further turns gave access to a magnificent burial chamber. The chamber, constructed out of a single sandstone quartzite monolith, weighed approximately 110 tons and contained a quartzite sarcophagus.

Undoubtedly, the most famous part of this pyramid complex was the pyramid temple, located to the south of the pyramid and known already from the account of Herodotus, who was astounded by its spaciousness and beauty:

'I have seen this building, and it is beyond my power to describe ... The pyramids, too, are astonishing structures, each one of them equal to many of the most ambitious works in

Greece; but the labyrinth surpasses them. It has twelve covered courts – six in a row facing north, six south – the gates of the one range exactly fronting the gates of the other, with a continuous wall round the outside of the whole. Inside, the building is of two storeys and contains three thousands rooms, of which half are underground, and the other half directly above them. I was taken through the rooms in the upper storey, so what I shall say of them is from my own observation, but the underground ones I can speak of only from report, because the Egyptians in charge refused to let me see them, as they contain the tombs of the kings who built the labyrinth, and so also the tombs of the sacred crocodiles. The upper rooms, on the contrary, I did actually see, and it is hard to believe that they are the work of men; the baffling and intricate passages from room to room and from court to court were an endless wonder to me, as we passed from a courtyard into rooms, from rooms into galleries, from galleries into more rooms, and thence into yet more courtyards. The roof of every room, courtyard and gallery is, like the walls, of stone. The walls are covered with carved figures, and each court is exquisitely built of white marble and surrounded by a colonnade. Near the corner where the labyrinth ends there is a pyramid, two hundred and forty feet in height, with great carved figures of animals on it and an underground passage by which it can be entered.'

(Herodotus, The Histories)

The temple has now, unfortunately, been completely destroyed, and thus we are unable to even approximately imagine its original appearance. We can only be certain that it consisted of many roofed rooms and courtyards and that perhaps it even had an underground part, dedicated to the cult of the crocodile god Sebek. During the modern excavations of the temple, undertaken in

Fig. 2.48 The pyramid of Amenemhat III at Hawara

the course of the last century by W. M. F. Petrie, only two granite sanctuaries were discovered, each of which contained two statues of the king. These sanctuaries stood at the southern face of the pyramid and originally may have been part of its cultic chapel.

Amenemhat III is the last in the line of significant Middle Kingdom kings, who played an important part in the shaping of relations with Syria–Palestine, Egypt's immediate neighbour. The history and development of this area, its importance for the understanding of Sinuhe's account, as well as its cultural heritage, are the theme of the next chapter.

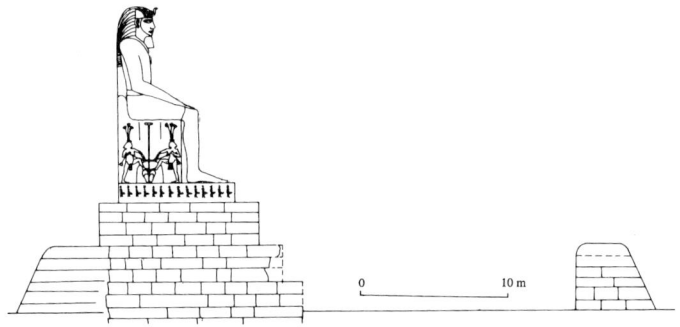

Fig. 2.49 a, b Remnants of the temple of Amenemhat III at Biahmu, Fayyum oasis, (above) and its tentative reconstruction (after W. M. F. Petrie, Hawara, Biahmu, and Arsinoe, London 1889, pl. 27)

Fig. 2.50 Amenemhat III as a priest (Egyptian Museum, Cairo)

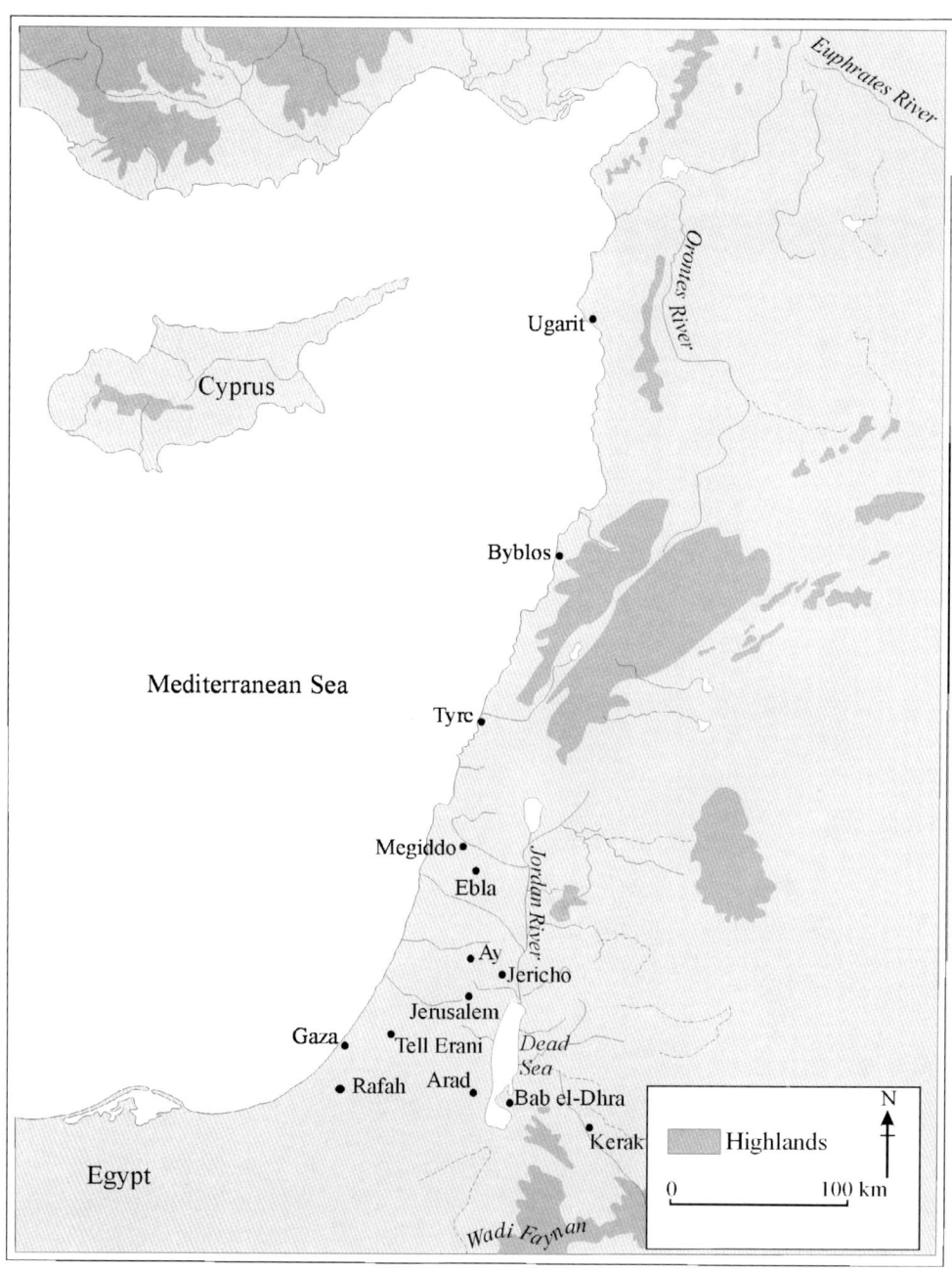

Egypt and Syria-Palestine in the Time of Sinuhe's Flight

Sinuhe's narrative clearly demonstrates that the Egyptians had detailed knowledge of the area of Syria-Palestine. This is understandable, since together with Nubia, to the south of the First Cataract, this territory played an important role in Egyptian foreign policy. The importance of this region should not be neglected or underestimated. At the time of Sinuhe's stay in Syria-Palestine, the area had already come through a long and troubled history with a thousand year tradition of relations with Egypt. As we will see later in this chapter, this relationship was usually a mutually advantageous symbiosis, which, especially in Syria-Palestine, stimulated further development.

Just as in Egypt and in Mesopotamia, we may trace the first indications of a spreading urban culture at the end of the fourth millennium BC in Palestine. Large fortified settlements were built and became centres of production and trade. Above all, they functioned as centres for the consolidation of power at the local level. They were controlled by rulers who governed their immediate sur-

Fig. 3.1 Buto, ancient site that played a key role in the exchange of commodities between Egypt and the Levant during the late Fourth and the early Third millennium BC

roundings and agricultural hinterland. Apart from the dynamics of social development, the growing importance of the area was at this period (i.e. the Early Bronze Age) increased by trade routes passing through it.

The Early Bronze Age is today divided into four basic phases, and lasted for approximately 1000 years – until the end of the third millennium. This period (abbreviated as EB/A + phase number) is divided as follows:

EB I – 3300–3050 BC
EB II – 3050–2700 BC
EB III – 2700–2300 BC
EB IV/MB I – 2300–2000 BC (this phase is either connected with the Early Bronze Age, or, alternatively, is classified as the first phase of the Middle Bronze Age – MB I. Often it is also regarded as an 'intermediate period'; we may, however, consider this phase as the beginning of the Middle Bronze Age).

The Early Bronze Age was followed by the Middle Bronze Age, which began around 2300 BC and lasted until approximately 1550 BC:

EB IV/MB I – 2300–2000 BC
MB IIA – 2000–1800 / 1750 BC
MB IIB – 1800 / 1750–1650 BC
MB IIC – 1650–1550 BC

In this chapter, we will concentrate mainly on the period between 2300–1800 BC, which is the most important for our understanding of the details of Sinuhe's account.

The very beginning of the third millennium BC was marked by a general change in Syria-Palestine. Nomadism and occasional agricultural production were abandoned in favour of the rapid development of intensive agriculture and trade. Thus circumstances became favourable for the foundation and growth of cities, which not only became the centres of power and administrative apparatus, but themselves stimulated further development in the area. The cities were a convenient environment for the expansion of crafts. Peasants from the surrounding areas were streaming in to exchange their produce for artefacts.

Increased systematization of specialized activities facilitated the demographic growth of the population, which was no longer limited by the nomadic way of life. The use of water sources, which were indispensable for agricultural activities, was also significant. The importance of water sources was enhanced by the fact that most of the great cities grew in their vicinity. A number of settlements were further constructed along the Mediterranean coast, which in the third millennium BC gradually became the artery of maritime trade, mostly with Egypt. Today, it is estimated that in the Early Bronze Age, the area of Palestine contained approximately 150 000 people and about 900 settlements. For comparison, Egypt had at that time around 1 500 000 – 3 000 000 inhabitants. The greatest Palestinian settlements covered the area of around 16 hectares (the contemporary Mesopotamian city of Uruk extended over 400 hectares.) In this connection, the concept of 'urbanism' can only be used with great care, since the scale was much smaller here than for example in Egypt or in Mesopotamia. With few exceptions,

Fig. 3.2 Recto and verso of the Narmer palette. On the left the king, wearing the White Crown, smites an Asiatic. On the right (at the bottom) the king is depicted as a bull demolishing the walls of an Asiatic town. It is quite possible that the scenes relate to the military control of the Ways of Horus and the area in southern Palestine

these settlements were not true cities, but rather partly fortified habitations, which in difficult times still functioned as centres of refuge, i.e. fortresses, where the surrounding village inhabitants took shelter in times of danger. The main settlements were concentrated around Upper Jordan, the Yezreel Valley and northern Syria-Palestine along the Mediterranean Sea coastline.

The Egyptians had maintained a busy trade with Syria-Palestine from the times of the First and Second Dynasties, as is proven by royal tombs in southern Egypt, in Abydos, approximately 700 km to the south of the Mediterranean coast. Their burial equipment contained Near Eastern pottery, in which wine and precious oils were imported. Moreover, cedar wood from the Lebanese mountains was often used for the construction of the subterranean burial chambers of the kings. At the same time, Egyptian annals record frequent expeditions against the Asiatics, which might explain the system of fortification of Asiatic cities. Military conflicts with Asiatics are reflected even on the ceremonial palette which bears the name of King Narmer, one of the Upper Egyptian rulers from pre-unification times. The king is depicted as a bull destroying the fortification of a city – probably Asiatic, since the following scene depicts him ritually slaying an Asiatic captive.

During the first two stages of the Early Bronze Age (EB I and II), that is until 2700 BC, the chief trade route led along the Mediterranean coast. The road began in the western Delta and continued to the east and northeast to the area of Gaza, southern Shephelah and the Negev Desert (the area of Arad). This track between Egypt and Asia is probably the one which later texts call the 'Ways of Horus'. It continued all the way inland to the site of copper ore sources in the

Fig. 3.3 Late Fourth – early Third millennium Bedouin tombs in Central Sinai (a type of tomb known as nawamis)

Fig. 3.4 The copper mines at Timna, Wadi Arabah (Israel)

area of Wadi Arabah, which connected the Dead and Red Seas. Rich sources of copper ore (greatly exploited in later times) were probably the reason for Egypt's strong political and military involvement in this area.

This is also true concerning the southern part of the Sinai Peninsula, where copper was found. Even here, however, the Egyptians had to back up their activities with military force, because the area was inhabited by the Bedouin. Evidence of the presence of nomadic tribes in this region is indicated by stone tombs of the *nawamis* type, above-ground circular structures with false vaults and dating as early as the end of the Chalcolithic – beginning of the Early Bronze Age (ca. 4000–3300 BC). They were built of smaller stones placed over one another without any connective material. Gradually, several hundreds of these tombs appeared in the area.

The importance of the road which connected the Dead Sea and the Red Sea at the beginning of Egyptian history is evident from the conclusions of the study of Ram Gophna, who analyzed the settlement patterns in southern Palestine, concentrating on the sites where the Egyptian presence had been recorded. He noted seven such settlements, dated to the time between 3050–2950 BC (EB IB). They were the following:

Tel Arad (Arad). Layer IV yielded Egyptian pottery from the time of the predynastic ruler Narmer and of the first king of the First Dynasty Hor Aha.

The small Tel Malhata, where many items of Egyptian pottery were discovered, as well as three fragments with a serekh (a schematic depiction of the royal palace) containing the name of Narmer.

At 'En Besor, ruins of an Egyptian settlement were identified in Layer III of this site. Among other finds were numerous Egyptian clay sealings, which were originally used to seal the transport jars containing wine, aromatic oils, etc. The Egyptian settlement rose over the ruins of a former Canaanite village (Layer IV).

At the Halif Terrace site, located on the edge of the northern Negev desert and the Shephelah, numerous Egyptian finds of pottery, including one vessel with the name of king Narmer prove yet another example of these settlements identified to date.

At Tel Ma'ahaz, Layer I of this tell was dominated by Egyptian pottery with only a few items of pottery of local production. The Egyptian ware came from the Predynastic period as well as from the beginning of the First Dynasty.

In Tel 'Erani, the importance of this tell lies in the fact that it was the first site on Palestinian territory, where Predynastic and First Dynasty material was discovered in a clear stratigraphic context, in Layer V. Lastly, in Afridar (Ashkelon) the discoveries of EBA finds come exclusively from the Egyptian Predynastic period.

Excavations in the aforementioned settlements seem to indicate that in at least five of them Egyptian merchants were living in symbiosis with the local population. The presence of Egyptian merchants on these sites was probably the result of mutual agreement, and we cannot exclude the possibility that in exchange for some agreement they might have been obliged to pay taxes from their activities. Two of the sites (Tel Ma'ahaz and 'En Besor) were probably exclusively Egyptian

Fig. 3.5 Tel 'Erani, one of the possible Egyptian settlements in southern Palestine during thirtieth century BC (Israel)

settlements, which played a significant role in the management of trade between Egypt and Syria-Palestine. Their existence was probably made possible by the fact that they were founded on unclaimed territories. Although both of these settlements were located on hilltops in the vicinity of water sources, they were quite different. Tel Ma'ahaz consisted of dwellings and storerooms, which were built of local stone collected from around the village. The site was very small and it seems likely that it was a seasonal encampment, as is also indicated by archaeological finds. They consisted almost exclusively of pottery, mainly of storage jars which were used for the transport of cereals and oil, the most commonly traded items in the area. The independence of these purely Egyptian settlements on the Canaanite population probably guaranteed them greater freedom of trade than in the case of the sites where the presence of Egyptian merchants was merely tolerated.

In 'En Besor the Egyptians built a mud brick settlement according to a regular plan. Its elevated location enabled them to control access to the springs at the foot of the hill, which are among the most abundant water sources in the region. The reason for the existence of the site was probably to supply water, bread and beer to the Egyptian caravans that were heading further north. Since the archaeological excavations revealed no storerooms or remains of large amphorae, we may assume that the local inhabitants were not engaged in trade.

The multidisciplinary investigation of the site of the Halif Terrace, situated along the interface of the northern Negev desert and the Shephelah also revealed a close association with Egyptian activities in the surrounding areas. One of the most significant recent discoveries here – besides some written documents with the name of the Upper Egyptian ruler, King Narmer – is that of a tomb built in the Egyptian style. This unique discovery was made in 1994. The tomb, which was undoubtedly built according to contemporaneous Egyptian practices, as, for example, the tombs at the cemetery of Helwan, belongs to the group of so-called stairway tombs. The subterranean chamber in Tel 'Erani was approached by a stairway and contained the burial of a woman in a contracted position, lying on her left side and facing southeast. Her age has been estimated at 25 – 30 years. The analysis of the pottery also yielded remarkable results. It showed that both Egyptian and Canaanite vessels were produced here. The distribution of the two types was highly differentiated. It is therefore likely that both an Egyptian and a Canaanite population lived simultaneously on the site, which was, however, divided, each group inhabiting its own appropriate area.

The information we currently possess about the history of the region indicates how important trade relations with Syria-Palestine must have been for the Egyptian state even as early as the Predynastic and Early Dynastic periods, but it was mainly in the time of the First and Second Dynasties that trade really escalated between these two countries. At the beginning, Egyptian activities were probably concerned merely with trade. Consequently, auxiliary support centres were constructed along the way to the north ('En Besor), and independent trade centres (Tel Ma'ahaz) or colonies were set up within indigenous villages.

The scene changed abruptly toward the end of the First and Second Dynasties. Most of the Egyptian outposts disappeared – probably due to the transfer of trade to the sea.

At the end of the second stage of the Early Bronze Age, maritime trade gained in importance, while that on land receded. This new trend had already been anticipated at the end of the Second Dynasty. The annals for King Peribsen mention the construction of ships, which may indicate that they were needed for maritime trade with the coast of Syria-Palestine. Despite the change in international trade routes, the development of urban civilisation and of city-state centres in Syria-Palestine was not interrupted. Every city state had a fortified urban or settlement centre, which was a base for the local administration and the residence of the king, who ruled the city and its immediate neighbourhood. These cities were above all centres of trade, exchange and production. They were enclosed within a network of smaller, mainly agricultural centres, which formed their rural background. In exchange for their produce, peasants obtained craft products and also gained military protection against the raids of greedy neighbours or foreign powers.

A relatively large number of fortified cities was discovered particularly in the eastern part of Syria-Palestine (the territory of contemporary Israel, Jordan, and possibly also Palestine). These cities may be divided into two groups. One of them consists of cities, which grew up around trade routes leading mostly in the north-south direction, as for example Dan, Hazor, Kadesh of Galilee, Beit Yerah,

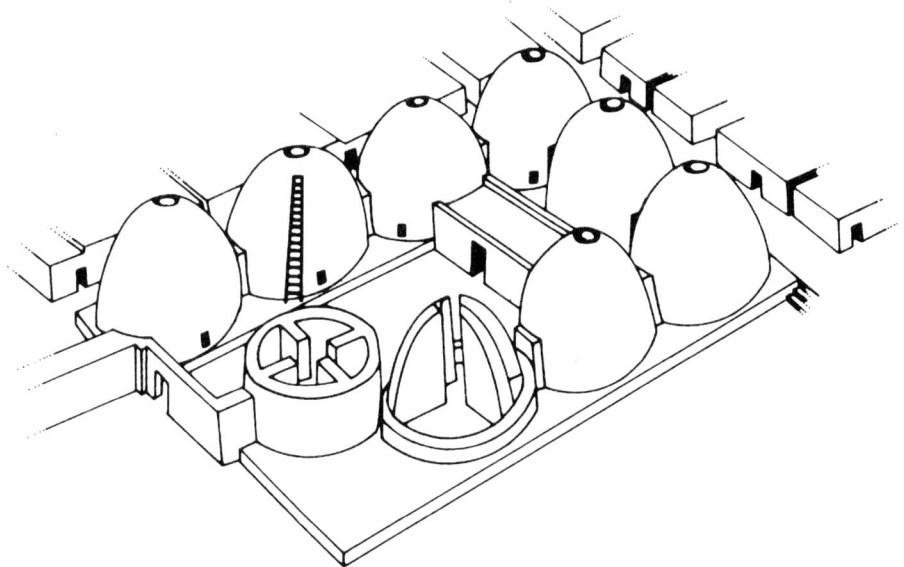

Fig. 3.6 Reconstruction of the granaries at Beit Yerah, Israel (after A. Mazar, Archaeology of the Land of the Bible. 10,000 – 587 B. C. E., New York 1992, p. 129, fig. 4.19)

Beit-Shean, Megiddo, Tel el-Far'ah, Tel es-Sa'idiyeh, Jericho and Lakhish. The other group consists of cities lying outside trade routes, and also in largely unfavourable climatic areas – Ay, Yarmut, Arad, Bab el-Dhra and Numeira.

The largest of these cities were Beit Yerah with 22 hectares, Yarmut with 16 hectares, Tel Hesi with 10 hectares, Ay and Arad with 10 hectares each. Then there were about thirty cities with 5 hectares each. The large centres were surrounded by approximately 160 smaller settlements amounting to approximately 1 hectare.

Besides handicrafts, these cities also practised agriculture, growing above all barley and emmer, legumes and flax. Other sites provide evidence for the growing of olives, figs, vine, pomegranates and dates, that is, of fruits that attest a highly developed cultivation. Mountainous areas show the first signs of growing vine and olives. The existence of horticulture and olive and viticulture may be one of the reasons for the relatively large cities in the highlands. It is also likely that a predominant proportion of wine and olive oil produce was intended for trade with Egypt. Flax was used for the extraction of oil and for the production of textiles. The discovery of gigantic granaries in Beit Yerah brought indisputable evidence of a highly developed agriculture and of an advanced organization of labour. A building extending approximately over 30 × 40 m was discovered here, which included nine granaries having a circular groundplan. Each granary was approximately 7 m high and could contain up to $200 - 250$ m^3 of grain. The total capacity of this storage area was estimated at $1400 - 1700$ tonnes of grain. The construction of a gigantic water container in the city of Ay, which otherwise had no source of potable water, contributes another piece of evidence for the highly developed organisation in Syria-Palestine. The cistern collected rainwater and could hold up to 1800 sq. m of water.

The settlements in the desert of Negev and in the Sinai peninsula were of a totally different character. Numerous remains of dwellings from Early Bronze Age II (3050–2700 BC) were preserved here. For example, in the area around the monastery of St. Catherine in the southern part of the Sinai, the Israeli archaeologist Beit Arieh discovered over sixty settlements. The dwellings, or rather temporary settlements, thus identified, were built of local stone and consisted of a central court around which other rooms were concentrated.

The existence of such settlements, which were constructed along trade routes in the main valleys of the peninsula, was probably connected with copper mining in the Sinai. According to the petrographical analysis of pottery, they were closely connected with the city of Arad, which could have been the centre of copper mining in the Sinai. This city may have been in some way involved in the organisation of copper mining in the Sinai and in the Wadi Arabah. All of these settlements were deserted at the beginning of the Third Dynasty, when the Egyptians probably achieved supremacy over the peninsula and thus also over the source of copper.

It may be estimated that altogether about twenty larger cities existed in the Negev area and close by. With the growing accumulation of wealth in the area of

Fig. 3.7 Arad (Israel)

Fig. 3.8 Arad, detail of the stone-built city and the fortifications (Israel)

Syria-Palestine and with its continuing social differentiation, new methods of fortification for the cities were developed, as is seen at some well-explored sites from the beginning of the Bronze Age. The settlement of Arad was fortified by a stone wall, which was strengthened by bastions set at regular intervals of 20–25 m. Since Arad had no natural water source, there was, moreover, a large and constructionally demanding network of cisterns for the collection and storage of rainwater. In Jericho, the ca. 1 m thick fortification wall was built on a stone platform. Toward the end of the Early Bronze Age, probably out of fear of growing danger from the outside, this wall was enlarged to a total thickness of 5 m and further strengthened by square bastions. The fact that at the end of the Early Bronze Age the cities of Syria-Palestine were indeed increasingly endangered, is confirmed by the fortification discovered in Tel Tanakh. The local settlement was enclosed by two walls with intervening free space. The outer was approached by an ascending ramp, and a third wall was built at its foot. The ramp was constructed in order to hinder raiders trying to penetrate the fortification. The outer side of the original fortification in Yarmut was covered by a stone wall constructed of large blocks. Both sides of the entrance gates of the cities were often protected by towers with a horseshoe-shaped groundplan. Approximately half of the total population lived either in these agglomerations or in their immediate vicinity. Most of the smaller settlements are located within 20 – 25 km from these centres. This evidence gives further support to the theory that several city-states existed side by side in this area, each having its own economic and agricultural background.

Hand in hand with growing urbanisation, the internal structure of the settlements was also developing. In Megiddo, Tell el-Far'ah and Khirbet Zeraqoun, the settlement was constructed as a network of streets crossing each other at right angles, which indicates that they were built according to a unified plan. Arad shows signs of profound social stratification. A wall divides dwellings from public buildings, such as offices, the palace, and two temples, which stood in the centre of the city. About twenty satellite villages, which constituted the agricultural background of the city, were located within a day's journey from Arad.

One of the latest interesting discoveries connected with the exploration of cities was made on the site of Tel es-Sa'idiyeh by the expedition of the British Museum, which was led by a British archaeologist, Jonathan N. Tubb. In the southern part of the tell, he discovered the remains of what may be considered the residential palace of the royal family. The complex of buildings consisted of several specialized construction units. Olive oil presses were discovered in the southeastern part of the palace, weaving mills in the southwestern part, and the central part of the area contained a wine production workshop. Even the residential area of the palace was found. However, the most interesting discovery was a small room, measuring 1.5×5 m, which can be interpreted as the palace kitchen. Pottery for altogether 11 people was discovered here, together with the remains of food which probably constituted the last supper of the ruling family before a fire broke out and destroyed the entire palace. There were four large trays with

Fig. 3.9 Sinai, area of the Monastery of St. Catherine

Fig. 3.10 Tel el-Far'ah, Early Bronze Age entrance to a fortified city (after A. Mazar, Archaeology of the Land of the Bible. 10,000 – 587 B. C. E., New York 1992, p. 123, fig. 4.15)

Fig. 3.11 Tel es-Sa'idiyeh (Jordan)

eleven semicircular bowls which served as plates, eleven fine flint knives and eleven long bone needles, which may have been used to roast meat. Apart from that, other items of tableware were found. One of the most important discoveries was that of emmer ears with grains of the wheat still attached. They enabled the archaeologists to date the burning of the palace to a period between June and July.

The above description should not make us believe that the people of that time lived only for the construction of their cities and their agriculture and handicrafts; on the contrary, they also appear to have been deeply involved in religious activities and they took refuge under the protection of their deities, to whom they built large temples. Naturally, some traces of these temples have also come down to us, although the details of everyday cult still remain a mystery. In the Early Bronze Age city of Megiddo, three temples were gradually constructed. Each of them was approximately 17 × 18 m large and their outer walls were almost 2 m thick. Each temple had a large open court with two columns at its one wall. The door in this wall led to a spacious room 14 metres wide and 9 metres long. At its rear wall was an elevated platform, on which a cultic statue of the god, who was worshipped here, may have stood. All three temples of Megiddo existed simultaneously and it is possible that they were dedicated to three different gods. Behind one of these temples was an elevated circular stone platform of 8 m in diameter. From similar remains elsewhere, we may presume that burnt offerings were presented on this altar. As for the interpretation of temple architecture, we can only suppose on the basis of distant parallels that the open courts were accessible to

Fig. 3.12 A cluster of three Early Bronze Age temples with a circular altar (?), Megiddo (Israel)

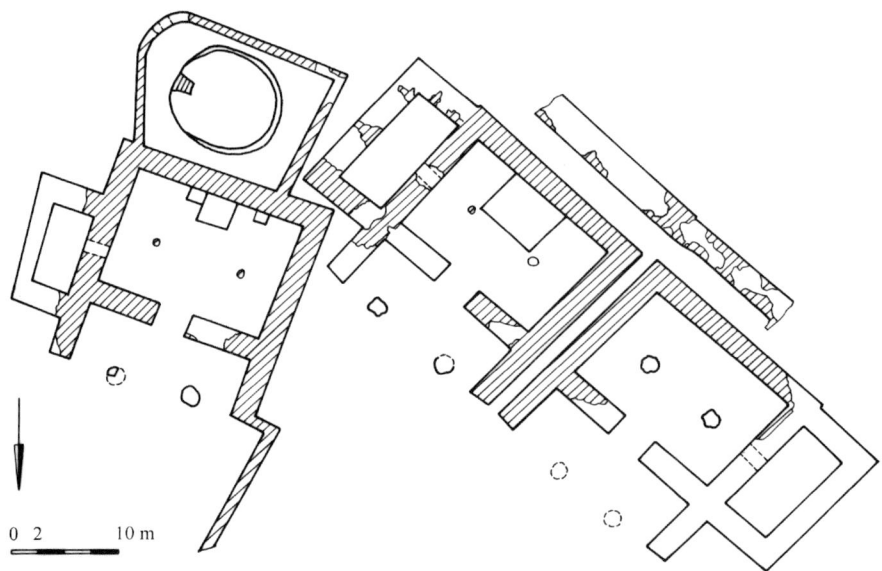

Fig. 3.13 Groundplan of the Early Bronze Age temples at Megiddo (after A. Mazar, Archaeology of the Land of the Bible. 10,000 – 587 B. C. E., New York 1992, p. 124, fig. 4.16)

everyone who wished to pay homage to their god, while the closed rooms in the rear part of the temple were reserved for the priests and for the ruler, who had the prerogative of direct communication with gods. Similar temple structures were discovered also in Ay and in Yarmut. In Arad, the temple stood on the highest place of the city and consisted of one transverse hall measuring 17.2×5.8 m, the roof of which was supported by a row of wooden columns. The sanctuary was approached from the east. From the outside it was encircled by a narrow corridor, which was later transformed into a complex of rooms.

The change of mercantile strategy and the emphasis on maritime trade in the course of the twenty-eighth century BC finally caused several cities in the area of Syria-Palestine almost overnight to become important economic centres. In these changing conditions the city of Byblos, which had already existed as a Mediterranean port in Neolithic times, became one of the most significant sites. Byblos undoubtedly belonged to the foremost cities of the ancient world, since its importance and leading position in international trade lasted, with some intermissions, for almost three thousand years. Thus it is worthwhile spending some time on this subject.

Byblos was of great importance for the Egyptians, mainly as a rich source of cedar wood for the construction of ships and buildings, and also of resin, copper and lead. Traces of contacts between Byblos and Egypt come from two main periods: the Third to the Sixth Dynasties and the Twelfth to the Thirteenth

Fig. 3.14 Byblos, the Temple of Hathor (Lebanon)

Dynasties. The city expanded to an area of approximately 5 hectares and was enclosed within a large stone wall with two gates: one facing the sea and the other towards the land. Around 2800 BC, the temple of the goddess Baalat – Gebal, 'Lady of Byblos' was built in the city. The temple, which was finally rebuilt in Roman times, appears to be a typically Egyptian construction, which even may have been built by an Egyptian architect. It was dedicated to the cult of the local goddess Baalat, who nonetheless shared many aspects of the Egyptian goddess Hathor. The city itself consisted mainly of houses, which were dominated by an open court around which there were rooms.

Subsequently, around 2600 BC, a second, L-shaped temple was constructed opposite the first one. During the Egyptian First Intermediate Period, contacts between Egypt and Byblos dwindled and it seems that the city fell victim to fire. Still later it was subdued by the incoming Anatolian population, who were called 'the torque-wearers', after the necklets with which they adorned themselves. In the course of the Middle Bronze Age, the L-shaped temple was superseded by a new one – the so-called 'obelisk temple'. Its main sanctuary was built on a large platform and its most important part was probably the stone base, which may have supported a cultic object (an obelisk?). Around it, no less than twenty six other obelisks were erected.

Fig. 3.15 Cedars of Lebanon (Lebanon)

The fact that the Byblite area provided the easiest access to the cedar woods in the Lebanon mountains east of the city was probably the reason for the enormous growth of Byblos, which became one of the greatest trade centres of its kind. Because of their exploitation in ancient times these woods have practically disappeared. In the beginning of the third millennium BC, Byblos also served as a reloading place for the trade route between Egypt and Sumer. The importance of this site is indicated by the numerous votive offerings – mainly stone vessels – of the Egyptian rulers, presented in the local temple. These vessels bore the names of the following Egyptian rulers: Khufu, Khafre, Menkaure, Sahure, Neferirkare, Neuserre, Djedkare, Unas, Teti, Pepi I, Merenre and Pepi II, that is, of the kings of the Fourth to Sixth Dynasties of the Old Kingdom (2575–2150 BC).

Around the year 2000, the city remained for some time under the supremacy of the Third Dynasty of Ur. Interestingly, the ruler of the city does not appear in the Egyptian execration texts, which indicates that he maintained friendly relations with the Egyptian kings. We know almost nothing about conditions in the time of the Twelfth Dynasty. Nonetheless, the city must have continued its trade policy, in which Egypt surely played a role. This was probably the reason why upon his arrival in Palestine, this was precisely the place which Sinuhe tried to reach. In the time of the reign of Amenemhat III, the city experienced one of the peaks in its development. In the course of several previous generations, Byblos had witnessed the construction of nine splendid rock tombs, belonging to local rulers. Almost all of them used hieroglyphic inscriptions in their tombs, in order to glorify themselves and their reigns. The inscriptions mention Egyptian deities, and the tombs themselves are decorated in Egyptian style. These chieftains even used the highest Egyptian official titles in order to emphasize their position and importance; these titles are chiefly *iri-pʿt* and *ḥȝti-ʿ*. The power of these rulers culminated during and after the rule of Prince Antin, the fifth of that name, who had himself called 'the ruler of rulers', and is even attested in the archives of Mari. The tombs of the kings who succeeded him (tombs VI–IX) are among the best examples of their kind. Some of them still contained stone sarcophagi and other items of burial equipment: golden jewellery, bronze objects, pottery, metal knives, ivory items, silver and bronze tableware and alabaster vases. Altogether, we know the names of ten rulers of Byblos, some of whom may be dated with a degree of certainty:

1. Ibdadi;

2. Abishemu I, the owner of royal tomb No. I. He was with all probability a contemporary of Amenemhat III;

3. Yapishemu-abi, the son of Abishemu I, a contemporary of Amenemhat IV;

4. Yakin-ilu, a contemporary of Sehetepibre II or III of the Thirteenth Dynasty. The shorter form of his name was Yakin;

5. Antin-ammu, a contemporary of Zimrilim in Mari. Probably identical with Antin. He was the son of Yakin and owner of tomb No. IV. A contemporary of Neferhetep I of the Thirteenth Dynasty;

Fig. 3.16 The boat of Khufu was built of cedar wood (Boat Museum, Giza)

6. Ilima-yapi, probably son of Antin and the likely owner of tomb No. III;
7. Hasrurum, son of Rum. Probably a contemporary of Sihathor of the Thirteenth Dynasty. It is likely that he was not an independent ruler of Byblos, but a governor of one of its parts;
8. Abishemu II, the owner of tomb No. IX;
9. Yapishemu-abi, son of Abishemu II;
10 a. Egel, also a son of Abishemu II;
10 b. Egliya/Akay, in all probability, identical with the aforementioned ruler.

With the exception of Hasrurum, who was not a true ruler of Byblos, we may allow for eight to nine rulers who reigned here at the end of the Egyptian Twelfth Dynasty and shortly after its gradual decline during the Thirteenth Dynasty. The most complete hieroglyphic inscription comes from the time of the reign of the last of these rulers, Egel/Egliya/Akay, and provides clear evidence that besides their own gods, the rulers of Byblos may have also worshipped Egyptian deities:

'*Offering which the King gives, and Nut, Ra-Harakhte, the Great Ennead and the Little Ennead. That they may give an invocation offering (consisting of) oxen and fowl, alabaster and clothes, oil, offerings and presents and all good and pure things, which heaven gives and the Nile brings, in the monthly and half-monthly festivals, to the ka of the hereditary prince and governor, who praises Nut every day on the monument that he made as renewal of the temple of Nut, built with Turah stone and cedar anew, as had been made by his father, the governor of Byblos, Akai.'*

(After R. Flammini, *'The ḥȝtyw-ʿ from Byblos in the Early Second Millenium BC, GM'* 164, 1998, 53)

The text allows us to make several conclusions which help us to better understand the nature of the Egyptian presence in Byblos. Above all, it is evident that the Byblite rulers worshipped, besides their own gods, the Egyptian deities, Nut and Hathor. The text also indicates that Byblos had a temple dedicated to the goddess Nut, which was built of Egyptian white Turah limestone and of cedar wood. It also suggests that the religious year in Byblos reflected the individual Egyptian festivals. All this evidence indirectly indicates that the Byblite ruler was not wholly independent of the Egyptian kings and that Byblos itself was greatly influenced by Egyptian culture.

The long-term strategic importance of Byblos is well documented, among others, in the somewhat later report of the journey of the official Wenamun to Byblos. This story contains a very interesting description of the entire journey to Byblos and back. The circumstances of such an expedition and the conditions that could have arisen in its course are equally intriguing. From this point of view, Wenamun's report may be considered timeless, since it describes the details of one of the trade missions for Lebanese cedars, which the Egyptians had already been organizing from Old Kingdom times.

The story of Wenamun unfolds almost a thousand years after Sinuhe's flight from Egypt, in the time of Ramesses XI, when the power over Thebes was main-

Fig. 3.17 Byblos, the Temple of Obelisks (Lebanon)

tained by the high priest of Amun Herihor. It was he who dispatched Wenamun to Byblos in order to fetch cedar wood for the building of the sacred barque of Amun.

The report begins with a description of the journey. Wenamun first reaches the city of Tanis in the eastern part of the Delta, where he hands his letter of authorisation from Herihor to the local ruler Smendes. He stays in the city until the summer season, which is favourable for setting out to the sea. Smendes gives him the Syrian captain Mengebet to assist him in this mission. The first stop on the way along the coast is the port city of Dor, which is located near today's Haifa (in Israel). This city is ruled by Beder, the chieftain of the Seker tribe, who welcomes Wenamun with fifty loaves of bread, a jar of wine and a haunch of veal. Immediately after landing, one of the members of Wenamun's crew escapes from the ship, having stolen one vessel of gold and four of silver, as well as a sackful of silver. Wenamun asks Beder to help him catch the thief; the ruler, however, denies any responsibility for what happened on the Egyptian expedition. Finally, Wenamun leaves for Byblos. On his way, he encounters a ship belonging to the chieftain of Dor and robs it of the equivalent of the gold and silver that he had lost in his city. Shortly thereafter he arrives on the Byblite coast, where he sets up his tent, which also hides a statue of Amun – the patron of pilgrims. For twenty-nine days, he waits for an audience with the ruler of the city, who refuses to hear him and suggests he should leave his city.

Finally, the ruler quite angrily admits him and accuses him of neither having a letter of authorisation from Herihor, nor presents to repay him for cutting

Fig. 3.18 Tomb with stone sarcophagus belonging to one of the Byblos rulers (Lebanon)

down his Lebanese cedar trees in order to build a barque for Amun. Wenamun dictates to his scribe a letter for Smendes in Tanis, including a request to send him the letter of authorisation and gifts via the messengers of the ruler of Byblos. After a few months, the messengers of the Byblite ruler indeed return with presents for their lord: five vessels of gold and five of silver, ten garments of royal linen and ten garments of fine linen, five hundred linen mats, five hundred haunches of beef, five hundred ropes, twenty sacks of lentils and thirty baskets of fish. Moreover, Smendes's wife, Tanetamun, sent Wenamun her personal gifts of ten garments of fine linen, one sack of lentils and five baskets of fish.

The ruler of Byblos is pleased and immediately orders three hundred men and three hundred head of cattle to go to the mountains to cut down cedar trees. Once cut, the trees are left lying on the spot for several months in order to dry out. In spring they are pulled down to the coast and loaded onto the Egyptian ships.

All seems to be going well for the Egyptian expedition but, at the moment of Wenamun's departure for Egypt, there suddenly appear eleven ships of the king of Dor, whom Wenamun had robbed. He asks the ruler of Byblos to extradite Wenamun to Dor. Unwilling to breach the rules of hospitality, the ruler refuses to do so and finds an ingenious solution – he lets Wenamun sail away and advises the Dorian messengers to catch him up on the sea, where he is no longer responsible for his safety. Wenamun saves himself by escaping to Cyprus, under the protection of its ruler Hatib.

The final part of the composition is missing, but there is no reason to think that Wenamun did not return to Egypt alive and well, bringing the load of wood. The entire account not only tells us how long such a trade journey could have lasted, but above all reports on the various sorts of hazards lurking along the coast. It particularly mentions how necessary it was to get on well with all the local rulers of the maritime cities. Most decisive, however, were favourable relations with the governor of Byblos, whose independence is evident from the fact that it was necessary to win his favour by a sufficient quantity of gifts. Thus Wenamun, who came without presents, found himself in trouble, since the angry governor refused to allow him to cut down the cedars until the gifts were given to him. The governor even ordered his servants to bring the archives with records of the presents, which each Egyptian ruler who had needed new cedar wood had sent to the previous rulers of Byblos. Among the favourite gifts, evidently, were vessels of gold and silver, garments of fine quality Egyptian linen and dried food – meat and fish.

The existence of the city of Byblos may be considered one of the most important aspects of the ancient history of this area. Byblos, particularly the cedar woods in the Lebanon mountains rising from the sea coast to the east, became part of the account of one of the most famous epic poems in human history, reporting on the life of the ruler of Uruk, Gilgamesh. In one of its tales, the Lebanese cedars are described as being both the property and hiding place of the monster Khumbaba. Gilgamesh and his loyal companion Enkidu set out to

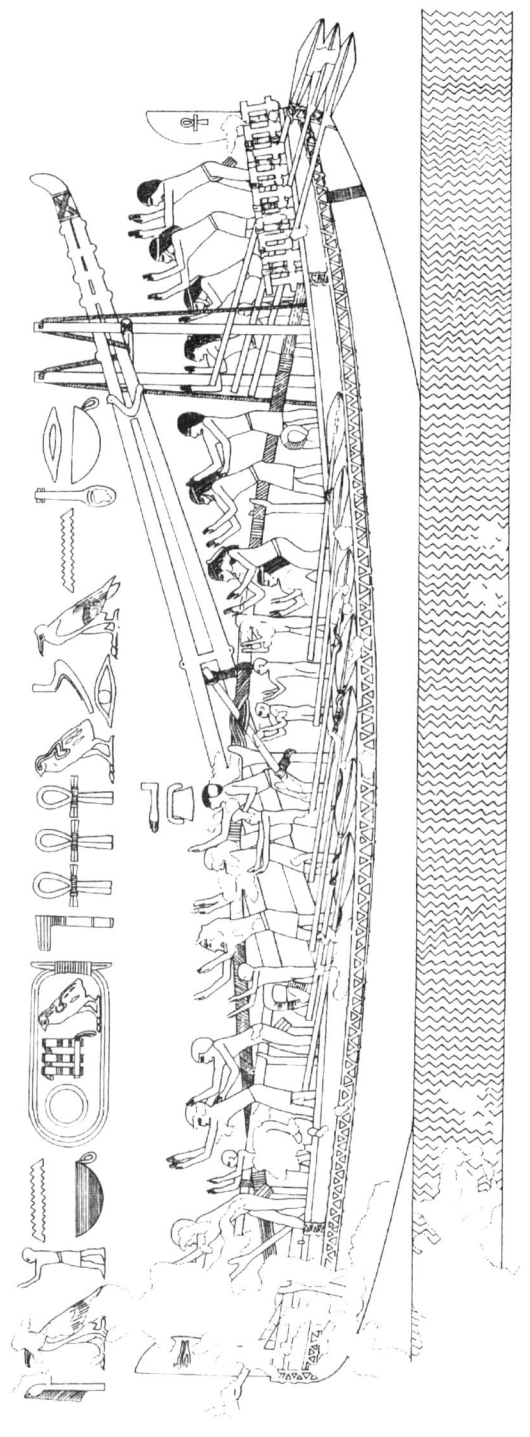

Fig. 3.19 Seafaring ship returning with Asiatics (mortuary temple of Sahure, Abusir; after L. Borchardt, Das Grabdenkmal des Königs Sahure. Band II: Die Wandbilder, Leipzig 1913, pl. 12)

defeat Khumbaba. When they arrived to the edge of the cedar woods, the text says, as follows:

'They stood at the border of the forest,
Staring at the cedar's height,
Staring at the forest's entry,
The place where Khumbaba used to walk and left a track,
The ways were kept aright, the path in good condition.
They looked at the mountain of cedars, seat of gods, dais of Irnini (Ishtar).
In front of the mountain of cedars, bearer of abundance,
Comfortable its shade, full of delight,
Entangled thorn was clothing [the forest,]
[...] cedar [...] ballukku-tree [...]'*

Finally in connection with Byblos we must mention the fact that it was the trees of Byblos that provided wood for the construction of the temple of Jerusalem, which was to contain the Ark of the Covenant with the laws of Moses. When Solomon succeeded David on the throne, he decided to build a temple for his God. When Solomon sent an order containing the request for building material to the Byblite ruler Hiram, he replied as follows:

'Praise be to the Lord today, for he has given David a wise son to rule over this great nation. So Hiram sent word to Solomon: "I have received the message you sent me and will do all you want in providing the cedar and pine logs. My men will haul them down from Lebanon to the sea, and I will float them in rafts by sea to the place you specify. There I will separate them and you can take them away. And you are to grant my wish by providing food for my royal household." In this way Hiram kept Solomon supplied with all the cedar and pine logs he wanted, and Solomon gave Hiram twenty thousand cors of wheat as food for his household, in addition to twenty thousand baths of pressed olive oil. Solomon continued to do this for Hiram year after year.'
(1ˢᵗ Kings, 5, 7–11)

Besides Byblos, another important site was that of el-Tel, the Hebrew Hai, located to the north of Jerusalem. According to the Bible, it was in the vicinity of this place, that is between Bethlehem and el-Tel, that Abraham set up his tent, built an offering altar and worshipped God (Genesis. 12, 8). A city was built at this very site, dominated by a stone fortress on the acropolis. Contemporary tombs were discovered on the northeastern slope, and on a lower terrace to the northheast of the acropolis archaeologists discovered an Iron Age settlement. The Early Bronze Age fortified city rose to the southeast of the acropolis. The city sanctuary was situated in its northwestern part, adjacent to the boundary wall. It may be estimated that the total area of the Early Bronze Age city was almost eleven

* *Translated by Tomáš Mařík, Department of the Near Eastern Studies, Charles University, Prague.*

Fig. 3.20 Entrance to the palace of Ugarit (Syria)

hectares. The town was built using monolithic blocks of stone, precisely according to Egyptian architectural tradition. We have further evidence of Egyptian influence in this area in the form of innumerable discoveries of Egyptian pottery. Other typical signs of an Egyptian presence are the alabaster vessels from the temple, among which was a model of a Nile hippopotamus. We may be justified in presuming the existence of an Egyptian settlement or even a trade colony at this site.

Another important port city was Ugarit in today's northern Syria. Most of the monuments of Egyptian origin found there come from the time of the Middle Kingdom. This site, which was originally one of the most important ports of the ancient world, located on the coast of Syria-Palestine, now lies several hundred metres from the sea coast, on a hill above the surrounding area. Even today, we can get some idea about the original character of the city and its fortifications. At the entrance of the city, the remains of magnificent fortifications have been preserved, together with a small postern gate, which enabled the besieged inhabitants of the city to surprise their enemies from behind. Apart from being an important port, Ugarit was also significant in its location close to the island of Cyprus, an important source of copper. At the beginning of the second millennium BC, Ugarit became, thanks to its trade contact with Cyprus, a leading centre for the production of bronze.

All that remains on the site today is the palace built on an area of over 6000 sq.m, a cemetery and an acropolis with two temples dedicated to the gods Baal and Dagan. All of these buildings come from the second half of the second

Fig. 3.21 Ebla, the royal palace with the archive magazines (Syria)

millennium BC, but they probably stood on the site of previous complexes, which had been originally built there. The palace was entered from the west, i.e. from the sea, through a large gate with two columns. The building itself consisted of several large courts, each of which was surrounded by a number of rooms. The courts were centres of administration as well as of private life. It is a peculiar trait of this palace that it contained five tombs for earlier rulers of the city. The subterranean tombs were approached by horizontal corridors, and the individual burial places consisted of a burial chamber with a stone vault. The tombs were part of the palace architecture and undoubtedly reflect the period of the history of Syria-Palestine when the dead were buried within the dwellings of their descendants. The importance of Ugarit for the Egyptian Middle Kingdom rulers is indicated by the discovery of two statues – a sphinx of Amenemhat III and a statue of the wife of Senwosret II, Khnumetneferhedjet Weret. Even non-royal statues were discovered in Ugarit: a statue of Senwosretankh, of his mother Teti, and daughter Sitamun, two female statues, one of a priest and several fragments of others of Egyptian origin.

Ebla, today's Tell Mardikh in northern Syria, was another site of great importance. Its greatest contribution to our understanding of the society corresponding to that of Abraham and Sinuhe lies in the written sources found here. Ebla became famous chiefly due to the discovery of an archive of texts inscribed on over 17 000 clay tablets, containing almost 2000 individual documents. These texts were written in the Eblaitic language, which belongs to the Semitic family of languages. The tablets date from the 24th and 23rd centuries BC. They contain numerous administrative, legal and religious texts, which richly illustrate the conditions of their time and contribute to the account provided by the Hebrew Bible (for example, on the problems of inheritance, succession, etc., that is on the topics of central importance for the tribal society of the Old Testament). The texts are also significant since they are the first to mention the later Hebrew names, such as Abram, Jacob, Laban, Ismael and Leah. Ebla's prosperity was terminated sometime around 2290–2250 BC by the invasion of the Akkadian ruler Naram-Sin, who conquered the city.

A visit to contemporary Ebla provides us only with a partial picture of the former monumentality of the city-state, which in its prime had around 30 000 inhabitants and whose fortifications were 30 metres thick and 20 metres high. The remains of the original Ebla, which flourished in the 24th–23rd centuries BC, include principally the royal palace with the administrative quarter of the city, where the clay tablets were discovered, the temple of Ishtar with the adjoining Northern royal palace, and finally, at the top of the central hill, the Amorite palace and temple of the god Shamash. No less magnificent are the city fortifications through which visitors enter the city.

The royal palace was accessible from the south by a large descending stairway of limestone and basalt blocks. To the east and north of this stairway were located rooms for servants and for the palace garrison. If the visitor turned left, i.e. to the west, he or she reached the very centre of the palace, the so-called audience hall, which adjoined the rooms of the state archives where its thousands of clay tablets were discovered. Later, in the course of the 19th–17th centuries, subterranean rooms under the archives were used to house the burials of the palace nobility, including the ruler Immeya (see below).

The unique temple of Ishtar was constructed in the shape of an oblong 15 metres high, stone terrace resembling the Mesopotamian ziggurats. In the middle of the terrace was a court, which extended over the area of 52 × 42 metres and was 15 m deep. Live lions, symbols of the goddess Ishtar, were kept in this court and regularly received offerings. The tripartite, so-called Big Temple, which is located in the vicinity of the Northern royal palace, is also of great historical importance. The sanctuary contained an offering altar, and the niche in its back wall held the cultic image of the goddess. The overall arrangement of the temple and its tight connection with the royal palace are features which allow us to consider this temple one of the oldest prototypes of Solomon's temple in Jerusalem, the description of which has come down to us in the Hebrew Bible.

Sporadic finds from Ebla indicate vivid contacts with Egypt in the time towards the end of the Old Kingdom (23rd century BC) and in the beginning of the Thirteenth Dynasty (ca. 1750 BC). From the Old Kingdom dates a fragment of an alabaster vessel with the name of Pepi I and from the time of the Thirteenth Dynasty comes the ritual sceptre found in tomb Q 78 C. This monument was dubbed the tomb of the 'Lord of the Goats' after the bronze goat statues that were discovered there. It was built in the underground area of the royal palace and in

Fig. 3.22 Mari (Syria)

all probability belonged to a ruler called Immeya. The sceptre discovered here belonged to Hetepibra Horhedjkheritef, a little known ruler from the Lower Egyptian city of Avaris, which later became the capital of the Hyksos. This ruler called himself 'the son of an Asiatic', and it is therefore possible that he could have had a close relationship with the Eblaite ruler Immeya. A recently published study by K. Ryholt provides us with a new interpretation of the sceptre. According to Ryholt's reading of the epigraphic evidence, it is possible that the sceptre originally belonged either to Amenemhat I from the Twelfth Dynasty, or to the Thirteenth Dynasty kings Hetepibra or Sehetepibra II. Two other roughly contemporary objects were discovered in the so-called Northern Palace in the vicinity of the temple of Ishtar, namely encrusted images of the deities Hathor and Sebek – the latter being a god whose popularity in Egypt was in its prime precisely at the time of the Twelfth and Thirteenth Dynasties.

Speaking about important settlements of this northern area, we must also mention Mari, a site in today's eastern Syria, which lies on the western bank of the Euphrates. This city was also a centre of international trade between Palestine and Mesopotamia, the Akkadian empire founded by Sargon and the Babylonian kingdom of the later king and lawgiver Khammurabbi. Mari maintained lively contacts with the area of southern Syria-Palestine and indirectly also with Egypt, to which it was connected via a desert route passing through the oasis of Palmyra.

Nowadays the tell, several metres high, is a tiny and sad reminder of the once mighty city state, whose palace was in its time one of the largest and most magnificent buildings in the area. The palace, the origins of which date back to the third millennium BC, reached its prime under the ruler Zimri-Lim (18th century BC). It contained almost 300 rooms which extended over 2.5 ha. Even today, however, the walls of the palace reach up to a height of almost 5 metres and the structure itself resembles a labyrinth. It was entered from the north via three rooms which led to a vast courtyard dedicated to the cult of Ishtar. This court was adjoined by a second, slightly smaller court, decorated with wall-paintings showing the king's coronation. The second court led to the sanctuary of the city's water goddess and to the east-west oriented throne hall with a throne at its western wall. Its location near the sanctuaries of Ishtar and the water goddess indicates the sacred nature of the kingship. From the west, south, and north, the throne hall, which was the heart of the palace, was flanked by industrial and living quarters. The south-eastern part of the palace was dedicated to other sanctuaries for the cults of Dagan, Ishtar and, in all likelihood, also other divinities. The objects which were discovered here may today be seen in the museums of Damascus, Aleppo and Paris (Louvre).

Besides archaeological evidence of an Egyptian presence in Syria-Palestine there are also reliefs, which come from the area to the south of Syria-Palestine, from the turquoise mines known as Wadi Maghara in the Sinai. These mines have preserved several depictions of Egyptian kings in a triumphant position, smiting Asiatics and foreign foes. The scenes, most of which are now displayed in the Egyptian Museum in Cairo, were carved as apotropaics, with the purpose of magically protecting the site of the mines, which the Egyptian rulers claimed for theirs own.

Fig. 3.23 The Citadel of Aleppo (Syria)

As a direct consequence of the development of the settled way of life, Syria-Palestine also witnessed the construction of large cemeteries. Because several subsequent generations stayed in one place, large family tombs emerged. These rock-cut tombs were accessible from a vertical shaft. Very often, they were virtually stuffed with the bodies of one family: each new burial caused the old ones to be removed to the sides or to the ancillary rooms of the tomb. Only the skulls, which were the objects of special piety, were lined along the walls. The burial equipment, which reflects relatively complex ideas pertaining to the afterlife existence, consisted primarily of pottery, which stored the commodities (above all foodstuffs and drinks) considered indispensable for an undisturbed life in the hereafter.

Any attempt at an exhaustive survey of the history of the area is hindered by the almost total absence of epigraphical sources. Nonetheless, it is likely that at this time the area was dominated by 'city-states', or eventually by larger settlements which governed their immediate surroundings, comprising mostly agricultural land and pastures. The idea of a unified state existing at this time is surely mistaken. Rather, the simultaneous coexistence of several city-states, each with its own sphere of influence, appears to have been much closer to reality. The period of prosperity was, however, filled with an atmosphere of continuous danger – as is endorsed by the numerous repair of damaged fortifications in Jericho – these being rebuilt no less than seventeen times.

The chief aspect of the relationship with Egypt was trade. The area exported chiefly Lebanese cedar wood from the port of Byblos, wine and olive oil. Besides maritime commerce, overland trade flourished, carried out by caravans of heavily loaded donkeys. However, the tomb of Inti at Deshasha in Upper Egypt, which comes from the Sixth Dynasty, includes a scene showing Egyptians besieging an Asiatic city. This tomb thus provides more evidence of the fact that the relationships between Egypt and Syria-Palestine were not always peaceful and that disagreement was often resolved by military force. The fortified Asiatic city is depicted in Inti's tomb as an oblong groundplan reinforced by bastions. In the area of Syria-Palestine, exactly the same type of city is also documented by archaeological evidence. The Asiatics are depicted with characteristic features, which are found in all similar scenes. They have beak-like and often big noses, long and narrow beards with curved tips, and long hair falling down to their shoulders tied with a black band around the forehead; they wear knee-length kilts. In Middle Kingdom times, Asiatics no longer have the band around the forehead and their dress is often of considerable length. Instead of a mere kilt, they now wear a long, hanging colourful tunic.

In connection with the tomb at Deshasha, it is appropriate to mention here the roughly contemporary account of Weni, a high Sixth Dynasty court official, who gives one of the most detailed reports of a military campaign in Syria-Palestine. His account surprises us with its extraordinarily detailed descriptions, as well as with the explicitly reported atrocities, which must have accompanied such campaigns.

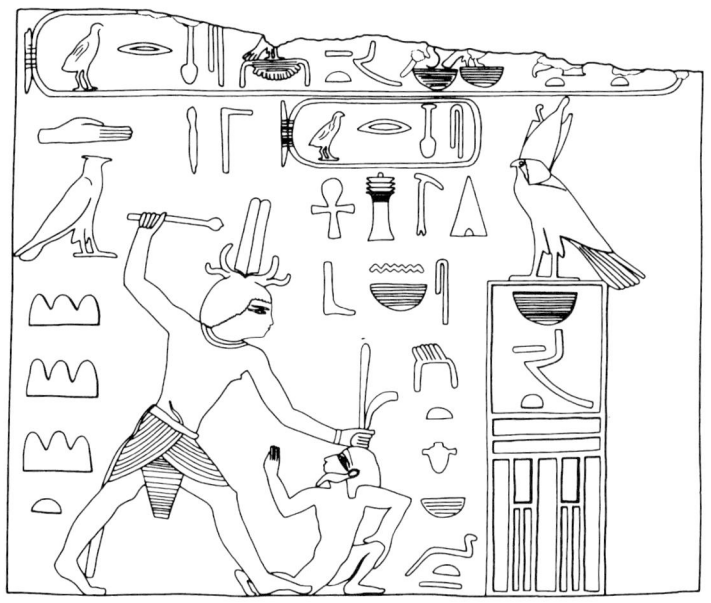

Fig. 3.24 King Sneferu smiting his enemies (Wadi Maghara, Sinai; after A. H. Gardiner, T. E. Peet, J. Černý, The Inscriptions of Sinai. Part I. Introduction and plates, London 1952, 2.5)

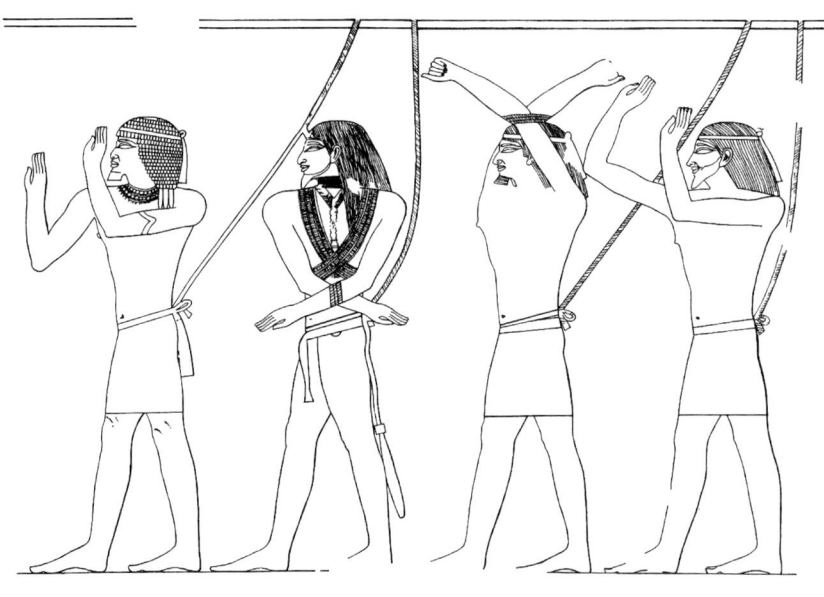

Fig. 3.25 Enemies of Egypt, Asiatic captive on the far right (mortuary temple of Sahure, Abusir; after L. Borchardt, Das Grabdenkmal des Königs Sahure. Band II: Die Wandbilder, Leipzig 1913, pl. 7)

'When His Majesty turned against the Asiatic Bedouin,
His Majesty summoned an army of several tens of thousands (of men)
from whole Upper Egypt, from Elephantine in the south
all the way to Medenit in Lower Egypt,
completely from the Two Sides of the House, from Sedjer and Khensedjeru,
of the Nubians of Irtjet, of the Nubians of Medja,
of the Nubians of Yam, of the Nubians of Wawat,
of the Nubians of Kaau and from the land of Irtjet.

His Majesty sent me at the head of this army,
there being princes, seal-bearers of the king,
confidants of the royal palace,
governors and mayors of royal domains
in Upper and Lower Egypt,
scout leaders and chief priests
from Upper and Lower Egypt,
chiefs of the nomes,
at the head of the squad of Upper and Lower Egypt,
domains and cities, which they governed,
and Nubians from these foreign countries.

I was also the one who was in command,
as the messenger of the king, overseer of peasants,
because I was righteous.
No one touched his comrade,
no one stole a loaf or sandal from a pilgrim,
no one took hold of a skirt in any city,
none of them seized anyone's goat.
I led them from the Northern Island to the gate of Iihetep
in the nome of Horus, the Lord of truth,
I assembled these troops,
that no servant (of the king) had ever compiled.

This army returned in peace,
having pillaged the Bedouin land,
this army returned in peace,
having trampled the Bedouin land,
this army returned in peace,
having destroyed its strongholds.
This army returned in peace,
having cut down its figs and its grapes.
This army returned in peace,
having set all their houses on fire.
This army returned in peace,

Fig. 3.26 Besieging an Asiatic fortress, tomb of Inti in Deshasha (after N. Kanawati, A. Mc Farlane, Deshasha. The Tombs of Inti, Shedu and others, Sydney 1993, pl. 27)

having killed tens of thousands of troops, who were in it.
This army returned in peace,
having brought hence numerous files of captives.
His Majesty praised me for it more than anything.'
(Urkunden des Alten Reiches I, Leipzig 1903, 101.13–104.4)

This section from the autobiography of Weni is of interest above all because it describes and elucidates various aspects of a punitive expedition against the Bedouin. The first part of this account describes the formation of an army, which was to march against the nomadic tribes. This force was comprised of soldiers from practically all over Egypt: from Elephantine in the south to the north of the country. Equally important is also the list of the individual groups of soldiers coming from various parts of Nubia which are named here: Irtjet, Dja, Yam, Wawat, and Kaa. As feared warriors, Nubian bowmen were much demanded in the Egyptian army. Even various frontier guards and the Egyptian police were recruited from amongst the Nubians.

The following section of the text describes the ranks of high officials, who probably organized the background of the campaign and the recording of the spoil, etc. It also mentions the priests, whose task was to guarantee that the Egyptian protector deities would provide the campaign with luck and success in battle. This could be guaranteed mainly by regular offerings and praise given to the individual gods.

The ensuing section first gives a list of everything that did not happen during the campaign. These collected misdeeds were probably an accompanying phenomenon of such campaigns. Therefore, Weni considered it laudatory to assert that nothing similar happened during his own campaign, or, in other words, that he was able to maintain law and order in his army. According to the testimony of Weni's account, the most common transgressions were the following: duels and skirmishes among the soldiers, robbing travellers, stealing clothes in the cities through which the army passed during its campaigns, and stealing animals from herds. At the end of his vivid account, Weni includes the result of his campaign against the Bedouin: plundering the land, the destruction of strongholds, cutting down trees (figs and vine), burning dwellings, murdering the population and taking the rest of the inhabitants into captivity. In Egypt, these people were then settled either on the land of the king, or on temple land, where they worked primarily as peasants.

Towards the end of the Early Bronze Age (EB IV, 2300–2000 BC), the area of Syria-Palestine underwent rapid change, sometimes accompanied by a sudden decline in the number of cities. Since this era is probably reflected in Sinuhe's account, we will consider it in some detail. The changes that influenced the culture of the Early Bronze Age were originally considered to have been a consequence of the invasions of new ethnic groups – the Amorites or even the Bedouin led by the Biblical patriarchs. The contemporarily prevalent view is that it was a natural development caused by the change of the economic situation and rapid development of the city-states. Together with the gradual decline of the Egyptian Old Kingdom in the end of the twenty-second century BC, the economic system of the city-states of Syria-Palestine was undermined. Since these city-states concentrated above all on the production of commodities that were required in Egypt, they lost their chief export market. The Egyptian market itself went through a period of crisis and for the ensuing two hundred years ceased to import the goods formerly so highly in demand. The total loss of the Egyptian market had a disastrous effect on the existence of the cities of Syria-Palestine. Most of them were deserted and, in order to find sustenance, their inhabitants returned to a semi-nomadic way of life, combined to a limited degree with agriculture. Most of the population moved into the contemporary Transjordan area and to the Negev desert. The Egyptian view of the situation of the First Intermediate Period is commented on by the sage Ipuwer:

'Today, no one travels north to Byblos. What should we use in place of pine wood for our mummies? Will, despite these facts, the priests be buried with objects coming all the way from Crete, and will the noble ones be embalmed with their resin? These products are, however, brought no more, since gold is lacking.'

The abruptness of the change in subsistence patterns of most of the area's population and the *de facto* regression to the nomadic way of life is proven, among other evidence by excavations in the area of the Negev desert and in the Sinai peninsula. Today, it is estimated that an area of approximately 70 000 sq. km was covered by more than 1000 smaller settlements, which were temporarily used by settled inhabitants. They practised sheep and goat herding and also, to a limited degree, hunting, agriculture, mining and the working of copper ore. They were, therefore, partly nomadic populations involved in semi-specialized activities – mining and trade with a highly valuable commodity, copper. These groups of inhabitants must have been mainly from the area of Palestine, since we have evidence that the existence of city-states on Syrian territory was not interrupted. Cities like Ebla on the territory of today's Hamma, and Aleppo were in their prime. The development of Byblos continued, while the situation in Ugarit resembles that at the end of the Early Bronze Age in Palestine. This difference may also have been brought about by the fact that the northern areas were not so exclusively dependent on trade with Egypt, and could export their goods to some other countries.

Despite the significant changes in Palestinian settlement patterns, it is still possible to find several cities which in one way or another persisted even at this time: Megiddo, Hazor, Beit-Shean, Jericho. The finds from Megiddo illustrate the character of such settlements (Layer XIV): a non-fortified village with simple huts and large open areas. A little temple was also found in the city, a small, one-room chapel where offerings were placed directly on the floor.

What evidence do we then have concerning the life of the populations in the end of the Early Bronze Age, after they left their cities and moved elsewhere?

The answer to this question can once again be sought in the archaeological excavations of Israeli scholars, chiefly in the area of the Negev desert. Their discoveries indicate that at this time the centre of settlement was transferred to the Negev lowland, to the northern and southern part of the Negev mountains, the area east of the Dead Sea, and northern and central Sinai. Mainly in the area of the Negev, seven great permanent settlements each of 100 – 200 buildings were found. According to their architecture, these settlements can be divided into three groups: the Ayin Zik group is characterized by circular dwellings built of large flat stones placed on their thin edges. In the centre of each of these circular rooms of 2 to 5 m in diameter stood one to three pillars, which supported roofs of large flat stone blocks. This group completely lacks enclosures for cattle, stables or cowsheds. The second group is called Har Yeruham and its typical houses are square, with roofs also supported by pillars. The rooms are often built around a small court. The buildings are placed on hilltops and the houses along the edge of the settlement are arranged so that their outer walls create a defensive fortification. Nahal Nizana, the third group of buildings, had large houses with rooms and spacious courts. Near these houses, excavators discovered large oval platforms of 7 – 20 m in diameter, paved with flat stones. A settlement similar to the third group was discovered in the western Sinai (Wadi Faukeia). Dwellings of the same size as those in the area of the Negev were also discovered in northern Sinai, from Rafah to the Pelusiac branch of the Nile. This was

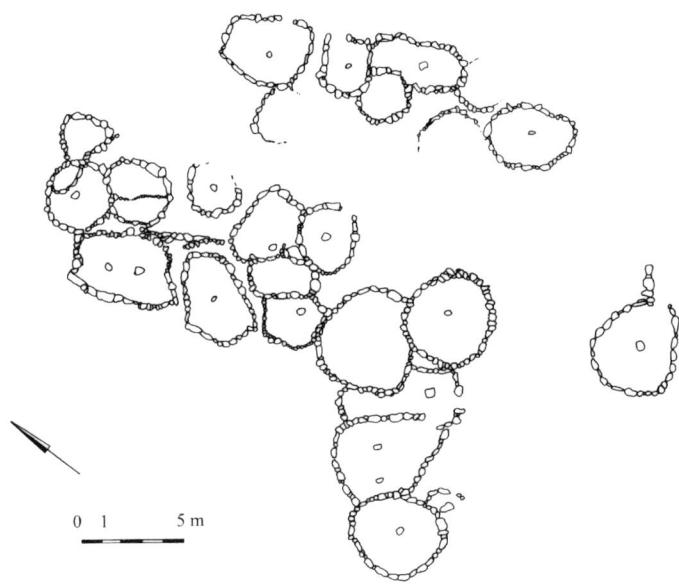

Fig. 3.27 Bir Resisim, plan of the settlement, the stone circles form several family clusters. The central pillars were supporting light roof construction, Sinai (after A. Mazar, Archaeology of the Land of the Bible. 10,000 – 587 B. C. E., New York 1992, p. 155, fig. 5.2)

undoubtedly the east-west route through which the Asiatic tribes entered Egypt in the course of the First Intermediate Period.

Besides large permanent settlements, it was also possible to excavate several small, temporary encampments, which were scattered at a greater or smaller distance around the large settlements. The encampments commonly consisted of 10 to 20 small one-storey houses and had many enclosures for cattle.

The pattern shows that towards the end of the third millennium BC there was continuous homogeneous settlement in the area between the Dead Sea and the eastern Egyptian frontier. As far as the material culture of this area is considered, it may be said that, apart from its homogeneity, it was very much like that in the area of Jordan. The connection of these two cultures is indicated chiefly by the presence of red polished ware. Other pottery groups allow us to presume a strong cultural relationship with the area of Palestine. The small encampments presumably belonged to herdsmen, who lived outside the main settlements with their cattle.

In order to learn about the subsistence patterns of the population living in this vast area, we must once again turn to archaeology. The evidence from excavations seems to indicate that practically no cattle was kept on long-term settlements. Most of these include the remains of dwellings with no sheds or enclosures suitable for household animals. Only on the sites of Bir Resisim and Nahal Nizana, covering the area of 80 and 8500 sq. m were enclosures discovered. They could have respectively contained approximately 40 and 4000 cattle. Otherwise, evidence for animal husbandry comes chiefly from temporary campsites, which is understandable, since the low potential of the pastures and large size of the herds forced their owners to keep moving on. For the total 250 temporary encampments, the enclosures traced so far covered an area of over 20 000 sq. m, and could house up to 10 000 head of cattle. It may also be estimated that these encampments with their habitable area of 8000 sq. m were occupied by 800 adult individuals, i.e. around 400 families. On average, each family would thus own 25 head of cattle, which shows that cattle herding was just an ancillary activity of these communities. In order for the group to rely exclusively on animal husbandry, 100 – 110 head of cattle would be necessary for each family, as is shown by contemporary anthropological parallels from the Middle East. The evidence for agricultural activities in the large permanent settlemets is almost nil, which means that wheat growing had no significance for their economy, and that they mostly relied on the exploitation of plants and fruits growing in the neighbourhood.

A totally different picture appears when we consider copper-working at these large sites. The most important evidence for these specialized activities can be found on the site of Har Yeruham, where about a third of the total area can be considered an 'industrial zone'. The archaeologists discovered here a considerable number of heavy stone hammers and millstones. Besides that, there were also thick layers of black ash and stone buildings filled with ash. Numerous copper fragments and small pieces of copper ingots were scattered over the entire

Fig. 3.28 Khirbet Iskander (Jordan)

settlement. It is therefore likely that copper was worked here, together with the production of copper instruments. The situation was similar within the settlement of Ayin Zik, where a substantial number of stone vessels were discovered. Each house also contained a large number of stone instruments – in some cases, archaeologists found over 40 stone hammers in one house. Moreover, the excavators also found sandstone blocks formed into large flat panels which were used for sharpening the tools. There were also large stone working tables and places with the remains of fire, as well as numerous copper ingots. A similar picture is indicated by the situation on the sites of Mashabe Sade and Har Zayiad. These finds indicate that the basic aspect of these economies of such large settlements was the processing of copper and the copper trade.

If we once again look at these three groups of settlements, it becomes clear that only the second and third, with complexes of rooms built around central courts, correspond to the traditional concept of a family house. However, the first group, typical for the site of Ayin-Zik, consisted of one-room houses, which were totally unsuitable for families. As was persuasively demonstrated by an archaeologist, Mordekhai Haiman, they were temporary encampments serving as shelters for copper merchants travelling from east to west, from the copper mines in Wadi Faynan south of the Dead Sea, to the eastern Nile Delta. It seems that the Egyptian trade hegemony from Old Kingdom times, which witnessed numerous seafaring expeditions to the coast of Syria-Palestine, was later, as a consequence of Egypt's decline, superseded by an Asiatic overlordship.

History often repeats itself, and this time too, the Asiatics renewed the land east-west trade route. This route connected southern Palestine with the eastern Delta and corresponded to the arterial road at the beginning of the third millennium BC, and to the Ways of Horus known from the historical sources at the beginning of the Middle Kingdom. In connection with long-distance trade, some modern calculations pertaining to trade caravans are of interest. The trade caravans of that time may have relied exclusively on donkeys. A donkey laden with 40 kilos of load (which is 60 copper ingots of the type usually discovered in the area), is able to travel at the average speed of 2.5 km per hour for eight hours a day. Each day, it can travel twenty kilometres. The distance of 300 km which divided Wadi Faynan from the eastern Delta could thus be covered in fifteen days.

It remains a mystery, however, who organized such demanding projects, which could not have been realized without an appropriate (chiefly agricultural) background and military protection. When we take into account the fact that at this time, the coast of Syria-Palestine was an area of secondary importance, the political and economic centre is most often sought to the south and east of the Dead Sea, where Genesis 14 already indicates the existence of five large city-states (Sodom, Gomorrah, Adma, Seboy, and Soar). Finally, archaeological excavations in this area have revealed agricultural, partially fortified centres – sites such as Iktana, Khirbet Iskander, Aroer and Ader – which could have formed the background for the mining activities. This system of copper mining disappeared towards the end of the Egyptian Eleventh Dynasty, when the reunified Egyptian state was once again able to organize and sustain expeditions to the copper mines on the Sinai and Arava and began to be self-sufficient again.

As far as the burial customs of this time are concerned, everything points to a type that was characteristic rather of a nomadic than for a settled agricultural population. The burials are mostly of one or a few individuals, which was in direct contrast to the preceding period, when the agricultural population buried their dead in family tombs containing numerous persons. Altogether, we know of three types of tombs. The first of these consisted of a shaft tomb with a burial chamber built in the wall at the bottom of the shaft and covered by a large stone slab. The second type includes stone tumuli, while the third consists of dolmens covered by a massive tumulus-like mound. Many cemeteries are concentrated in the vicinity of erstwhile important city centres – Megiddo, Jericho, Hazor, Lakhish, Beit-Shean. A number of new cemeteries were discovered in the mountains of Hebron, such as eg. Khirbet Kirmil with 900 shaft tombs. The tumuli and dolmens are, on the other hand, concentrated in the mountains of Negev. In contrast to the preceding periods, both primary and secondary burials were now practised. A primary burial means that the deceased is interred shortly after his death and he is transported no further. A secondary burial typically involves firstly a temporary burial, after which the body is gathered up (as a consequence of natural decay, by this time usually only bones remain), and carried to another cemetery. This custom is characteristic of nomadic populations who, as a rule, prefer to bury the members of their tribe in the tribal cemetery.

If they are too distant from it, they are forced to bury their deceased in a temporary site and return for them only when they are on their way back to their ancestral cemetery.

Most of our information about this period comes from the excavation of cemeteries, which were maintained in the vicinity of former settlement centres (Jericho, Lakhish). Although rock shaft tombs continued to be built, a new style of burial slowly became predominant. In contrast to previous periods, each tomb contained – as we have already seen – only one deceased, which was a direct consequence of the nomadic way of life. It is very interesting to note that these burials are in most cases secondary, perhaps due to the fact that the individual nomadic groups always eventually returned to their customary cemeteries.

The indisputable fact is, that towards the end of the Early Bronze Age, Negev and Sinai became centres of intensive settlement and dwellings for numerous populations – this is evident from archaeological sources, as well as from the Bible, from the account of Abraham's departure from Kharran after the Lord promised to give him a new land. Abraham set out to the area of the desert of Negev (Negeb):

'He took his wife Sarai, his nephew Lot, all the possessions they had accumulated and the people they had acquired in Haran, and they set out for the land of Canaan, and they arrived there. Abram travelled through the land as far as Shechem. All that time the Canaanites were in the land. The Lord appeared to Abram and said: "To your offspring I will give this land." So he built an altar there to the Lord, who had appeared to him. From there he went on towards the hills east of Bethel and pitched his tent, with Bethel on the west and Ai on the east. There he built an altar to the Lord and called on the name of the Lord. Then Abram set out and continued towards the Negev.'
(Genesis 12, 5–9)

Until recently, most authors were puzzled by the fact that a settled population of the Early Bronze Age, which practised trade and agriculture, could regress to a cattle herding and nomadic way of life. A plausible explanation is provided by the currently prevailing theory of anthropologists and economists, according to which the nomadic way of life relying mostly on cattle herding is one of the consequences of the gradual settlement of the population and their transition to agriculture. As a consequence of this process, the population density in the area increased, and it was necessary to take the cattle herds further and further away from human dwellings. The people who relied exclusively on cattle herding were thus gradually more and more independent of these settlements, and finally, they became nomads herding cattle, goats and sheep. Another theory, based on the observation of the Bedouin in the Middle East and Africa in our century, maintains that the process which finally led to nomadisation may have been initiated as a consequence of the growth of herds in the possession of several families. Their large herds then forced these families to travel and search for ever new sources of pasture. In the light of these theories, the subsistence patterns of the

Fig. 3.29 The Bedouins accompanying the return from a stone expedition in the desert (causeway of Sahure, Abusir)

end of the Early Bronze Age may no longer seem so primitive and surprising. Finally, studies of Bedouin populations indicate that their subsistence pattern is a lot more reliable, less demanding and less hazardous than that of specialized agriculturalists.

In ancient times it was, however, often the case that, due to adverse climatic conditions, these tribes were not able to sustain their herds. In such cases, they made use of the weak eastern Egyptian frontier, and penetrated the Nile Delta, which provided sufficient pasture for their herds. The characteristic attributes of these tribes are revealed to us by the literary work called the *Instructions for King Merikare*, which dates from the Heracleopolitan period (Kheti III) and includes the following descriptions of such nomadic populations:

> *'They say of the barbarian:*
> *Indeed, the Asiatic is wretched and evil*
> *because of the place where he is,*
> *lacking water, inaccessible due to numerous trees;*
> *its ways are impenetrable because of the mountains.*
> *He is unable to stay in one place,*
> *his legs drag him away for lack of sustenance.*

He has been fighting since the time of Horus.
Not conquering, but neither conquered,
he does not announce the day of battle
like a robber whom his people cast out.'
(The Instructions for King Merikare, 91 – 94)

This text provides a concise picture of the life of the nomadic Bedouins, although it must be admitted that it is a very Egypto-centric one. Its main theme is the description of the environment, since Bedouin tribes were always simply barbarians for the Egyptians. The text describes the hostile and poor highlands, which were inhabited by these groups. These characteristics may hold good even for the entire area of the Sinai. The account emphasizes the fact that it is due to the lack of sustenance that the Bedouin are driven to nomadism. The passage quoted ends with an allusion to the invincibility of the Bedouin, which was probably a consequence of their being scattered over a large area, their tremendous mobility, as well as their fine knowledge of their terrain. Finally, the text mentions the 'barbaric' art of war as practised by the Bedouin, who never announced the time of battle in advance.

The Egyptians had a number of synonyms for the Bedouin. Ever since Middle Kingdom times, the Egyptians had named these Asiatics after several of their characteristic features, as e.g. 'people with the knot on their shoulder', since they tied their clothes with a knot on the shoulder, 'the pigtailed ones', for those who often tied their hair into a pigtail, or 'kilt-wearers' after that type of garment. Often they were also called the 'bowmen' or 'people of the bow', after their predominant weapon. Geographical classification perhaps also played its role, since for the Bedouin living beyond the Sinai were referred to as 'those who dwell on the sand'. 'The sand' in this case referred to the Sinai peninsula, and in the third millennium BC, this name was frequently used for any population from Syria-Palestine. The nomads living immediately beyond the eastern border of Egypt were also called 'Easterners'.

The penetration of the Bedouin, i.e. of Asiatics, into Egyptian territory is also mentioned by the *Instructions for King Merikare*. The account directly describes the expelling of the Asiatics from Egypt and the constructions of strongholds to defend Egypt against the Asiatics:

'But while I lived and was here,
the bowmen were inside the fortress, which was open.
I drove them out of it
and I made the Northern land defeat them.
I captured their people,
I seized all their nourishment
and killed...
so that Asiatics detest Egypt now.

*Do not worry about it:
the Asiatic is like a crocodile on the bank,
he attacks on a barren road,
but does not make assault on the place of a populous city.*

*Dig a ditch (in Wadi Tumilat)...
and fill one of its halves with water all the way to the Bitter Lakes:
it will be a defense against the bowmen.
The strongholds there are prepared for the fight, the soldiers are numerous
and the subjects know how to use weapons.'*
(after B. Vachala, The Wisdom of Ancient Egypt, Prague 1992, 81)

The presence of nomads in Egypt was not an uncommon phenomenon, and even Sinuhe mentions in his account that he met a sheikh who had visited Egypt, perhaps in the time of the reign of Amenemhat I. This form of contact between the two cultures is also confirmed by the famous scene from the tomb of Khnumhotep II at Beni Hassan, which depicts the Bedouin chief Abishay with his family. This scene comes from the sixth year of Senwosret II, and shows the Bedouin chief together with his suite, comprising eight men, four women, three children and donkeys (the accompanying text states that altogether there should be thirty seven individuals), as they pay homage to the tomb owner, bringing him powder for eye-paint as a present. Actually, this scene is very difficult to explain. In no way does it depict wretched Bedouin pleading for permission to pasture their cattle on Egyptian territory. The possibility of a trade expedition is also a little unlikely, since the number of people is rather high for a trade caravan, and would make its sustenance burdensome. The group includes women and children, who usually did not take part in trade expeditions. Furthermore, the commodity brought by the Asiatics is black cosmetic powder, which was commonly exploited in Egypt or in the Eastern Desert. These two facts exclude the interpretation of the scene as one depicting a trade caravan from Asia. The accompanying inscriptions over the scene state: 'The arrival for the bringing of black powder' and 'he (i.e. Abishay) brings thirty-six Asiatics'. These labels are complemented by a document held in the hand of 'the scribe of the royal documents' Neferhetep, who ushers the entire group led by Abishay into Khnumhotep II's presence. The text of the document runs as follows:

'Year 6 under the Majesty of Horus Leader of the Two Lands, King Khakheperra: list of the Asiatics, whom the son of the nomarch Khnumhotep brings because of black eye powder: Asiatics from Shu: 37.'

Besides Neferhetep, the scene includes another royal official, the overseer of hunters, Kheti, who may have accompanied the Asiatics on their journey through Egypt all the way to Beni Hassan. The circumstances seem to indicate that the scene depicts Asiatics, who have come to Egypt in order to settle here and take

Fig. 3.30 Bedouins from the tomb of Khnumhotep II at Beni Hassan (after P. E. Newberry, *Beni Hassan I*, London 1893, pl. 31)

part in the mining of black eye powder. The act of accepting the nomads takes place under the cautious supervision of royal deputies, the scribe of the royal documents and the overseer of hunters, Neferhetep and Kheti.

Sinuhe's account strongly implies that numerous Bedouin tribes were located immediately beyond the Egyptian frontier and that in Egypt's unstable times during the First Intermediate Period, they even penetrated the Delta. The reason for such an undertaking, which was not without risk, was both simple and extremely important. Sufficient irrigation in Egypt guaranteed the Bedouin sustenance for their herds, for these beasts were their chief source of livelihood. These facts are mentioned in the Hebrew Bible, since the legendary Abraham, the forefather of the Jewish people, despite certain danger, had already been forced to find refuge in Egypt in the time of drought:

'Now there was a famine in the land, and Abram went down to Egypt to live there for a while because the famine was severe. As he was about to enter Egypt, he said to his wife Sarai: "I know what a beautiful woman you are. When the Egyptians see you, they will say, "This is his wife." Then they will kill me but will let you live. Say you are my sister so that I will be treated well for your sake and my life will be spared because of you."'
(Genesis 12,10–13)

Besides the fact that the passage describes how the Bedouin were taking refuge in Egypt in order to survive, it is also important to note that there are absolutely no indications of the eastern Egyptian border with Syria-Palestine being fortified or watched, as was the case in later times, as well as in the time of Sinuhe's flight. Therefore, we may only hypothesize that the Biblical Abraham might have stayed in Egypt in the time of the interregnum of the First Intermediate Period.

It is probably not by chance that the Arab Khushmaan tribe gave the same reasons for their settling in the Egyptian Eastern Desert between the Nile valley and the Red Sea, which happened almost 4000 years after Abraham:

'In Arabia the acacias and other trees had been cut. The ibex had all been hunted, and there was little pasture. In Egypt, there was water in the interior. The mountains were full of ibex. We used to come from Arabia to buy grain and other supplies in Qena. We made acacia charcoal to sell in the Nile Valley and brought provisions there. People returned to Arabia saying, 'Egypt is rich'. So, we started coming. In Arabia there was always warfare, raiding, and killing. Raiders came from as far away as Syria to attack us. In Egypt there was peace.'
(T. Hobbs, Bedouin Life in the Egyptian Wilderness, Cairo 1990, 17)

When, however, the Bedouin prospered too much, the land could consequently no longer sustain their large herds, and the tribe was split. Evidence for such events has come down to us even from the times of Abraham's migrations:

'So Abram went up from Egypt to the Negev, with his wife and everything he had, and Lot went with him. Abram had become very wealthy in livestock and in silver and gold.

From the Negev he went from place to place until he came to Bethel, to the place between Bethel and Ai where his tent had been earlier and where he had first built an altar. There Abram called on the name of the Lord.

Now Lot, who was moving about with Abram, also had flocks and herds and tents. But the land could not support them while they stayed together, for their possessions were so great that they were not able to stay together. And quarrelling arose between Abram's herdsmen and the herdsmen of Lot. The Canaanites and Perizzites were also living in the land at that time.

So Abram said to Lot, "Let's not have any quarrelling between you and me, or between your herdsmen and mine, for we are brothers. Is not the whole land before you? Let's part company. If you go to the left, I'll go to the right; if you go to the right, I'll go to the left."

(Genesis 13, 1–9)

One of the most frequent names that the Egyptians used for the Asiatics was the term ˁ3mw, which can be pronounced as a'amu. This term comes from the end of the Old Kingdom, and may have been first used by Weni in his description of his campaign against the Asiatics. The phoneme *ayin* (ˁ) was in West Semitic languages pronounced as a sharp guttural tone. *Aleph* (3) was used by the Egyptians to record the West Semitic *l* in their texts. The presence of *l* in the West Semitic languages of the Third millennium BC is also documented in the Eblaitic dialect from northern Syria, which was discovered on the tablets from the palace archives from Ebla, to the south of Aleppo. Therefore, we must search for a common West Semitic word, which would be composed of the following consonants: *a – l – m*. This is not difficult at all, since all West Semitic languages contain the stem 'alamu, which means 'young man' or – in the usual sense – 'man'. That means that the Asiatics called themselves 'men' with as confident an ethnocentrism as the Egyptians, who called themselves *remetj*, 'people'.

The rise of the Middle Bronze Age was contemporary with the consolidation of the situation in Egypt and the reunification of the Egyptian state at the end of the Eleventh and beginning of the Twelfth Dynasties. The renewal of trade relationships with the area of Syria-Palestine led to a gradual return to the situation of the Early Bronze Age (except for its terminal stage) and to the revival of the cities which had been deserted for almost two centuries. Some epigraphic evidence for the renewal of trade relationships with Byblos comes even from the Eleventh Dynasty, as early as the time of Nebhepetre Mentuhotep II. This is made clear by the autobiographical inscription of the official Henenu from his tomb built in the vicinity of Deir el-Bahri (tomb no. 313). In this text, Henenu states that he undertook a journey to the 'cedar plateau', where he cut down cedars and transported them to Egypt.

However, the consolidation of Egyptian interests in the area of Syria-Palestine was gradual and lasted throughout the entire first stage of the Middle Bronze Age (MB IIA, 2000–1800/1750 BC). This period was marked by the existence of numerous nomadic groups, as well as by the gradual reoccupation of city-states, which were at first regenerated primarily in the area along the coastline of the

Mediterranean Sea. As in earlier periods, the most eloquent testimony for social development comes from the cemeteries, which reflect the growing social differentiation between the people buried there. Apart from the return to multiple burials in rock shaft tombs, an entirely new type of burial appears. These new tombs are panelled with stone blocks and after the burial, they were covered with limestone plates. They commonly have much richer burial equipment than the shaft tombs, consisting of large collections of elaborately decorated pottery, as well as of metal weaponry. These tombs may have been reserved exclusively for high-ranking members of society, who were perhaps of foreign origin. The discoveries of statues of Egyptian officials on several sites in the territory of Syria and Palestine are also worth mentioning. They belonged to the official Djehutihotep from Megiddo (his tomb is located at el-Bersha), and to Senwosretankh from Ugarit; other finds come from Tel el-'Ajjul, Gezer, Byblos and Qatna. These other monuments belonged mostly to men and women ranking lower in the social hierarchy, about whose activities and presence in this area we know absolutely nothing. They may have been involved in the organizing of certain trade activities on behalf of Egypt.

Further evidence of a renewed settlement of the population of Syria-Palestine are the so-called execration texts coming from the Twelfth Dynasty Egypt, which mostly date to the period of 1850–1750 BC. These texts were believed to guarantee the magical destruction of Egypt's enemies. The enemies were either directly modelled as single figures of fired clay, or else were models made of stone or wood. A third alternative was to have their names inscribed on clay vessels. An execration formula was then pronounced over these objects, which were subsequently ritually smashed. The purpose of this sympathetic magic was to destroy the individuals, cities, or tribes in Syria-Palestine, Nubia and Libya, which were mentioned in the texts on the figurines or vessels. These texts do not aim at the cities or territories themselves, but at the individual chiefs of cities or tribes. When toponyms are mentioned next to them, it is in order to better particularize a chieftain. It is noteworthy that these texts do not include the princes of Byblos, but only regular inhabitants of the city, which indicates that Byblos must have been within the Egyptian sphere of influence. Neither do these texts mention Megiddo, Ugarit or Qatna. Their importance lies in the fact that they provide us with a detailed picture of the geopolitical situation in Syria-Palestine, of the existent cities, their approximate number, as well as of the nomadic populations in this Bronze Age period. These texts thus indirectly continue the Old Kingdom tradition, reflected in the numerous figurines of tied Asiatics and Libyans sculpted in stone or wood that have been discovered in the royal funerary complexes of Egyptian kings.

Among such texts and models from the Middle Kingdom are the following: uninscribed figurines from Helwan from the beginning of the Twelfth Dynasty, figurines and inscribed sherds from the Nubian fortress of Mirgissa dated approximately to 1900–1850 BC, pottery sherds of unknown provenance located now in the Berlin collections and dated to the time of Senwosret III, and

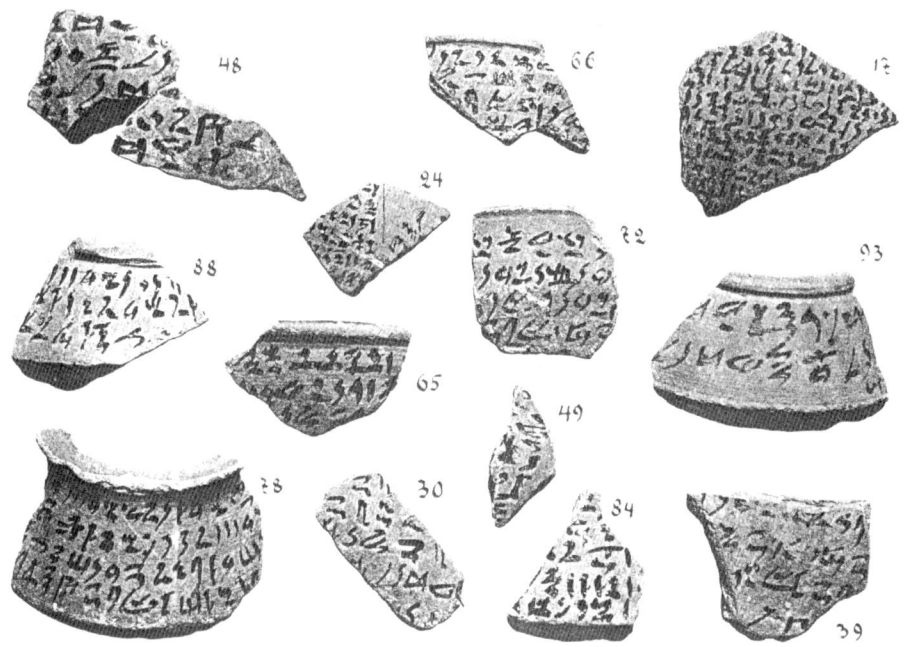

Fig. 3.31 Execration texts from the Middle Kingdom (K. Sethe, Die Ächtung feindlicher Fürsten, Völker und Dinge auf altägyptischen Tongefässscherben des Mittleren Reiches, Berlin 1926, pl. 33)

Amenemhat III, and finally clay figurines discovered in Saqqara (today in Brussels). The Mirgissa and Berlin group are divided from the Brussels texts by a gap of approximately fifty years, and these two groups differ substantially as far as the recorded situation in the area is concerned.

The early Twelfth Dynasty group of texts from Mirgissa mentions only a few cities – five altogether, while the Brussels corpus includes over sixty. The texts of Mirgissa and Berlin associate several local chieftains with a single place. In the later Brussels group of texts, each site is connected with just a single leader. Another difference lies in the fact that while the toponyms in the Berlin texts are ordered at random, the Brussels group arranges the toponyms according to geographical areas. Further, the Berlin texts place little emphasis on the identification of the chieftains according to areas, while the Brussels texts do this rigorously. This fact provides us with new evidence that the population of the area of Syria-Palestine was not completely settled at the beginning of the Middle Bronze Age. While the Berlin and Mirgissa texts date to the beginning of the Middle Bronze Age (MB I), the Brussels texts belong to the second stage of the Middle Bronze Age (MB II).

The Mirgissa texts mention only four sites, which were located along the coast of the Mediterranean Sea: Byblos, Ulazza, Anaki and Mugar. Only a single site from the Transjordan area is mentioned: Shutu. The inland of Syria-Palestine, with a very low density of population, was completely out of the picture. The sites mentioned indicate that the Egyptians were interested above all in contacts with the coastal areas. The Berlin texts list four sites on the Mediterranean coast: Arkata, Ashkelon, Ulazza and Byblos, and other three in its vicinity: 'Anaki, Mugar and S'apa. Of the sites on the Palestinian territory, Jerusalem, Ashkelon and Rehab are mentioned. The toponyms in both groups are spelled in such a way that they indicate and even make probable the theory that not only the sites themselves are meant, but also their surroundings. This further corroborates the presumption of archaeologists and historians that city-states were gradually developing here, out of which local rulers governed the surrounding areas from their centres of power. These chieftains are, moreover, referred to by the common term *nekhet*, 'strong man', a term which usually refers to Bedouin chieftains. This term also appears in the story of Sinuhe, when he is challenged to fight a foreign chief.

On the other hand, the Brussels group of texts mentions many more cities, and most of the rulers occurring in these texts are uniquely identified by a toponym which cannot be explained otherwise than as a name for a city. This too testifies to the gradual settlement of the area and the return to the original Early Bronze Age patterns. The individual place-names are grouped as follows: the coastal plain in southern Syria-Palestine and in the area of Shephelah, the sites along the trade route connecting the coast with Sekhem, and Pella in the Jordan

Fig. 3.32 Remains of a monumental doorway built by Amenemhat I at Ezbet Helmi (Tell ed-Daba'a)

valley, the plain in the surroundings of Haifa and to the east of Mount Karmel, the caravan route through the northern part of the Jordan valley to Bikaa, the Transjordan route, the area along the upper Orontes River and the area of Damascus in the southern part of today's Syria and, finally, the Phoenician coast. Among the places identified with certainty are Jerusalem, Akko, Shamkhuna, Lakhish, and Beit-Shemesh. In a rather simplified way, we may say that the Brussels texts describe the same area as the Berlin corpus, but the list of the Brussels group is a lot more detailed, mentioning individual kingdoms and indicating the population growth in the area. This growth was mainly connected with the area along the long-distance trade routes, which connected Egypt with the areas to the north and east. In contrast with earlier texts, this corpus uses the term 'nekhet' to refer to a foreign chief or ruler much less frequently. Other terms are used instead, such as the equivalents of 'city dwellers' and 'collectors of crops'.

The existence of the aforementioned execration texts certainly does not exclude the possibility that the Egyptians and the population of Syria-Palestine may have lived in a peaceful symbiosis. Persuasive evidence in favour of this view was discovered at the site of Tell ed-Daba'a in the eastern part of the Nile Delta, which played an important role mainly in the time of the Second Intermediate Period and the Nineteenth Dynasty of the Egyptian New Kingdom under the reign of Ramesses II.

In sector F/I of the site, archaeologists discovered a settlement from the beginning of the Middle Kingdom. It consisted of dwellings measuring 5×5 m, which were built of mud bricks. The individual houses were separated by 5 m wide streets, and it is likely that the entire settlement might have been enclosed within a boundary wall. The eastern part of the settlement area was free and may have been used as a night shelter for cattle, goats and sheep. The total area of the settlement is unknown, but its population may have exceeded a thousand inhabitants, including both men and women. The city was deserted in the time of the reign of Amenemhat I, when the inhabitants were moved to a recently founded site, which was called (according to the surviving sources) 'The settlement of the beginning of the two ways of Amenemhat, justified'. The pottery from this site included mainly imperfectly-fired cooking pots, which typologically belong to the nomads of the early Middle Bronze Age (MB I) in Syria-Palestine. The relationship of these nomads to the settlements may have been twofold. Perhaps they indeed temporarily lived here at a time when they also inhabited the eastern Delta, or they at least often visited this Egyptian location. The importance of the site grew in the time of the reign of Senwosret III, perhaps in connection with the growing number of expeditions to the Sinai and Syria-Palestine.

A further development of foreign settlements took place toward the end of the Twelfth Dynasty. A loose agglomeration of houses belonging to the cultural and architectural tradition of Northern Syria was set up south of the original settlement F/I. Their basic types included the 'house with a central hall' and the 'house with a wide hall'. The former resembles the architecture of the roughly

Fig. 3.33 Remains of what once used to be the Hyksos capital of Egypt (Austrian excavations at Tell ed-Daba'a)

contemporary palace of Mari. The settlement also includes a cemetery with tombs that are, unlike those of the Egyptian cultural tradition, next to the houses of the living. This custom is typical mainly for the area of Syria-Palestine in the time of the Middle Bronze Age. The tombs discovered here were mostly lined and covered with mud bricks. Their burial equipment, above all weapons of Asiatic provenance, indicates that they belonged mostly to Asiatic warriors in the service of the Egyptian crown. Their typical weapons included two lances, a battle axe and a dagger. Whilst the previous inhabitants were nomads, now we are concerned with a settled urban population, which is attested above all by cemeteries constructed close to houses. According to the director of excavations Manfred Bietak, this settlement was a base for expeditions to the Sinai, and Asiatics from the land of Retjenu may have lived here (Retjenu was at that time a toponym which referred to the wider area of Syria-Palestine). Tell ed-Daba'a was probably also inhabited by Asiatics, who were employed by the Egyptian state to lead expeditions to the Sinai, and above all to Serabit el-Khadim. This fact is attested for example by the stele of Imeni, the 'royal envoy and commander', which states that he was the son of an Asiatic, and depicts him as an official with the typical Asiatic elongated beard. On the whole, it appears that the Egyptians trusted the Asiatics even as leaders of expeditions.

In the ensuing stage of the Asiatic settlement, in the beginning of the Thirteenth Dynasty, we encounter some new evidence regarding the influence of

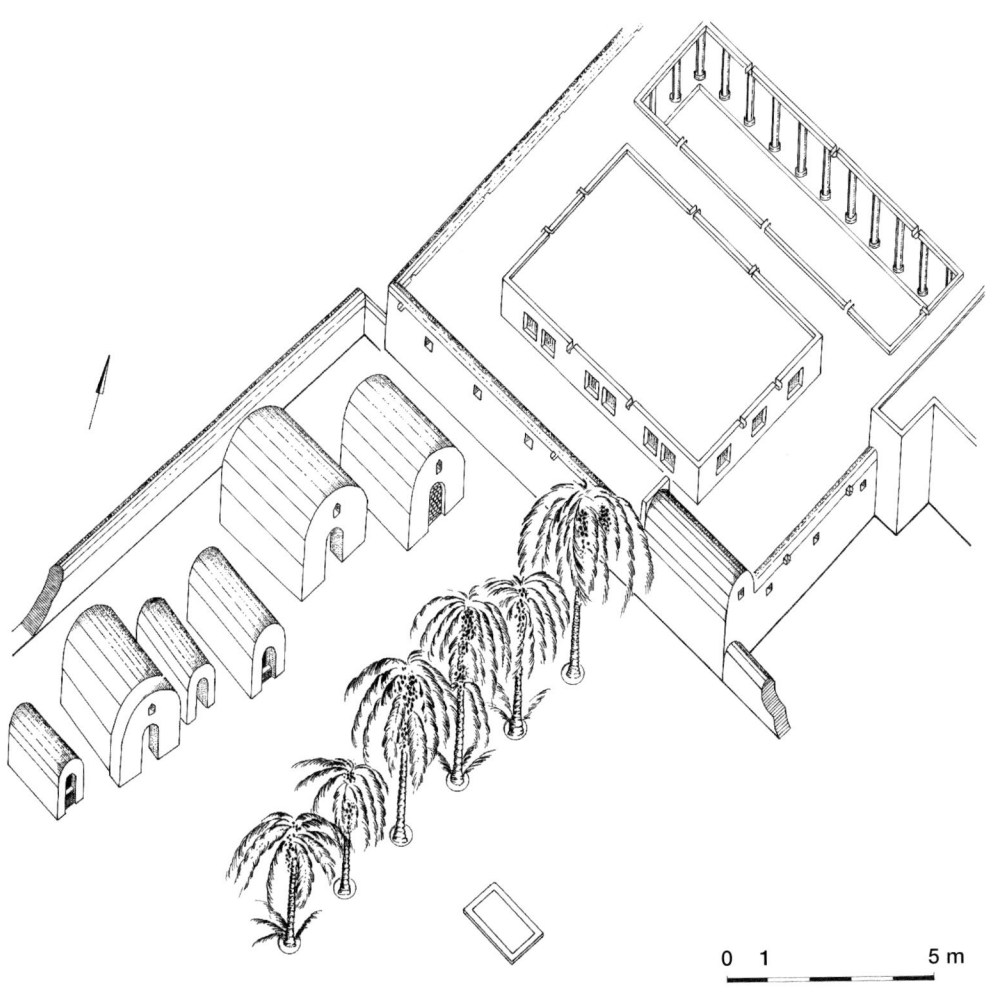

Fig. 3.34 Reconstruction of the palace and graveyard of an Asiatic official, Tell ed-Daba'a (after M. Bietak, Zwischen der beiden Ewigkeiten. Festschrift Gertrud Thausing, eds. M. Bietak, J. Holaubek, H. Mukarovsky, H. Satzinger, Vienna 1994, p. 18, fig. 11)

Syria-Palestine. A large palace for a local Asiatic chief was constructed within the settlement. This palace had a typically Egyptian groundplan and structure, and included an audience hall with four columns, a bedroom, magazine, dressing room, and a large court with a lake and a garden, which was located to the south of the palace. In the garden, archaeologists discovered a cemetery with six tombs.

These tombs had subterranean burial chambers and at ground level chapels with brick vaults. A tree was planted in front of every tomb, so that the overall plan was reminiscent of the cemeteries of the Lower Egyptian rulers of Buto. In the pits in front of the tombs, a pair of donkeys, a sheep and a goat were buried according to a typically Near Eastern custom. Above all, the burying of donkeys before the houses was a typical Mesopotamian custom, which in the course of the third millennium BC spread to Syria. It is characteristic mainly for populations whose basic source of subsistence was caravan trade. In Palestine, this subsistence pattern appears in the Middle Bronze Age (Jericho, Lakhish, Akko, Hazor). It is therefore likely that the tombs at Tell ed-Daba'a belonged to the caravan leaders, who lived in the palace. The Asiatic origins of these tomb-owners are attested by the weapons discovered inside the tombs, which were looted in antiquity. The most important types of weapons are the bronze dagger with a central rib and handle decorated with engraved lotus flowers, lance tips of silver, the axe, and the curved knife. In the end, however, the palace was hastily deserted, as is indicated by the tools scattered on the floor of the court and by its walled-up entrance. It is thus likely that the owner fell into disgrace and consequently the entire complex was abruptly abandoned.

As was already mentioned before, one of the most important Middle Kingdom sites in the Sinai was Serabit el-Khadim, the place of the turquoise mines, which was, in the course of the Middle Kingdom, increasingly gaining in importance. There is no reason for believing that the expeditions to the Sinai were of an exclusively military character. On the contrary, our sources indicate that the relationships between the Egyptians and the Asiatics in this area were peaceful and calm. Either individually, or in groups of six, ten or twenty men, the Asiatics were coming to this place in order to work in Egyptian service. Several scenes from the votive offerings from this site even depict a man riding a donkey. The accompanying inscription labels the man as 'Khebded, brother of the chief of Upper Retjenu'. However, he certainly did not visit these mines in order to work there, but rather to indirectly pay homage to the Egyptian ruler. One more inscription discovered here is also worth mentioning. It records the number of Asiatic men present in the mines during one expedition: 20 men, together with 200 stone-miners, 20 sailors, 14 carpenters and 30 peasants. This seems to indirectly imply that if Asiatics worked here, they were probably employed in specialized tasks, since they had detailed knowledge about the surrounding area. They knew how to travel in it, were familiar with the water sources and were able to successfully hunt in these very unfavourable conditions. Even Sinuhe's account demonstrates that the relationships between Egypt and Syria-Palestine were, apart from a few exceptions, peaceful.

Fig. 3. 35 Khebded, Serabit el-Khadim, Sinai

The temple at Serabit el-Khadim was first founded by Amenemhat I, perhaps in connection with the consolidation of the Egyptian position in South Palestine. This irregular temple of unique groundplan was dedicated to the goddess Hathor, Lady of Turquoise, Sopdu, Lord of the Foreign Lands, and also to the deified founder of the Fourth Dynasty Sneferu. One of the greatest expeditions to Serabit el-Khadim was organized by Amenemhat III. It comprised 735 individuals. Altogether, Middle Kingdom rulers left behind them over 200 glorification stelae and inscriptions, more than all other Egyptian rulers. The temple itself consisted of two small rock sanctuaries. Since these sanctuaries were placed beside one another, the temple was atypically constructed along two axes. The rooms in front of the sanctuaries were divided by courts and other cultic rooms, within which members of the expeditions then erected stone stelae dedicated to the deities of the temple. These stelae often include lists of expedition members, their numbers as well as the names and titles of the expedition leaders. Since the temple is situated in a remote area of the Sinai peninsula, most of these monuments were preserved in good condition, and they provide a detailed picture of these expeditions. In the vicinity of the temple, archaeologists also discovered quarries and quarters of the workers employed here during the various expeditions.

Against this cultural background, that is the late Early and ensuing Middle Bronze Age, we may reconstruct the environment of Sinuhe's hypothetical flight from Egypt, and his stay in Syria-Palestine. The arrival of the patriarchs headed by Abraham is dated to the same period. Our only source of information on Abraham is outlined in the Old Testament, the reliability of which will probably never be verified with certainty. Be that as it may, it is significant that there is evidence for the cultural and social situation that is described in the Hebrew Bible. Had Abraham really existed, then he must have lived in a society corresponding to that of the transition between the Early and Middle Bronze Ages, one of nomadic groups and the contemporaneously developing city-states.

* * * * * *

Until now, our attention has been directed mainly to the historical and archaeological sources that form the background of Sinuhe's story. Our survey of the mutual influence between Egypt and Syria-Palestine would not be complete, however, if it did not at least shortly mention the cross-fertilization that took place between the Egyptian deities and those of Syria-Palestine. In the Old Kingdom, foreign deities were practically unattested in Egypt. The cult of Egyptian deities outside Egyptian territory is much better documented, although it should be stressed that these deities were worshipped above all by Egyptians who were dispatched on missions beyond the frontiers of their homeland.

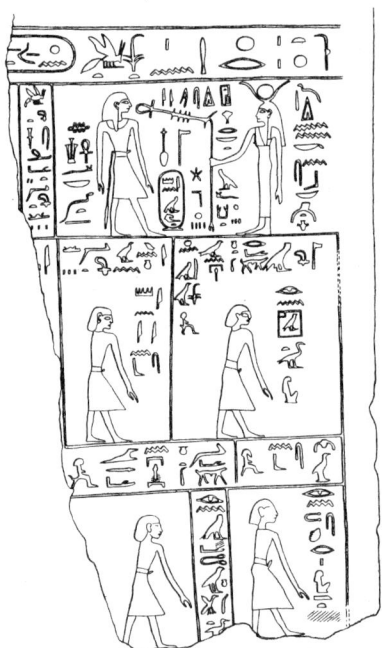

Fig. 3.36 Stela from Serabit el Khadim dated to the second year of reign of Amenemhat II, who receives life from the goddess Hathor. Below: officials who took part in the expedition (after A. H. Gardiner. T. E. Peet, J. Černý, The Inscriptions of Sinai. Part I. Introduction and plates, London 1952, pl. 26)

Since the Fourth Dynasty, it had been chiefly the god Thoth who was worshipped as the 'Lord of the Foreign Lands' by the miners sent to the Sinai to quarry stone. Besides him, the goddess Hathor also appears in the Sinai, with the epithet 'Lady of Turquoise'. The Egyptians regarded Hathor as a goddess who was worshipped in the regions where mineral resources were present and exploited by the Egyptians. Later in the time of the Middle and New Kingdoms, she was worshipped in the Sinai in a small rock temple at the site of Serabit el-Khadim. Here, she was also worshipped as the 'Lady of Lapis Lazuli', a stone which was imported from the Near East. In the quarries of Wadi el-Hudi, she was worshipped as the 'Lady of Amethyst'. It appears that in all these cases, Hathor was not so much connected with the actual sites where the minerals were exploited, but directly with the precious stones. Hathor was also worshipped as the 'Lady of Punt', the country from which all incense and myrrh were imported. Besides that, she was also the 'Lady of Silver' and the 'Lady of Gold' (silver was because of its relative scarcity in Egypt, until the time of the New Kingdom, valued at a higher rate than gold). Hathor's close connection with the precious stones may have been a consequence of the character of her cult, where she was regarded as a goddess of feasts and beauty, and also as the goddess connected with materials used for the production of items of personal adornment and jewellery.

One exception, which proves that some deities of the area of Syria-Palestine were known in Egypt already at the time of the Old Kingdom, is the god Khaitau, who was also worshipped in Byblos. He is mentioned in the Pyramid Texts (§ 518, § 242 and § 423). Spell 518 a – d identifies the Egyptian king on his journey to heaven with this god. The king is described as the one who passes through the gates of various fortifications. The identification can, according to Stadelmann, be explained by the fact that these gates were built of cedar wood, that is, of wood from Lebanon, where Khaitau was worshipped:

> '*Open is the sky and open is the earth,*
> *open are the enclosure gates for Horus.*
> *Open are the gates of the bush fortification for Seth.*
> *You will be destroyed for him who is "the first of his fortification".*
> *The ruler passed through you like Atum,*
> *because the ruler is Khaitau within the Nega mountains.*'

The situation did not change much in the Middle Kingdom. The only exception was the goddess Hathor, who was worshipped in Byblos as the 'Lady of Byblos'. The city and its surroundings were in this time governed by princes whose very titles expressed utmost loyalty to the Egyptian rulers. Hathor, the 'Lady of Byblos' is also once mentioned in the Coffin Texts, where she is connected with the oars, which were of wood from the Lebanese mountains (CT I 262b): 'May Hathor, the Lady of Byblos, make the oars for your boat.'

The tradition of the cult of Hathor continued beyond the limits of the second millennium BC, as is proved by the inscription of King Yehawmilk, the ruler of

Fig. 3.37 Serabit el-Khadim, the Temple of Hathor

Byblos at the time of the Persian supremacy in the fourth century BC. His inscription is filled with great respect for this goddess:

'I am Yehawmilk, King of Byblos, the son of Yeharba'al, the grandson of Urimilk, King of Byblos, whom the Mistress, the Lady of Byblos, made king over Byblos. I have been calling my Mistress, the Lady of Byblos (and she heard my voice). Therefore I have made for my Mistress, the Lady of Byblos, this altar of bronze, which is in this (courtyard) and this engraved object of gold, which is in front of this inscription of mine, with a bird (?) of gold that is set in a semiprecious stone, which is upon this engraved object of gold, and this portico with its columns and the (capitals), which are upon them, and its roof: I, Yehawmilk, King of Byblos, have made (these things) for my Mistress, the Lady of Byblos, as I called my Mistress, the Lady of Byblos, and she heard my voice and treated me kindly. May the Mistress of Byblos bless and preserve Yehawmilk, King of Byblos, and prolong his days and years in Byblos, for he is a righteous king.'

(N. Jidejian, Byblos through the Ages, Beirut 1986, 97.)

There is no evidence for the cult of any deity of Syria-Palestine on Egypt's territory in the Middle Kingdom. Only the communities of Asiatic captives, who were settled in Egypt after having been captured during Egyptian campaigns, may have formed exceptions. Some evidence may be found in the names of these people which are related to divinities. We may presume the cults of Baal and Baalat, Reshef, Shamash, and Anat. However, even these theophorous names cannot be considered clear evidence for the worship of foreign deities in Egypt.

The situation changed abruptly in the time of the Second Intermediate Period after the decline of the Middle Kingdom, when the Delta was penetrated by large groups from the Near East under the leaders of the Hyksos. Some indirect evidence for foreign deities has come down to us in the form of scarabs, which have been discovered in the Delta. Some of them show depictions of a naked goddess resembling Hathor. This goddess is holding a branch or lotus flowers in her hand, which indicates that she is in fact the goddess Kadesh. The style of the accompanying, purely decorative hieroglyphic signs, indicates that these objects may have been produced in southern Palestine. Kadesh was later often identified with Astarte, and she was considered the goddess of fertility and healing. In the New Kingdom and later, she was depicted standing on a lion, either naked or wearing a transparent dress.

Another deity that appears on the scarabs is a standing god in a long dress, wearing a tall crown decorated either with big horns or with a gazelle head (the low quality of the depiction makes it impossible to tell). This is Baal who, in the Egyptian Delta, was often identified with Seth. Their association was probably a consequence of the fact that the Egyptian god Seth was considered the god of the deserts and foreign lands.

Fig. 3.38 Depiction of the god Seth from the Tanis stela of 400 Years. The god is shown with attributes of the Levantine god Baal

Sinuhe's Afterlife

The end of Sinuhe's account makes explicit his strong desire to be buried in the land of Egypt, in the country of his ancestors. The fulfilment of such a wish meant not only building a tomb according to his status as a high royal official and having a traditional burial following Egyptian customs, but above all securing for himself the maintenance of his mortuary cult by priests. Mortuary priests were called *hemu ka*, which literally means 'servants of the spirit (of the deceased)'. The task of these priests was to regularly bring offerings to the altar in the tomb and present them to the soul of the deceased tomb owner. Equally important was the location of Sinuhe's tomb in the immediate vicinity of the final resting-place of his lord and ruler, Senwosret I. For it was the king of Egypt, deified after his death, who guaranteed the appropriate afterlife existence to his subjects. As will become clear later in our narrative, the Egyptians considered a properly designed and equipped tomb, the body preserved by means of mummification, the correctly performed funerary ceremony and perennial funerary cult to be the decisive conditions for their dwelling and existence in the afterlife. Perhaps the best wording of this concept comes from Sinuhe himself: 'For what is more important than to bury my body in the land where I was born?' (B 159–160).

The purpose of securing an existence in the afterlife appears towards the end of Sinuhe's account, and can rightly be considered as a major theme of the whole composition. The fact that the ruler himself assumes responsibility for the organization of Sinuhe's burial as well as for the building of the tomb, gives particular meaning to Sinuhe's unbroken loyalty to the king – despite his prolonged stay beyond the borders of his homeland. The royal gifts can thus be considered an expression of the king's strong favour and respect for Sinuhe. The passage from the end of Sinuhe's account deserves to be repeated at this place:

> *'They built for me a pyramid of stone among the pyramids.*
> *The workers of the necropolis, who build pyramids,*
> *measured out its foundations.*
> *The overseer of draughtsmen drew it,*
> *the overseer of sculptors sculpted in it,*
> *And the overseer of the works in the necropolis himself worked on it.*
> *(B, 305) The entire burial equipment, which was to be placed in the burial shaft,*
> *the need of it was satisfied.*
> *Funerary priests were assigned to me,*
> *a funerary estate was allotted to me.*

Fig. 4.1 Scarab – dung beetle – symbol of the rising sun and of resurrection in ancient Egypt

*There were fields in it and a garden in its place,
as it was done for a best friend.
My image was overlaid with gold,
the apron with electrum.
It was His Majesty
who ordered this to be done.'*

This passage illustrates the chief aspiration of the Egyptian official in his earthly life: to be a loyal servant of his king, and to be in return awarded by the ruler, who would assign to him a place for his tomb in the vicinity of the pyramid and perhaps would also take care of its construction. In the case of Sinuhe, the ruler supervised even the decoration of the tomb, the fashioning of Sinuhe's statue (or statues), the preparation of the equipment to be placed in the chamber and, finally, also the burial itself. All preparations were believed to be indispensable for the existence of the deceased in the afterlife. Some contemporary written sources do actually reflect this deeply rooted belief. The Instructions of Hardjedef, for example, show how important the construction of a tomb was in the minds of the ancient Egyptians:

'*When you build your house for your son,
you make a dwelling for yourself.
Establish your house in the necropolis
and make excellent your place in the west.
Remember that death means nothing to us,
remember that we think of life,
the house of death is precisely for life!*'

The autobiography of Weni, another written source dealing with the king's support of his loyal official, comes from the Sixth Dynasty, from a time toward the end of the period of the famous pyramid-builders of the Old Kingdom. It includes an account of how the ruler partook in the construction of the tomb of Weni from Abydos:

'*When I asked His Majesty to bring to me a limestone sarcophagus from Tura, His Majesty dispatched the royal seal-bearer together with a group of sailors, who were under his command, in order to bring to me this sarcophagus from Tura. It was brought in a ship of the court, together with the lid, tomb-entrance, lintel, two doorjambs and an offering table. Never had the like been done for any servant; but then, I was excellent in the heart of His Majesty.*'

Sinuhe, who introduces himself in the beginning of his narrative as a *hereditary noble and prince, governor of royal estates in the lands of the Asiatics, true and beloved friend of the king, servant in the royal chambers, and (servant) of the princess, one greatly praised, the royal wife of Senwosret, the praised lady Neferu,* could also hope for royal

Fig. 4.2 Osiris, Lord of the Egyptian Netherworld

assistance in securing his existence in the afterlife. One of the acts of royal favour was to grant official permission to be buried in the immediate vicinity of the final resting-place of the king, for this was considered a prerogative of the upper échelons of society.

This, however, was not so from the very beginning. In the most ancient times, the site next to the royal tomb was assigned to servants, to make sure that they would be at the king's disposal even after his death. The situation at the royal necropolis of Abydos makes it clear that in the First Dynasty, the servants of King Den were buried forcibly. On the day of the king's burial (or death), they were violently killed and buried in tiny graves. This barbarous custom has, however, soon disappeared from Egyptian history. The neighbourhood of the royal tomb was to become the final resting-place of several members of the royal family and some high officials of the country, who were all interred only after their natural death.

A burial in the royal necropolis guaranteed the king's protection for a nobleman, even in the hereafter. During the Middle Kingdom, when the king was subordinated to the gods, high officials were permitted to join him in worship in his funerary complex. A comparison of the Pyramid Texts from the pyramids of the rulers at the end of the Fifth and Sixth Dynasties with the Coffin Texts found on wooden coffins of high officials of the Middle Kingdom also reveals significant changes in the religious concept of life beyond death. In the Old Kingdom, the posthumous existence of the subjects depended to a great extent on the will of the king, who was the only one who could be identified with Osiris, the god of the ancient Egyptian afterlife. In the Middle Kingdom (and *de facto* already towards the end of the Old Kingdom), even a commoner could become Osiris. The Sinuhe narrative is explicit enough when referring to the attitude of the king where the afterlife of his subjects was concerned. A further examination of the importance of the royal tomb for the concept of rebirth will allow us to understand the nature of the afterlife, as it was envisaged by Sinuhe himself at the beginning of the Twelfth Dynasty.

The nucleus of the royal funerary complex, which is critical for the correct understanding of its meaning and significance for posthumous existence, is the pyramid itself. The pyramid of the Egyptian king was primarily conceived as his tomb. Its construction and most importantly its existence were connected with numerous concepts, which are of profound importance for the understanding of ancient Egyptian religious views about the afterlife. The beginnings of these concepts can be traced back to the tombs of the First and Second Dynasty rulers, who were buried in the necropolis of Umm el-Qaab, close to the Upper Egyptian

Fig. 4.3 The Early Dynastic cemetery at Abydos, subterranean part of the tomb of Den (c. 2850 BC)

city of Abydos. Their tombs consisted of two parts, below and above ground. The underground section was built in an open pit. Inside were the burial chamber and magazines, constructed out of unfired bricks, wood and mats. The magazines contained burial equipment, which was supposed to satisfy the needs of the deceased during his posthumous life. The upper part of the tomb consisted of a low embankment, which symbolized the so-called primeval hill. As a symbol for the rebirth of life, this hill was of particular significance in Egypt. This concept can probably be associated with the annual floods, which filled the Nile valley with water and fertile mud for a few months every year. When the floodwater began to recede, the first mound of earth appeared above water as a symbol of renewed life.

Starting in the Second Dynasty, some kings had already been buried in the necropolis near the capital of the Old Kingdom, called the White Walls. This city was founded by Hor Aha at the beginning of the First Dynasty and lay on the border line between the two united lands, Upper and Lower Egypt, in the area to the east of today's Saqqara necropolis. From the very beginning, ancient Egyptian architects strove to build these complexes as true copies of the earthly residences, which would serve the king in the afterlife. One of the oldest complexes of its kind, the enclosure of Djoser's step pyramid, illustrates this point very well.

Djoser is the first Egyptian ruler whom we know to have built his final resting place in stone. His complex includes numerous structures, which appear to be stone copies of the king's earthly residence. This we must imagine as a symbolic fortified palace (there is evidence that even the palaces of Early Dynastic rulers

Fig. 4.4 The pyramid complex of Djoser (Saqqara)

Fig. 4.5 The mortuary temple and the pyramid of Sahure (Abusir)

were forts), a posthumous residence where, as tradition would have it, the king met with individual Egyptian deities. Later, during the Fourth and Fifth Dynasties, royal tombs become standardized in form. A more symbolic approach prevails, with particular focus on the construction of the burial chamber to house the bodily remains, and on the chapel, the place of the funerary cult of the deceased, which was gradually becoming the centre of posthumous existence.

The beginning of the Fourth Dynasty witnessed the establishment of the geometrical shape of the pyramid, which had undoubtedly evolved from Third Dynasty step pyramids. The Third Dynasty royal funerary temple is located to the north of the pyramid, at the site next to the exit from the pyramid's interior. Here the king began his journey to the sky, where he was to become one of the stars 'who do not know destruction'. In the Fourth Dynasty the temple was relocated to the east of the pyramid – in connection with the developing cult of the sun god – and the entire complex was oriented from east to west, to correspond with the course of the sun. The increasing importance of solar religion is also reflected in the fact that the king began to call himself 'son of (the sun god) Ra.' The pyramid complexes consist of several invariable functional units: the valley temple, the ascending causeway, and the funerary temple with the pyramid. Possibly the most illustrative example of a pyramid complex of the Old Kingdom is the early Fifth Dynasty complex of King Sahure in Abusir, which is one of the best preserved structures of its kind. Its appearance and design became a kind of matrix that was imitated as long as kings were building pyramid complexes.

The main entrance to the complex was in the valley temple at the edge of the Nile valley, between the cultivation and the semi-arid desert. A waterway – a channel with a port in its vicinity – led to the temple. This channel was also the highway for transporting of the individual commodities destined for the everyday cult of the king in his funerary temple and for the sustenance of the priests who were in its monthly service (priests in the funerary complexes of the Old Kingdom kings worked in monthly shifts, and got paid in kind, mainly with provisions). In the two entrances to Sahure's valley temple (the main entrance was presumably oriented toward the port) stood papyriform columns, which represented the sacred palm groves of the Nile Delta, the symbols of rebirth. The floor was of black basalt, as black as the rich soil of the Nile Valley, which, being annually fertilized by deposits of Nile mud, was the source of ever new crops. The decoration of the inner walls of the temple was intended to accentuate the divine nature of the king, as can clearly be seen in the scene where the king is being suckled by the goddess Nekhbet. Scenes such as the king smiting numerous enemies reflected the victorious aspect of his reign.

The roofed ascending causeway connected the valley temple with the funerary temple. The inner walls of the causeway were also covered with relief decoration. One of the scenes located here was that of the king in the form of a sphinx, smiting enemies and evil powers. However, there are also scenes of an utterly secular character, such as the completion of the construction of the pyramid complex, festive games etc. During recent years the Egyptian expedition led by Zahi Hawass has uncovered several huge limestone blocks from the causeway, which bear unique decoration. They substantially enlarge the motifs and the decoration programme of this part of the complex and their forthcoming publication will undoubtedly significantly modify our knowledge of this subject.

The transition between the causeway and the funerary temple was formed by the entrance hall, which was called 'the room of the great ones'. It is likely that high officials of the country gathered here during Sahure's funeral to pay homage to the king on his last journey. The hall led into an open court lined with papyriform columns, which were – just as the black basalt pavement – intended to represent the idea of rebirth in the papyrus thicket. The columns were inscribed with the titulary of Sahure and decorated with representations of the protective goddesses of Upper and Lower Egypt – the vulture goddess Nekhbet (in the southern part of the court) and the cobra goddess Wadjet (in its northern part). The northwestern corner of the court originally contained an alabaster altar, on which offerings were presented. The court was enclosed in a roofed corridor, with blue-painted roof blocks dotted with yellow stars to imitate night sky.

Behind the open court was the so-called 'intimate' section of the temple, which was divided from it not only by a higher floor-level, but also by a transverse, north-south oriented corridor. The corridor gave access to the chapel with five niches, which contained five statues of the king. Further to the west corridors led to the east-west oriented king's chapel located at the foot of the eastern wall of the pyramid. This was the site of daily offering rituals for the king's soul. The west wall

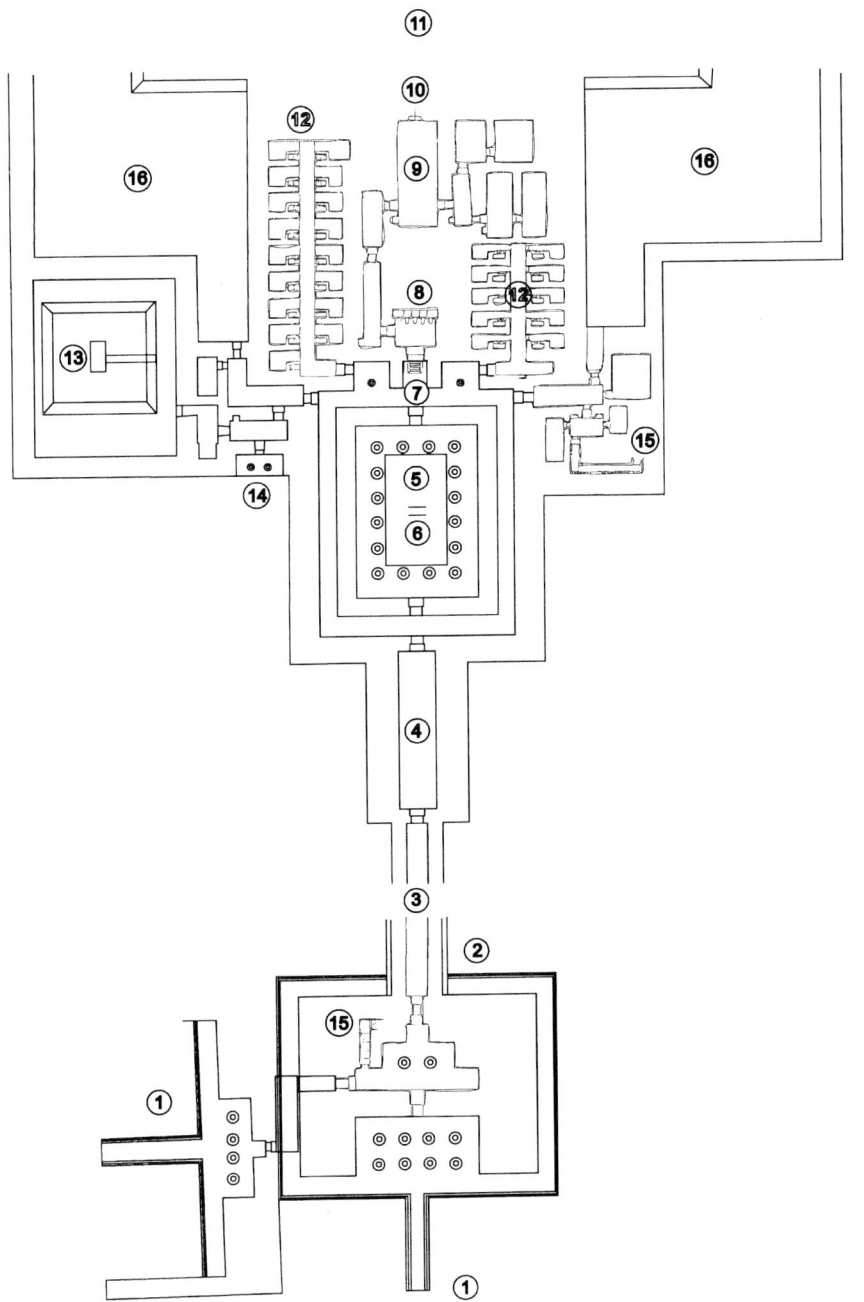

Fig. 4.6 Groundplan of the pyramid complex of Sahure: 1 – landing ramps, 2 – valley temple, 3 – causeway, 4 – entrance hall, 5 – open court, 6 – altar, 7 – transverse corridor, 8 – chapel with five niches, 9 – offering room, 10 – false door, 11 – pyramid, 12 – magazines, 13 – cult pyramid, 14 – southern entrance, 15 – roof entrance, 16 – pyramid courtyard

of the chapel included the so-called 'false door' of red granite which resembled a real door in shape. Through it, the spirit of the king was believed to enter the chapel during offering ceremonies and leave it again to go to the west, to the realm of the dead. This door, then, was the magical frontier between the world 'here' and 'there'. The walls of the chapel were decorated with offering scenes, showing the king seated on his throne and receiving heaps of offerings. Over the offering-bearers extensive lists of offerings were inscribed. Together with the representations, they guaranteed that the king was to be well provided for life in the hereafter. To north and south, the chapel was flanked by numerous storerooms, which housed cult equipment and the individual items of offerings. The small 'cult' pyramid stood in the southeastern part of the complex. Its character was presumably symbolic, but its precise significance remains a mystery.

The burial chamber is located approximately in the centre of the pyramid. At its western wall stood the sarcophagus of black basalt which contained the royal mummy. After the funeral, the descending corridor that leads to the burial chamber was blocked with stones, in order to hinder unauthorized entry into the pyramid. The entire pyramid was enclosed in a large open court. We should also bear in mind that the pyramid complexes did not stand isolated within the necropoleis. An entire economic infrastructure was created around them, including houses of priests, archives with written records pertaining to the temple cult and its administration, etc. These buildings were concentrated mainly in the vicinity of the valley temples. The entire necropolis was thus a world of the living, a realm of a strictly organized and controlled business.

The description shows that Egyptian society already considered the construction of the royal tomb an event of utmost importance. This was because the ruler was first chosen by the gods to rule the world created by them, and later, himself a god, joined the divine suite of the sun-god Ra. He was thus the only link between the world of humans and that of gods, between the profane and the sacred realms. The construction of the royal tomb brought to the Egyptians a reassurance that the king would ceaselessly maintain the order and course of things called *maat* in Egyptian, and thus protect his subjects.

As far as the shape of the pyramid is concerned, we may mention several theories that attempt to explain its significance. One of these theories that interprets the pyramid's shape as a symbolic ladder, by means of which the king ascended to heaven to join other gods, finds support in the Pyramid Texts. This extensive collection of religious texts, incised since the end of the Fifth Dynasty on the walls of the inner rooms of the Egyptian pyramids (and later even of the pyramids of queens), provides us with a vivid illustration of the Egyptian concept of the king's afterlife. The spell in question is No. 304, which likens the pyramid to a heavenly ladder, by means of which the king ascends to heaven and joins the gods:

'Welcome, daughter of Atum, who is above the eyebrow of the sky,
Friend of Thoth, who presides over the bars of the ladder,
Open the way for Unas, let Unas pass!'

Fig. 4.7 Pyramid Texts (mortuary literature) (pyramid of Unas, Saqqara)

Much more probable is, however, the view according to which the final shape of the pyramid was a compromise between the Upper and Lower Egyptian conceptions of the tomb, i.e. a combination of the primeval hill and posthumous fortress – the residence and place of encounters with gods. This is best illustrated by the successive building stages of the Step Pyramid of king Djoser at Saqqara. This pyramid was built in six main stages. The first three (M1-M3) strictly reflected the Lower Egyptian conception of the tomb as a royal funerary palace with all the necessary components for such a structure, including, besides the burial place, also the court for the celebration of royal jubilees, chapels of gods, the funerary temple, the South and North houses expressing both the duality and union of the land, and the symbolic place of burial, the so-called South Tomb. This concept was based on the legendary palaces of predynastic sovereigns of Lower Egypt, who ruled in Buto. In stages M1-M3, the superstructure over the king's burial had the form of a large rectangular platform. Subsequently, in stages P1, P1´ and P2 was this platform, a mastaba, transformed into a monumental four- and still later six-step pyramid. Together with the change of shape came also a shift of meaning assigned to the structure. The pyramid became an abstract symbol of the primeval mound. In the course of the Fourth Dynasty, this concept was further developed into that of the true pyramid.

James Allen's analysis of the Pyramid Texts from the tomb of Unas makes it possible to trace the connection between the individual underground sections of the pyramid and their significance for the king's rebirth. The western part of the burial chamber contains mainly spells for the protection of the king against dangerous animals and enemies. Similar spells are also located on the eastern wall of the vestibule in front of the burial chamber – the king is thus magically protected from both sides. The royal sarcophagus can be considered as the goddess Nut, who each morning gives birth to the sun coming out of her womb. The sun travels the sky all day, and by night it is swallowed by the goddess, only to reappear on the eastern horizon by dawn. The burial chamber itself is conceived as the netherworld, *dat*, where the king's body lies. The soul of the deceased king leaves this area and travels first through the vestibule, which signifies the *akhet*, the morning sky where the sun rises as a symbol of life and rebirth. The walls of the corridor between the vestibule and the burial chamber often contain spells that describe the passage through the thickets on the edge of *akhet*, the place of daily rebirth of the rising sun, the god Ra himself. These thickets (understood as papyrus thickets) were the mythical birthplace of the god Horus. One purpose of the thickets was therefore to assist the symbolic rebirth of the king after his physical death. Finally, the king's soul travelled through the ascending corridor leading north from the vestibule out of the burial chamber, to join the sun god Ra. The conception of 'rebirth' which is documented in the pyramid of Unas can be compared to the journey of the sun, i.e. the death/setting of the sun in the west and its subsequent rise in the east. The direction of motion, from west to east, symbolizes the regeneration of the sun at night before its new rise in the east, i.e. its rebirth.

Fig. 4.8 Obelisk of Heliopolis, the most important remnant to survive from the temple built by King Senwosret I for the sun god Ra

One of the basic religious compositions explaining the origin and role of the Egyptian king as a representative of the gods on earth is the Heliopolitan Cosmology. As for the concept of the primaeval mound, its identification with the pyramid poses no problems for this cosmogony, which comprehends the creation of the world and the birth of gods. It is well attested already in the Pyramid Texts (Spell 600):

'Atum-Khepre, you have come in order to raise yourself on the mound, you have come out on the benben stone in the palace of the benben stone in Heliopolis. You spat out Shu and Tefnut and you embraced them in your arms as in the arms of the symbol (of the soul) ka, so that your power is within them. O Atum, put your arms around the king, around his building, around his pyramid like the arms of the symbol ka, so that the power of the king's ka can be within them.'

The Heliopolitan cosmogony may also be quite reliably reconstructed from allusions to it in other, often much later, texts. The creator god (or 'Demiurge', as he is sometimes known) of these texts is Atum, who gives birth to two elements, the air-god Shu and the moisture-goddess Tefnut. This pair then creates the earth-god Geb and the sky-goddess Nut, the symbol of the sky vault traversed by the sun during its daily course. Geb and Nut themselves conceive two pairs of children – the brothers Osiris and Seth, and sisters Isis and Nephthys. Seth cunningly kills his brother and cuts his body into pieces, which he scatters throughout the entire land. He then assumes kingship over the world. Isis, the sister and wife of Osiris, manages to gather his dispersed members and reassemble them in the marshes of the Nile Delta. Osiris is temporarily revived and impregnates Isis. Thereafter he dies again and becomes the ruler of the netherworld, the realm of the dead. In a papyrus thicket in the mythical landscape of the Egyptian Delta called Khemnis, Isis gives birth to Horus. Horus challenges his uncle Seth and, after numerous struggles, regains his inheritance, the kingship over the world. The conflict of Horus and Seth is one of the most often repeated themes in Egyptian mythology. It reflects the antithesis of the life-giving Nile Valley (represented by Horus) and the barren desert (represented by Seth). On another level, however, this fight represents a parable of the struggles for Egyptian unification, where the antagonists were Upper and Lower Egypt. The final victory belongs to Horus, who was born in the thickets of Lower Egypt. He thus becomes the living ruler on the Egyptian throne.

The office of the king, Horus, was thus necessarily – following the Heliopolitan concept of the creation of the world and kingship over it – considered a divine one, immortal and guaranteed by the gods. The king, since predynastic times entitled Horus, was its mortal representative. After his death the king became Osiris, and the new king on the Egyptian throne became inevitably his son. Thus, the unchanging order of rebirth was to be repeated forever. A clear testimony about this relationship can be found on the Shabaka stone in the British Museum, which describes the link between Osiris and Horus thus: *'And his son*

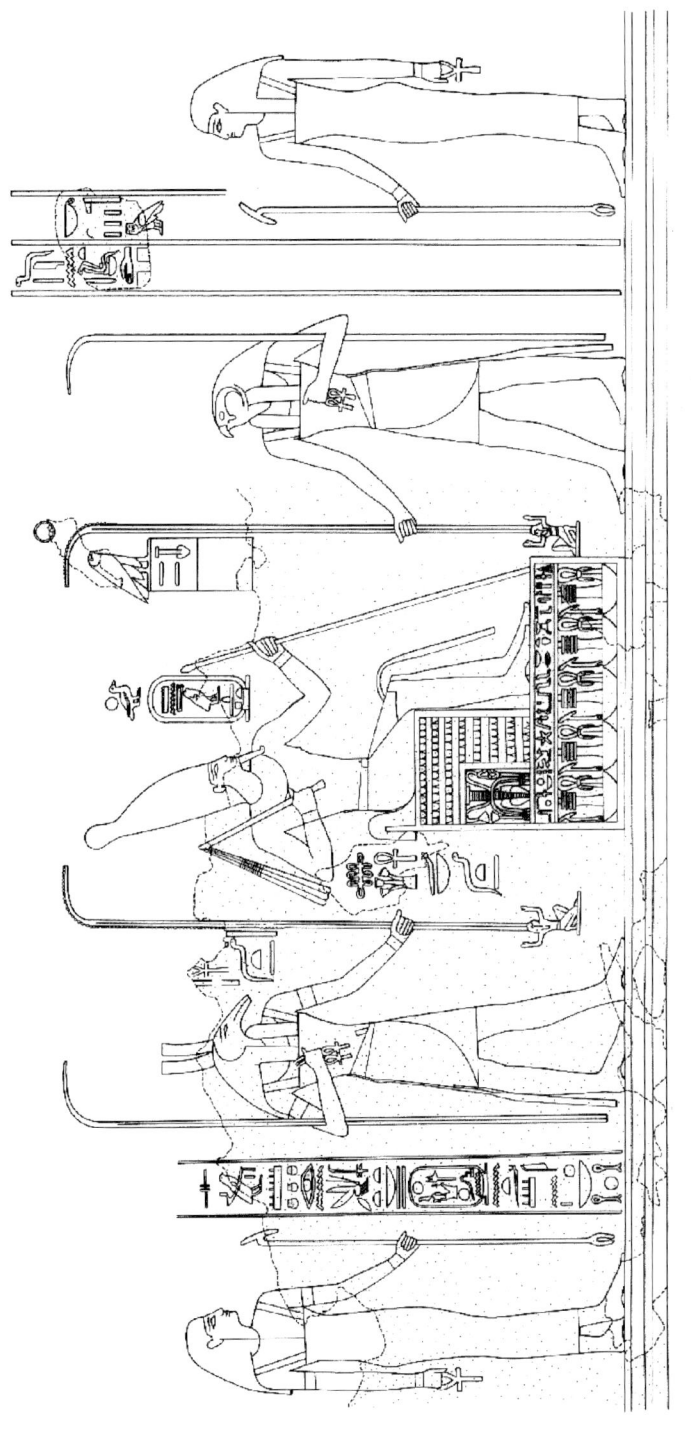

Fig. 4.9 Mentuhotep II receiving symbols of eternal rule (palm fronds) from Horus and Seth, unifiers and patrons of Upper and Lower Egypt (Deir el-Bahri)

Horus rose as the king of Upper Egypt, he rose as the king of Lower Egypt, in the embrace of his father Osiris and the gods before and behind him.' The status of the king in the Old Kingdom is also described in the Pyramid Texts. The king is depicted as a god who rises to the sky, joins other gods and the stars, becomes a member of the suite of the sun god Ra and crosses the sky together with him in his barque. The meaning of the individual spells is often contradictory, since these texts were not compiled simultaneously, but appeared during the course of several centuries. Thus, for example, Spell 337 describes how the king rises to the sky as Osiris:

'The sky cries, the earth trembles
Out of the fear of You, Osiris, in your coming.
O you cows who give milk here, o you cow-nurses here,
Turn to him, cry for him, mourn him, pity him,
When he rises and goes to the sky
To his brothers, the gods.'

Another important aspect of the cult of the king was his filiation with the sun god Ra, one of the most important deities of the Egyptian pantheon. The king was regarded as his son. This is clearly shown in Spell 407:

'Teti purified himself:
May he assume his pure place which is in the sky!
Teti is eternal, may his beautiful places also be eternal!
Teti will assume his pure place at the stern of the sun-barque of the god Ra.
The sailors, who row for Ra, will row for Teti,
The sailors, who travel the horizon with Ra,
Will travel the horizon with Teti.
Teti's mouth has been split,
Teti's nostrils have been opened,
Teti's ears are stuffed no more,
Teti will judge matters,
He will judge the two,
Teti will command for one greater than himself,
Ra will purify Teti,
Ra will protect Teti from all evil!'

The status of the king underwent several modifications during the Middle Kingdom period. The first evidence for a change can be found in the mortuary temple of Mentuhotep II in Deir el-Bahri in Western Thebes. The king's chapel now contains also a cult statue of the god Amun-Ra, and the king was thus no longer the sole receiver of offering ceremonies within his own complex. He even assumed an active role in them by worshipping Amun-Ra. The typical representation of the king on his throne, accompanied by the main deities of Upper and Lower Egypt: Nekhbet, Wadjet, Horus, and Seth, also underwent significant changes in this period. From now on, the representation of the king to whom these gods give palm branches with incisions symbolizing the infinite number of regnal years becomes a common motif in temple decoration. Thus, the king – unlike the Old Kingdom custom, when he was equal to the gods and one of them – finds himself inferior to the gods and becomes a mere executor of their will during the Middle Kingdom. The best expression of this new relationship is recorded in a slightly younger representation on a gateway from the temple of Medamud. It depicts the King Amenemhat Sebekhotep enthroned during the celebration of the thirtieth anniversary of his reign, while Horus and Seth present him with symbols of eternal reign.

Thus we have established why being equipped for the afterlife by the king was of the utmost importance for Sinuhe. Apart from the fact that he desired to be buried close to the king, Sinuhe's account tells us of other necessary precautions which needed to be fulfilled to secure one's afterlife. King Senwosret himself calls Sinuhe's attention to them in his letter, which describes the time when his last moment comes and it will be necessary to think about his burial:

'(B, 190) *Today you have begun to grow old,*
you have lost virility.
Consider the day of your burial,
when you shall join the revered ones!
The night is assigned to you
with oils and bandages from the hands of Taiet.
The burial procession will be prepared for you on the day of death.
Your mummy will be covered with gold,
the head with lapis lazuli,
the sky above, facing you.
You will (also) be given a sarcophagus.
Cattle will drag you
and singers will go in front of you.
(B, 195) *The muu-dancers will be made to dance at the entrance of your tomb.*
One will recite the ritual giving sacrifices to you.
One will make offerings for you in front of the entrance to your chapel.
Your pillars will be made of white limestone.'

This passage begins with an allusion to the need for securing the mummification of the body. The importance of this was because in the afterlife the preserved physical features guaranteed the identification of the deceased. Without this identity there would have been no eternal existence. To overcome the natural processes the Egyptians designed several techniques. In the beginning of the second millennium BC, they already had a few centuries of experience with the mummification process. The origin of mummification can be traced to the end of the fourth millennium BC, when it was the custom to bury dead bodies in a contracted position in dry desert sand. The bodies were wrapped in skin or just

Fig. 4.10 Contemporary local community cemetery near Wadi Shatt el-Righal in southern Egypt, a model for the reconstruction of prehistoric graves that underwent a natural mummification process

in a reed mat. Dry desert sand, wind, and the stable Egyptian climate then took care of everything else. By the influence of weather, the bodies were dried and conserved, their muscular tissue stiffened and the body resisted all decay. The bodies were perfectly dried out, and thus the graves have been preserved to our times.

Already at this early stage, the Egyptians were aware of the importance of proper burial for the afterlife. Together with the expansion of tomb-construction and rapidly improving architectural methods, it was necessary to continue developing the art of preserving the physical body after death, the art of mummification. Once bodies were buried in tombs, however, it was no longer possible to rely on the effects of hot sand for dessication, and it was of utmost importance to design artificial methods that would imitate the effects of natural phenomena. Naturally, only the wealthy families of officials and artisans could afford this service; the common peasant had to rely solely on the help of nature. The importance of mummification in the life of the ancient Egyptians is described in some detail in the account of the Greek author of the fifth century BC, Herodotus – we have to say that the Egyptians themselves were silent at this point for the most part of their history maybe because of a simple reason – the art of mummification was considered 'trade secret':

'As regards mourning and funerals, when a distinguished man dies, all the women of the household plaster their heads and faces with mud, then, leaving the body indoors, perambulate the town with the dead man's female relatives, their dresses fastened with a girdle,

and beat their bared breasts. The men too, for their part, follow the same procedure, wearing a girdle and beating themselves like the women. The ceremony over, they take the body to be mummified.

Mummification is a distinct profession. The embalmers, when a body is brought to them, produce specimen models in wood, painted to resemble nature, and graded in quality; the best and most expensive kind is said to represent a being whose name I shrink from mentioning in this connexion; the next best is somewhat inferior and cheaper, while the third sort is cheapest of all. After pointing out these differences in quality, they ask which of the three is required, and the kinsmen of the dead man, having agreed upon a price, go away and leave the embalmers to their work. The most perfect process is as follows: as much as possible of the brain is extracted through the nostrils with an iron hook, and what the hook cannot reach is rinsed out with drugs; next the flank is laid open with a flint knife and the whole contents of the abdomen removed; the cavity is then thoroughly cleansed and washed out, first with palm wine and again with an infusion of pounded spices. After that it is filled with pure bruised myrrh, cassia, and every other aromatic substance with the exception of frankincense, and sewn up again, after which the body is placed in natrum, covered entirely over, for seventy days – never longer. When this period, which must not be exceeded, is over, the body is washed and then wrapped from head to foot in linen cut into strips and smeared on the under side with gum, which is commonly used by the Egyptians instead of glue. In this condition the body is given back to the family, who have a wooden case made, shaped like the human figure, into which it is put. The case is then sealed up and stored in a sepulchral chamber, upright against the wall. When, for reasons of expense, the second quality is called for, the treatment is different: no incision is made and the intestines are not removed, but oil of cedar is injected with a syringe into the body through the anus, which is afterwards stopped up to prevent the liquid from escaping. The body is then pickled in natrum for the prescribed number of days, on the last of which the oil is drained off. The effect of it is so powerful that as it leaves the body it brings with it the stomach and intestines in a liquid state, and as the flesh, too, is dissolved by the natrum, nothing of the body is left but the bones and skin. After this treatment, it is returned to the family without further fuss.

The third method, used for embalming the bodies of the poor, is simply to clear out the intestines with a purge and keep the body seventy days in natrum. It is then given to the family to be taken away.'

(Herodotus, The Histories)

Even Herodotus' description clearly implies that, far from being an easy procedure, mummification was a privilege of the wealthy, the more so during the Middle Kingdom period. The development of this art began in the course of the third millennium BC. The whole sophisticated art of mummification underwent considerable development during the three thousand years of Egyptian history and consisted of several main stages such as washing, removal of the brain, removal of viscera, drying the body, packing, anointing and cosmetic treatment, wrapping the body, external trapping and masking. From the Old Kingdom period comes the first evidence of extraction of viscera from the bodies of the dead to prevent

Fig. 4.11 Anubis, ancient Egyptian god of mummification

their decay. Extracted were the stomach, lungs, intestines and liver. The body cavity was cut on the left side, and the internal organs were then extracted through this incision, which was subsequently sewn up. Originally, in the Fourth Dynasty, the viscera were dried in natron and wrapped in special linen packages. Only later were they placed in special vessels, known today as the canopic jars. Each of these vessels was under the protection of one of the sons of Horus: the human-headed god, Imset guarded the liver, baboon-headed Hapi the lungs, jackal-headed Duamutef the stomach, and falcon-headed Kebehsennuf protected the intestines. The four sons of Horus appear already in the Old Kingdom Pyramid texts, where they assist the deceased king in his ascent to the sky. In contrast to the Old Kingdom fashion, when the canopic jars were typical by their flat, disc-shaped lids, during the Middle Kingdom a tendency appeared to shape each of the four containers' lids into four distinct heads of the sons of Horus. Consequently, even today, when canopic jars are found, it is possible to identify the contents of each jar.

The dead body was covered with natron powder, which came mostly from Wadi Natrun in the Western Desert. The powder was left to work on the body and thus completely dry it. This stage of mummification was not a cheap one, since the complete drying out of the body required an amount of natron many times larger than the volume of the body itself. The body was then cleansed of all impurities and anointed with oils, which functioned both as perfumes and as disinfectants. To resemble the living person as much as possible, the body was stuffed with sawdust and linen. Once thus prepared, it was wrapped in linen. While in the Old Kingdom the individual bodily parts – arms, legs, trunk and head – were wrapped separately, in Sinuhe's time the preferred method was to wrap the body in linen strips as a whole. Thus the resulting cocoon shape of the mummified body with arms along the body and legs together, obscured the main bodily features. Instead, to secure the tomb owner's identity, the facial features were captured – mostly in an idealised manner – by means of linen layers. Additional details such as eyebrows or male moustache, were painted on the outer layer of linen bandages.

A study of the Middle Kingdom mummy of the chief overseer Wah provides a very detailed picture of contemporary Egyptian mummification procedures. For this mummy alone, the embalmers used around 375 sq. m of linen. Numerous jewellery pieces and necklaces of semi-precious stones and protective amulets were concealed in the wrappings.

In the early Middle Kingdom, many mummies were not eviscerated and thus had no canopic jars in their burial equipment. At this stage the brain could have been extracted in some cases – instead of left nostril perforation, the eye-socket was broken and the brain pulled out with special hooked sticks. The cerebral cavity was subsequently washed out with hot resin.

The precise duration of mummification still remains a mystery. According to later sources (Herodotus) the entire procedure lasted seventy days. Most of the written resources at our disposal relating to mummification are very late in date. Therefore, in trying to understand the process in some detail, one has to reach for earlier allusions hidden in Old Kingdom tombs. Thus in the Fourth Dynasty case of Queen Meresankh buried at Giza, there was a 273-day long period between 'the resting of her ka, its departure to the funerary workshop' and 'her departure to her beautiful tomb.' The case of vizier Senedjemib from the twenty-third century BC who oversaw the burial of his father indicates that mummification could have lasted even longer:

'I asked my Lord to bring for him (Senedjemib's father – author's note) a sarcophagus from the Tura (mines) for this his tomb, which I built for him in the course of a year and two thirds, while he was in the funerary workshop in the house of his estate, which is located in the (cemetery called) Beautiful is (King) Isesi.'

A more recent source, one of the Rhind papyri from the first century BC (discovered in 1856 by Alexander Rhind, a Scottish lawyer), however, state, in accordance with Herodotus that mummification lasted seventy days. Therefore it seems that the seventy days were most probably the average period during which the dead body was exposed to the mummification. The preserved evidence from Ancient Egypt provides many examples showing the perseverance and stability of

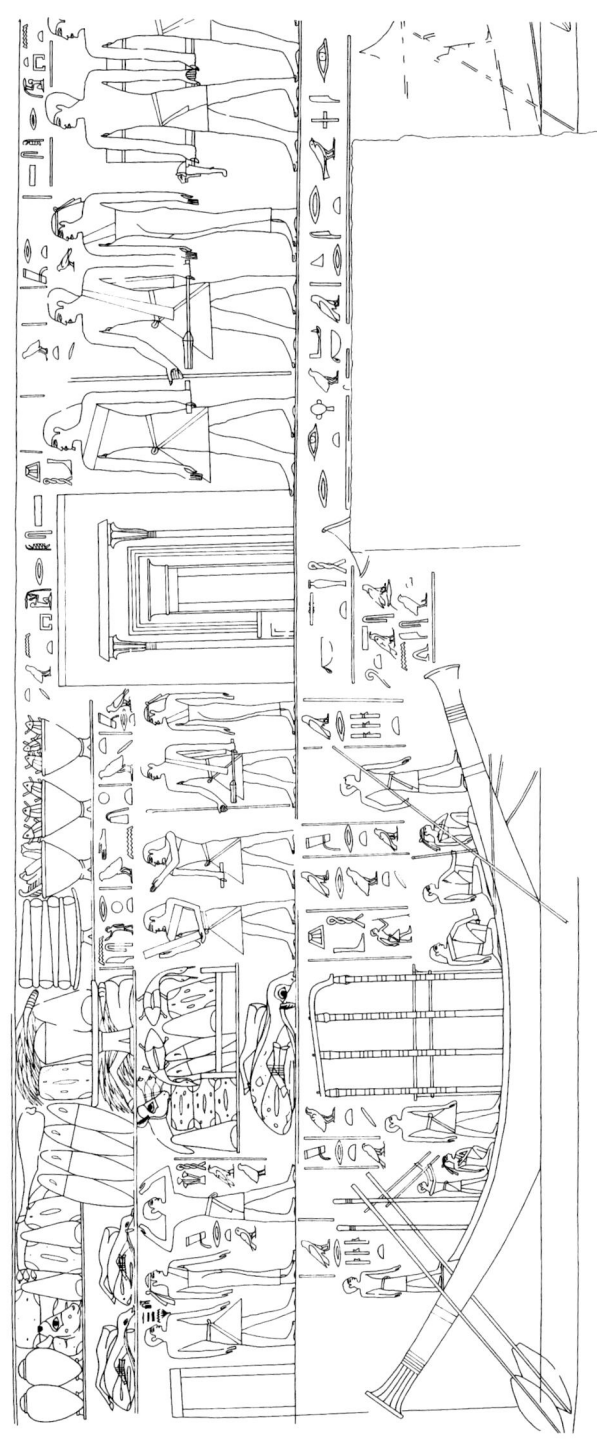

Fig. 4.12 Procession heading towards the embalmer's tent of purification (tomb of Pepiankh, Meir; after A. M. Blackman, M. R. Apted, *The Rock Tombs of Meir, Part V*, London 1953, pl. 42)

the culture when religious concepts and rituals were concerned. This may also apply to mummification. The Rhind papyri mention that the dead body was first ritually cleansed in 'the basin of Khons'. It was then left in a 'purification place' for thirty days. According to this papyrus, eight different religious rituals were performed during the first thirty-six days of mummification. These were followed by a ninth. On the seventieth day, the mummy was placed in the tomb.

The cleaning and mummification procedures were carried out in installations called *ibu* and *wabet*. First of all, the body of the deceased was ritually cleansed in a tent called *ibu*. After that, mainly for practical reasons, the body had to be quickly transferred to another workshop called *wabet*. Here the body was submitted to the proper process of mummification which started with the removal of the internal organs. The location of these funerary workshops is as yet unknown. As far as the Egyptian kings are concerned, their funerary workshops must have been located in the vicinity of the valley temples of their funerary complexes. The only evidence for the equipment of royal mummification workshops, in the form of two alabaster tables, was found in the underground rooms of Djoser's pyramid at Saqqara. The tables were shaped to resemble lion bodies and their backs are slightly inclined towards the waste containers that were placed at their feet. This precaution enabled the flow-off of excess liquids during mummification. Their size suggests that they were used only for the mummification of the king's extracted internal organs; they were not large enough for the entire body. Similar tables with lion heads and paws are also known from later

Fig. 4.13 Possible royal mummification workshops discovered by Zahi Hawass in front of the valley temple of Khafre in Giza

Fig. 4.14 Departure of the funeral procession from the house of the deceased (tomb of Ankhmahor, Saqqara, after N. Kanawati, A. Hassan, The Teti Cemetery at Saqqara. Vol. II. The tomb of Ankhmahor, Sydney 1997, pl. 56)

representations. They are depicted with a human body lying on them, while a priest with the mask of Anubis, the god of the dead and of mummification, is leaning over it. A deeper understanding and identification of the remains of royal mummification workshops was made possible by the discoveries of the Egyptian archaeologist Zahi Hawass east of the valley temple of Khafre in Giza. In 1995–1996, archaeological excavations revealed traces of ramps, roads and even of structures, which could be related to the royal burial and mummification.

As far as 'non-royal' workshops are considered, some depictions suggest that they must have been situated close to the course of the Nile, since a great amount of water was required during mummification. Furthermore, the concerns of hygiene would make a location further from a water-source unacceptable. Some scenes indicate that the workshops were light shelters, constructed of organic materials. The fact that the location of these workshops was indeed close to the Nile was recently endorsed by the examination of one of the mummies in the Kestner Museum in Hannover. On the back of this mummy traces of several plants were found: tamarysk, hazel, various grasses, and marigold flowers. The Egyptian embalmers probably placed the mummy on its back in the grass, the remains of which have thus been preserved for us. The most likely hypothesis is, therefore, that these workshops were constructed on the eastern edge of the necropolis, and were accessible by a waterway of some sort – most probably a canal.

The hypothesis that these structures were not far from the cemetery may be confirmed by an indirect archaeological evidence. The most recent comes from Abusir South. During the 2002 archaeological campaign the Czech team worked in the tomb complex of the vizier Qar and his sons dating to the Sixth Dynasty. During the course of excavation there were discovered, near the burial shafts of some members of this wealthy family, two smaller shafts. They were only about two metres deep and at the bottom contained a rich accumulation of broken pottery and complete vessels with unused straps of linen. Pre-eminent among them were large bowls containing traces of their original content of resin. At the bottom of one there were trapped carrion beetles that had adhered to the glutinous surface of the hot resin.

Once ready, the body departed for its last journey to the necropolis, where it would be placed into the burial chamber of the tomb, which the deceased official had built for himself during his lifetime. If he had not managed to do so (in case of sudden death or for other reasons), the responsibility for his burial passed to his eldest son, as is clearly testified, for example, in the account of the Old Kingdom official Meriaa:

'I buried my father with the help of royal gifts, and I buried him in the beautiful West. I embalmed him with oils from the royal residence and with red linen from the House of Life. I inscribed his tomb and erected his statues, as a conscious son, beloved by his father, who buries his father and whose arm is strong.'

Undoubtedly, the purification and mummification were the necessary beginning of the whole burial ceremony, which was designed according to the wealth and social position of each individual. Some of the steps that followed after mummification are mentioned in the story of Sinuhe:

'The night is assigned to you
with oils and bandages from the hands of Taiet.
The burial procession will be prepared for you on the day of death.
Your mummy will be covered with gold,
the head with lapis lazuli,
the sky above, facing you.
You will (also) be given a sarcophagus.
Cattle will drag (you)
and singers will go in front of you.
(B, 195) The muu-dancers will be made to dance at the entrance of your tomb.
One will recite the ritual, giving sacrifices to you.
One will make offerings for you in front of the entrance to your chapel.'

The German scholar Jürgen Settgast amply demonstrated that Old and Middle Kingdom sources may be used and even combined in order to tentatively reconstruct the stages in the burial ceremony. Earlier Old Kingdom and Middle Kingdom documents (the latter being contemporary with the time of Sinuhe) show that the funerary procession started at the house of the deceased and terminated in the necropolis in front of his tomb. The beginning of such a procession is depicted in the tomb of Ankhmahor at Saqqara (twenty-third century BC). Below on the left, one can see the groundplan of the house from which the funeral procession departs. Many mourning women are represented. Some of them lift up their arms as a sign of their grief, others are fainting and the women around them are holding them up. The accompanying inscription labels the scene as *'departing from the house of the estate to the beautiful West'*. Pepiankh from the provincial cemetery at Meir is even more precise at this point when he mentions not only the purpose of the whole procession but even gives the chronology for the first stage. *'Procession to the purification tent on the first day after having attained a nice old age with the well-provided under the Great God, the Lord of the West.'* The deceased is then carried on a litter and accompanied by high officials who pay homage to their dead colleague on his last journey.

This stage of the funeral ceremony is illustrated in the tomb of Pepiankh at Meir. In the bottom register we can see a boat that has just arrived at the necropolis. The crew consists of (from right to left) the captain, the female mourner, the chief embalmer and the lector priest. In the middle there is a light construction protecting the coffin containing the deceased. On the stern there is an embalmer, another female mourner, the helmsman and another captain. The top register shows, on the far right, men carrying a litter which bears the wooden coffin with the mummy of the deceased. In front of them walks a female mourner and two men are protecting the body – the lector priest and the embalmer. The woman wears a long hanging dress and a shoulder-length wig; she is a professional mourner, called *djeret* – one of the two mourners who took part in funeral processions and substituted for the goddesses Isis and Nephthys, the sisters of Osiris. According to religious concepts from the end of the Old Kingdom, every deceased was symbolically equal to Osiris, and these goddesses would thus protect him on his last journey. She is preceded by two officials. The first one wears a pointed skirt and a band of linen over his body. He is holding a sceptre in the right hand and a staff in the left. The accompanying inscription labels him as 'embalmer'. The second one wears skirt pointed in front and also a band of linen over his body. He is labelled as a 'lector priest'. The lector priest is holding a papyrus roll in his left hand, an indispensable item for his role in the funerary procession. It was he who read aloud the religious texts that were supposed to secure for the deceased a successful burial, an undisturbed afterlife existence and an uninterrupted transition to the other world. Next to this scene we can see the embalmers' workshop façade, decorated with two slender columns. To the left of it, in front of heaped-up offerings, the priest performs ritual actions connected with the ceremony.

Other stages of the funeral procession are detailed in the scenes from the tomb of Sneferuinishtef in Dahshur (twenty-third century BC). At the top left of two horizontal bands of decoration (registers) which have been preserved we can discern a barque. In the centre of its deck is a shelter which contains the body of the deceased. At the prow and stern sit the two mourners. At the stern stand also three officials; the last of them is labelled as the lector priest. A chest with his cultic instruments, chiefly papyrus rolls with the individual religious texts and spells lies in front of the priest. At the prow stands the helmsman. The scene is probably set on the canal which led to the necropolis, because the funerary boat has neither a sail to sail upstream nor rudders to sail downstream. On the contrary, the boat is being pulled by others which can be seen to the right and are equipped with rudders.

When the boat reached the edge of the necropolis, the body was lifted out. At this point, after landing at the west bank, the body was ritually cleansed in

Fig. 4.15 Inyotefiker and his wife on the pilgrimage to the tomb of Osiris at Abydos (tomb of Inyotefiker at Thebes, after N. de Garis Davies, The tomb of Antefoker, vizier of Sesostris I, and of his wife, Senet, London 1920, pl. 18)

a purification tent called *ibu* and transported to the embalmer's workshop which must have been located in the vicinity. After the period necessary for embalming was over, symbolic rituals had to be performed. They related to the journey of the mummy to the sacred places in the Delta. During the Middle Kingdom the symbolical journey to the tomb of Osiris at Abydos in southern Egypt became one of the main prerequisites for undisturbed existence in the afterlife. In all probability the mummy did not actually undertake all these visits. They were performed only indirectly by representations on tomb walls. One of these scenes can be found in the early Middle Kingdom tomb of Inyotefiker, the vizier of Amenemhat I. This scene shows two boats: the one on the left shows a boat with a canopy with the seated figure of Inyotefiker in the company of his wife Senet. Both of them are depicted in close-fitting dresses. On the prow there is a male figure cutting off the front leg of a cow. Behind him there is an offering table laden with offerings. The second boat, propelled by several oarsmen, is, as the label makes clear, heading towards Abydos to worship Osiris, the Great God and Lord of the West.

The last stage of the funeral ceremony is also illustrated in this tomb. We can see a procession with the litter carrying the deceased official, after the boats landed at his tomb. The litter bears the wooden coffin and the mummy of the deceased. At his head and feet stand two female mourners. Further on there are three men protecting the body – the lector priest, the embalmer and the sealer of the god. The sledge is organised and dragged by eight men and a couple of bulls. Next to this scene we can see the *tjekenu* scene which shows a pair of smaller sledges, each of them being dragged by two men. The one is loaded with

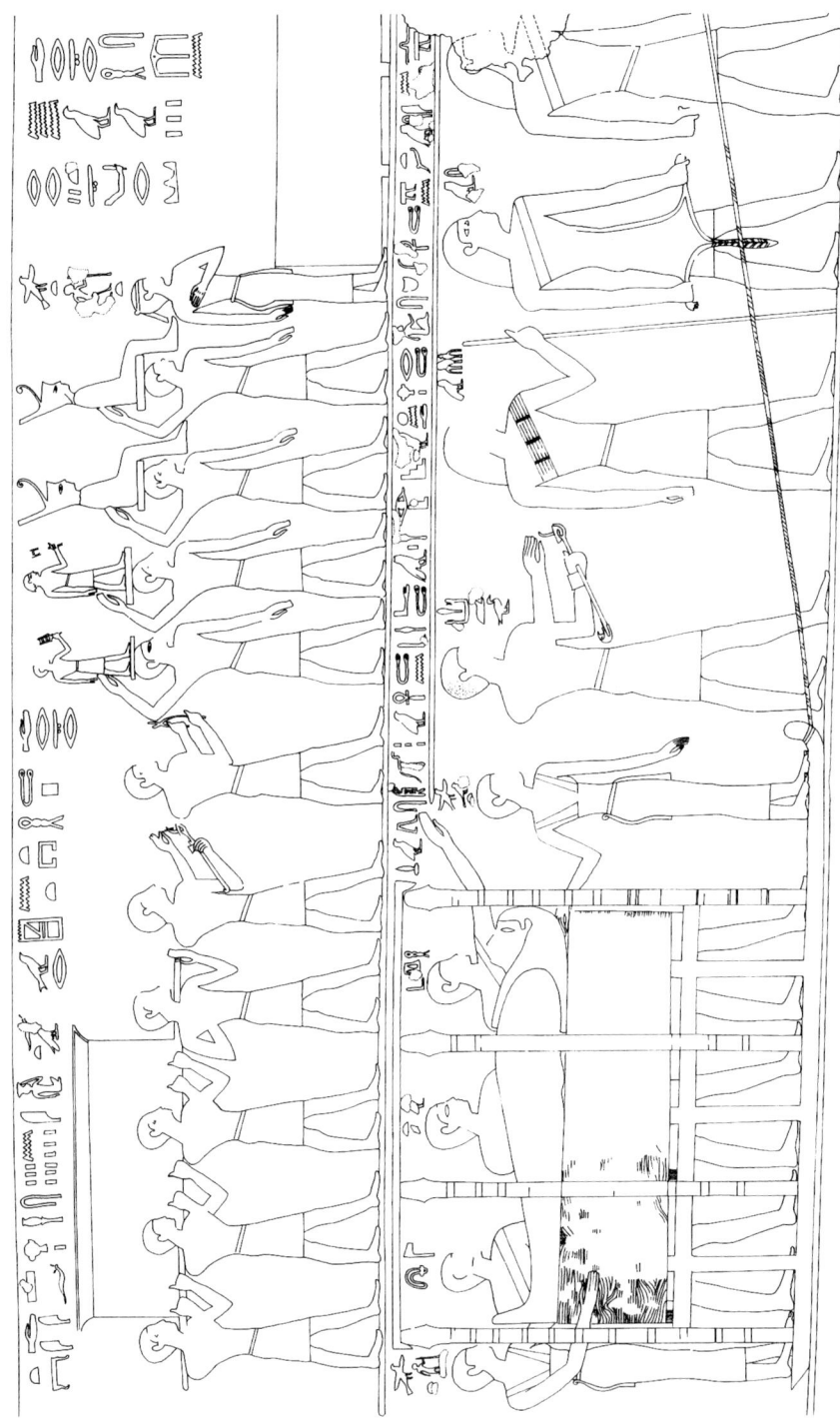

Fig. 4.16 Arrival at the tomb: the burial of Inyotefiker (after N. de Garis Davies, *The tomb of Antefoker, vizier of Sesostris I, and of his wife, Senet*, London 1920, pl. 21)

a canopic box containing four vessels with the mummified viscera. The second one probably contained the remains of the embalming ritual, which are personified as a kneeling human being. When the procession reaches the tomb, the lector priest performs the last ritual actions connected with the burial. To the right we can see the four ritual *muu* dancers receiving the funeral procession.

Most of the final actions at the tomb were probably performed in front of its entrance, in the funerary chapel and on the roof, where the mouth of the shaft leading to the underground burial chamber was located. One of the most significant rituals at this point was the opening of the mouth. It was performed on a statue – the earthly image of the tomb owner, and later on the mummy itself. In the course of this ritual, the *sem* priest touched the mouth of the deceased with several instruments (above all with a stone knife called *peseshkef*). The aim of this action was to revive the statue, respectively the mummy, to renew its ability to speak, hear and see, and thus to bring the deceased back to life in the hereafter. After the completion of the ritual, the deceased was lowered through the vertical shaft into the burial chamber and placed into the sarcophagus or wooden coffin. The burial chamber was filled with offerings and funerary equipment, which were to serve the deceased in the afterlife. The entrance to the burial chamber was subsequently walled up with bricks or large stones and the vertical shaft was filled with sand. Thus, the burial ceremony was concluded. From now on, offerings would be regularly brought to the chapel of the deceased, which was usually located at the eastern side of the tomb to face the rising sun. The regular performance of these ceremonies was the task of professional funerary priests, who recited religious texts and presented offerings, consisting mainly of food and drinks, to the soul of the deceased.

The funerary ceremony of Sinuhe's time must have looked similar. We should not, however, forget that it was preceded by more than a thousand years of development and changes in tomb construction and design as well as in the general concept of afterlife existence. Had Sinuhe indeed lived, he would certainly have built for himself a tomb which would reflect precisely this development and the traditions passed down for generations.

In the earliest times of funerary practices, the tomb was designed as a simple pit hollowed out in the desert and equipped with only a few offerings. A low mound was heaped over it, and the location of the grave was marked by an erected stone, from which the later stelae with the name and sometimes also the titles of the deceased developed. These stones/stelae not only marked the place of burial, but also allowed the relatives of the deceased to identify the site of their ancestor's burial. This was very important, since it enabled them to come to the grave to present offerings to his soul, which dwelt in the hereafter.

Apart from the burial itself, burial equipment was also of essential importance. In the most ancient times it consisted of pottery containers with food and drink to satisfy the needs of the deceased. There were also items of daily use, such as stone palettes, often decorated (which were used for the preparation of cosmetics), weapons, and stone and copper tools. In the course of the centuries, even the composition of the burial equipment was subjected to many changes. The inventory depended mainly on the social status of the deceased and on his financial situation. To generalise somewhat, it can be said that the richer a man was, the more expensive and variegated burial equipment he could afford. This was of course true of the design and decoration of the tomb itself as well.

In the beginning of the third millennium BC, a new type of burial appeared near the capital of unified Egypt, later Memphis. High officials of the country started to build mud-brick tombs whose height can reach up to five metres and whose walls can exceed fifty metres in length. The tombs resemble the low benches that stand in front of modern Arabic village houses, and are therefore called mastabas (Arabic word for 'benches'). These tombs consisted of a superstructure and a substructure. The superstructure could contain up to 45 inaccessible rooms or magazines, which were filled with objects for the afterlife of the deceased, including board games to occupy his free time. In the substructure of the tomb was the burial chamber, which contained a stone (mostly limestone) or wooden sarcophagus within which lay the dead body of the tomb owner. In some cases more storerooms with burial equipment surrounded the burial chamber. One of the First Dynasty Saqqara tombs contained a complete 'funerary banquet' for the soul of the deceased, which consisted of the following items: a slice of bread, barley porridge, boiled fish, boiled pigeon, boiled chicken, two boiled kidneys, bovine ribs and legs, fruit, fresh nabk berries, little

Fig. 4.17 Eastern façade of the late Third Dynasty tomb of Hetepi in Abusir. Hetepi is depicted seated in front of a table of offerings, with titles and name above his head

honey cakes, cheese, and a jug of wine. According to ancient Egyptian conceptions, the soul of the deceased continually partook in such banquets, and lived from them in the afterlife. Like the tomb and its burial equipment, even these dishes were supposed to last eternally, and thus to be forever at the disposal of the deceased.

The tombs are oriented with their long axes in the north-south direction. The façade of the tomb, visible from the world of the living, was turned to the east where the sun, the personification of Ra and the symbol of rebirth, rises. Below ground, the body of the deceased was placed in the western part of the burial chamber, the west being the symbolic region of the dead and of the netherworld. The deceased faced the east, where he could every morning witness a symbolic rebirth – the sunrise. In the course of the Second Dynasty the above ground storerooms began to recede. They were gradually transferred to the substructure. It seems likely that already at this time tomb robbers threatened the afterlife existence of the deceased. Since the Egyptians considered the tomb a real dwelling place for the soul and for the hereafter, at this period they regularly constructed several rooms as exact copies of those in their earthly residences. The individual rooms were conceived as entrance halls, kitchens, bedrooms and even bathrooms. From the Third Dynasty on, we can trace a gradual decline in the number of storerooms and underground rooms in the tomb and the growing importance of the funerary cult itself.

The cult was performed as follows: the family of the deceased travelled to the tomb, where they gathered in front of the niche in the southern part of the eastern façade. They offered for the deceased and pronounced spells that were supposed to facilitate his afterlife existence. Food and drink were mostly presented as offerings to the *ka* soul at this place. The *ka* received the symbolic aspect of the offering, from which it derived its subsistence in the afterlife (just as it could use the funerary equipment in the burial chamber and in the storerooms of the tomb). This niche was considered a link between this and the other world, between the world of the living and that of the dead. Through its western wall the deceased entered this world to take part in various rituals and then, after their performance, returned to the hereafter

In the Fourth Dynasty the main focal point lay in the construction of the superstructure of the tomb, which thus became the true centre of the mortuary cult of the deceased. Above all, a new material – stone, mainly limestone – became more common in tomb construction instead of mud bricks. Already in the course of the Third Dynasty, the original offering niche had been transformed into a roofed chapel, an independent room with an entrance in the eastern side. The walls of this chapel were decorated – covered with wall paintings or reliefs cut in stone showing scenes from the life of the tomb owner, with the objective of guaranteeing for him a similar life in the hereafter. The western wall of the chapel contained the so-called false door, a stone stela imitating a real door. This item had evolved from the original offering niche. The false door marked the boundary between the world of the living and that of the dead. The fact that the funerary chapel housed a stone – and therefore in the eyes of the Egyptians

Fig. 4.18 False door, a gateway to the Netherworld, embedded in the west wall of the offering chapel of the vizier Qar (Abusir)

eternal – gateway between the world of the dead and the world of the living, only intensified its role and importance in the cult.

The false door was inscribed with the name and titles of the deceased. The focus of its decoration was the scene representing the deceased seated at a table laden with slices of bread, and with jars of beer standing below. The list of offerings to be presented to the deceased was also an integral part of this scene, including commodities such as cloth, alabaster, poultry, wine, fruits, sweet cakes, milk, or items of funerary equipment, etc. Towards the end of the Fifth Dynasty, the slices of bread on the table were transformed into the representation of reeds, which symbolized resurrection. This belief was based on the story of the birth of Horus in the thickets of the Delta. In the Sixth Dynasty, the idea of resurrection in a reed thicket was considered as the basic symbol for the wish of the deceased: to be reborn, even as Horus was, in a sense, reborn Osiris.

In front of the false door stood an altar on which offerings were presented to the deceased. This altar frequently bears the name and titles of the deceased. Sometimes it was also decorated with reliefs representing the most important ancient Egyptian offerings. Richer families could often afford to commission and pay funerary priests to maintain the cult of their ancestor. The various cultic rituals consisted not only in the bringing of offerings, but also in the recitation of formulae, which guaranteed the deceased a steady supply of offerings, an undisturbed existence in the afterlife, the attainment of bliss, etc. In the time of Sinuhe, these formulae commonly address Osiris, the Lord of the Afterlife, and ask him for various favours. Another god who frequently appears in these formulae is Anubis, who was as the guarantor of burial often asked for assistance in funerary matters. Some of these formulae, which have been passed down to us in writing on tomb walls and other Egyptian monuments, went as follows:

'May you receive a beautiful burial in the western desert of the cemetery, in peace, in peace!'

'May (gods) make offerings to you, according to this prescript which was composed by Thoth in the House of the god's book!'

'May he give you water, beer, incense, ointment, all things, all sweet kinds of fruit, all offerings due on yearly festivals and all heneket-offerings!'

'May you walk beautifully on the beautiful ways of the cemetery through which the blessed are led!'

'May he sail in the morning solar barque!'

'May he (Osiris) cause that both arms with offerings be extended to him in the time of the festivals of the cemetery, together with the companions of Osiris and the ancestors who have existed before!'

'May he cause that you may land on the pure places which are in heaven!'

'May he cause that you rise to the Great God, lord of the West!'

Fig. 4.19 Entrance into the tomb of judge Inty, with his biography and obelisks, symbols of the sun god Ra (Abusir)

We have already mentioned that the chapel walls were decorated with paintings or reliefs cut in stone. They were virtually entirely covered with inscriptions and scenes which bear witness to the work, religion and favourite pastime of the tomb owners. The fact that these scenes depict contemporary life with great precision is above all a consequence of the basic belief of the ancient Egyptians, namely that the world after death is similar to that on earth. Hence the apparently paradoxical fact that tombs, although they are funerary constructions, are among our foremost sources for our knowledge of life on earth.

The walls in the tomb entrance were most commonly decorated with a standing figure of the tomb owner dressed in his official attire, usually consisting of a long kilt reaching down to the calves and forming a flap in the front. As a symbol of his authority, he is usually seen holding a sceptre in his hand, and he leans against a staff. His head is covered with an ornate wig. Above his head we may read the titles that describe his position in the society. In the early periods of the Egyptian state, it was common for one official to hold different functions at the royal court, in state administration and as a priest. Thus, an Egyptian tomb may include for example a warden of the royal palace, who served simultaneously as a priest in the funerary temple of one of the Egyptian rulers, or a vizier, whose duties included, aside from the maintenance of the royal palace, the collection of taxes and overseeing of the funerary complexes of the Sixth Dynasty kings. Only much later, during the time of the New Kingdom, appear specialized groups of high state officials and the division of priestly and state power.

The tomb chapel was situated either immediately behind the entrance, or divided from it by a series of rooms. The individual rooms could have had different functions, such as magazines, vestibules, big courts which housed gatherings of relatives during various celebrations in the tomb, etc. The tomb could also have included several chapels simultaneously, since it often served as the burial and cult place of several members of one family. The decorated walls of these rooms reveal an incredibly rich world, into which all the individual scenes on the tomb walls fit precisely like pieces of a jigsaw puzzle. The first scene, on the right in the tomb entrance, shows the figure of the tomb owner standing in a reed boat. The boat is passing through reed thickets and the tomb owner is depicted hunting different species of animals, mainly hippopotami and crocodiles in water. Fowling in the thickets and fishing are also depicted. The tomb owner is often accompanied by his wife, who represents Isis and thus accentuates the role of rebirth for the spiritual world of the ancient Egyptians. Near the official, other boats may be carrying fishermen and other servants, ready to assist their master. The importance of this scene has been already indicated in connection with the explanation of the offering scene: it is the motif of rebirth while passing through the papyrus thicket on the journey to the hereafter. The tomb owner must constantly be on guard, since there are many dangers lurking on this path, such as hippopotami and crocodiles. It was thus necessary to destroy such animals.

After the rebirth, we find ourselves in the heart of the tomb. The deceased becomes a resurrected being who lives his life in the hereafter. The visitor is thus

Fig. 4.20 Khnumhotep II fowling in the papyrus thicket (Beni Hassan)

transferred from his own world directly to the one where the tomb owner once lived and now lives again. Common scenes of 'this world' meet the visitor's eye, since life goes on exactly the same way as it did before. We can see agricultural scenes being inspected by the tomb owner, such as the breeding of poultry, fishing with fishermen arguing and fighting for their catch; or the nobleman himself approached by a file of humble servants carrying numerous offerings to facilitate his life in the hereafter. Furthermore, we can find numerous depictions of craftsmen building papyrus boats, jewellery, wooden furniture, stone vessels or metal products, scenes of animal husbandry and leading cattle herds across the river, of agricultural work including the harvest of crops, transport and threshing of wheat, market scenes, where artisans exchange their products with the peasants, and of the preparation of food, mostly baking bread and brewing beer. Less frequent, but more interesting, are scenes depicting the tomb owner being carried by servants in a litter while overseeing the construction of his own tomb or the fashioning of statues for his funerary cult.

Among the most important scenes are those of slaughtering cattle. This motif belongs to the oldest activities documented on tomb walls and can be seen as taking up the tradition of prehistoric hunting rituals, which consisted of catching and killing antelopes and gazelles in the desert. Their death symbolized the destruction of enemy forces represented by the god Seth, who incessantly strove to gain might over the world with the help of the forces of evil and chaos. The animals' death symbolized the victory of benign powers and the preservation

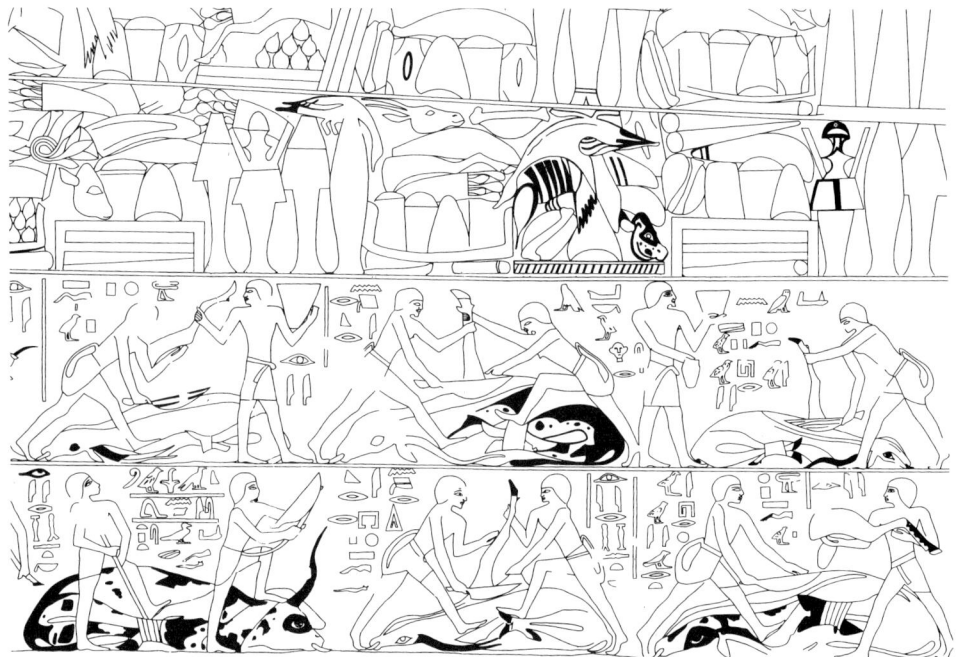

Fig. 4.21 Butchers slaughtering cattle (tomb of Niankhpepi, Meir; after A. M. Blackman, M. R. Apted, The Rock Tombs of Meir, Part V, London 1953, pl. 35)

of the world order. In historical times, cattle were slaughtered in precisely the same way. First, the animal's legs were tied, then it was thrown to the ground and, finally, its throat was ritually cut. To this end the slaughterers used archaic flint knives. Once killed, the animal was cut up into portions, which were presented to the tomb owner as offerings. The most valuable parts, the heart and the haunch, symbolized the animal's power and were thus offered upon the tomb owner's altar immediately after the slaughter.

Another important commodity was the animal's blood. The death of the animals was not only a kind of 'dramatisation' depicting the victory of the forces of order and the divine system; it was also their redemption for having served the evil powers. In a way we may also speculate that the death of an animal was supposed to deliver the tomb owner, from all his potential sins. In Egypt, just as in the Old Testament, animals played a very important role in human redemption.

Another motif that deserves our attention is the scene depicting the so-called journey to the 'beautiful west' by boat. The boat crew either mans the oars, or manages the sails. The tomb owner is depicted twice, once standing in the ceremonial skirt and watching the course of the journey toward the cemetery ('the beautiful west'), and once as a mummified body lying on the catafalque at the stern of the boat. The meaning of this scene is clear – the deceased is travelling in a boat to the cemetery, to the realm of the dead, to the hereafter where new life begins. The importance of this journey is attested by the location of the most famous burial sites containing tombs of Old Kingdom nobles: Giza, Abusir, Saqqara and Dahshur. All these cemeteries were accessible by water. Virtually the same characteristic applies to the later Middle Kingdom cemeteries.

Finally, we should also mention the scene depicting the tomb owner performing his duties. Mainly due to the fact that only high state officials could afford to build large decorated tombs, these tombs include numerous scenes of collecting taxes. Just as in all other cases, the tomb owner is depicted on a much larger scale than all other persons, so that his superiority is evident. He is mostly seated and inspects the collection of taxes.

Aside from the aforementioned scenes, the tomb chapel itself could also include large scenes with bearers of offerings and funerary equipment. The bearers face the tomb owner who is depicted in a sitting or standing position while inspecting and receiving their procession. Both men and women approach him with reed baskets, tables laden with fruits and vegetables, meat and bread loaves, herdsmen bring herds of cattle, sheep and goats, men and women carry fowl, ducks and geese, wooden furniture with funerary equipment, etc.

In the western wall of the chapel stood the false door, the focus of the cult of the deceased and a symbolical gate between the worlds 'here' and 'there'. Behind it could hide a closed, inaccessible room called *serdab* in Arabic, which contained a statue or statues representing the tomb owner. The purpose of these statues is also to be sought in the securing of the afterlife existence of the deceased. They served as bodies to which the soul of the deceased could return

Fig. 4.22 Tax collecting in the tomb of Mereruka (Saqqara)

Fig. 4.23 Mo'alla, burial place of Ankhtify

while funerary rituals were performed in the chapel. Other statues of the tomb owner could be located in various parts of the tomb, for example in the large courts where offerings were commonly presented to the spirit of the deceased.

The end of the 23rd century BC was marked by the final downfall of the Old Kingdom, the glorious era of the pyramid builders. Current research indicates that the ancient Egyptian state had exhausted its resources by the building and maintenance of gargantuan pyramid complexes, which swallowed much of the economic potential of the country. Since the end of the Fifth Dynasty, officials gained more and more independence, and accumulated great power at the expense of the sovereign. Indicative of this situation is the fact that King Pepi I was married to two sisters of the high-ranking vizier Djau of the Upper Egyptian Abydos nome for political reasons. These two queens later became mothers of the two subsequent rulers on the Egyptian throne – Merenre and Pepi II. Significant changes in the religious sphere presented another factor that enabled the gradual rise of the power of the officials. Since the time of the reign of the Abusir sun-king Neuserre, the right of post-mortem identification with Osiris, lord of the Netherworld, was no longer reserved to the king. The idea of mythical resurrection found yet another expression. In the traditional scene of the funerary repast, which depicts the deceased seated behind an offering table, the table is covered with reed leaves instead of the previous bread loaves. The reed thicket implied the concept of resurrection in the thickets of the Delta (connected with Osiris) and symbolised a kind of gate to the netherworld. The rising independence of officials in this time is indicated also by the fact that they began to build their tombs in the provinces of their origin.

In consequence of the character of the terrain – Nile valley enclosed by rock massives – the rock-cut tomb (which was in limited numbers already known at the cemeteries of Giza, Saqqara, Abusir, etc.) becomes the predominant tomb type. These tendencies reached a peak in the First Intermediate Period, when several cemeteries grew in Upper Egypt, attesting the independence and power of local dignitaries. We may mention for example sites such as Mo'alla or Gebelein. Probably the most famous tomb of this period is that of the official Ankhtify in Mo'alla, dated approximately to 2140 BC. This tomb can still today be seen to the left of the road on the journey from Luxor to Assuan, approximately 35 km south of Luxor. It was entirely cut out of the rock massif and it is peculiar on account of the irregular shape of the individual columns and walls inside the tomb. The interior of the tomb comprises a single transversal room, the ceiling of which is supported by thirty columns arranged in three rows running approximately parallel to the façade of the tomb. These columns, or rather buttresses, are of various shapes – rectangular, polygonal, rounded, etc. The walls of the tomb are plastered and decorated with provincial paintings, which depict motifs from the everyday life and the afterlife of the tomb owner.

The tomb acquired even more importance after the British-German expedition to Mo'alla in autumn 2002. The preliminary reports seem to indicate that the tomb included a valley temple and ascending causeway. This would mean that Ankhtify imitated the basic structure of royal pyramid complexes similarly like the owners of the Middle Kingdom tombs at Qaw el-Kebir.

Fig. 4.24 Interior of the tomb of Ankhtify in Mo'alla, the room being divided by several forms of pillars

Fig. 4.25 Reconstruction of the tombs at Qaw el-Kebir, Wahka I on the left and Ibu on the right (after H. Steckeweh, Die Fürstengräber von Qaw, Leipzig 1936, frontispiece)

Fig. 4.26 Qubbet el-Hawa with tombs of the Old and Middle Kingdom officials (Assuan)

Middle Kingdom tombs follow the same basic rules and principles that were developed and observed in the Old Kingdom period. In contrast with previous development, most of the Middle Kingdom cemeteries concentrate in the provinces of southern Egypt. One of the more profound differences can be seen in the fact that now the majority of tombs are cut in the rocks enclosing the narrow Nile valley. As far as significance and decoration are concerned, we are faced with a similar thinking and analogous themes to those of the Old Kingdom. This holds true for the main themes on the tomb walls. What seems to be accentuated from now on is the idea of a journey to the afterlife. This idea is reflected in the architectural design – the individual rooms are arranged along the central axis, thus follow one after the other. When visiting some of these tombs today, one can see along the entire structure from the entrance. Whereas during the Old Kingdom it was only the cult chapel proper that had to be oriented in an east-west direction, in the Middle Kingdom the whole tomb incorporates the notion of the journey to the West. New items and elements appear in tomb equipment, such as *ushabti*, tomb stelae instead of the false door, the so-called Coffin Texts inscribed on wooden coffins, tomb statues that were no longer concealed in closed rooms but displayed in the tomb, and model estates. All these elements modify and develop the basic concepts of the previous periods.

In consequence of their considerable independence, provincial officials of the Middle Kingdom began to build their splendid tombs close to their hometowns, far from the capital of the state and the sovereign. Despite the fact that these tombs preserved certain features that connect them to the development of

Fig. 4.27 Open courtyard in front of the tomb of Sarenput I at Qubbet el-Hawa

the royal complexes and the decoration of the tombs of high Old Kingdom officials, in general they represent an entirely new, independent type and development stage.

The most imposing Middle Kingdom cemeteries are located in Upper and above all Middle Egypt. These cemeteries were founded in prominent places in the rocks overlooking the banks of the Nile, which enhanced their splendour. The first fleeting encounter with these tombs leaves no doubt that these were the tombs of powerful local rulers. In the course of the Eleventh and Twelfth Dynasties, necropoleis were founded in the rocks façades on the eastern bank of the Nile in Beni Hassan and further south at el-Bersha and Qaw el-Kebir. On the western bank, cemeteries appeared at Asyut, Deir Rifeh, and at the very southern frontier of Egypt, at Qubbet el-Hawa opposite Assuan.

Despite their relatively independent development, the individual cemeteries share several general traits. The first stage of their common development is based on the tradition of the Old Kingdom rock tombs, which preferred relatively simple rooms, wider rather than deep. The concept of the tomb as a house for eternal life is gradually strengthened by the use of elements of secular, everyday architecture. At first columns are integrated into the tomb design and begin to divide the interiors of the tombs. Then the façade of the tomb itself is transformed into a portico with several columns. In the course of the Twelfth Dynasty the interior of the tomb is divided into several rooms, which are arranged behind one another along a central axis. Thus an impression of a journey leading to the other world is created, which in tomb architecture is expressed by the distance that the visitor must negotiate from the entrance of the tomb to the cult chapel itself.

In the Middle Kingdom, the powerful nomarchs buried at the site of Qaw el-Kebir imitated the structure of the royal pyramid complexes. Their tombs contained the main features of the pyramid complexes of Old Kingdom kings – the valley temple, ascending causeway, and the 'mortuary temple' – i.e. a cultic area with a chapel. The site of Qaw el-Kebir lies in the vicinity of Asyut in the rocks on the eastern bank of the Nile, and belongs to a larger cemetery which contains tombs from prehistorical times all through the Graeco-Roman period. The cemetery was located in the immediate vicinity of the capital of the Tenth nome of Upper Egypt, which extended on both banks of the Nile, the left-bank side being called 'The City of Wadjet' and the right-bank side 'The City of Sandals'. The location of the cemetery was far from accidental, for according to an Egyptian legend it was precisely here that Horus and Seth fought their battle.

We will, however, concentrate on the large tomb complexes of a noble family, the tombs of Wahka I, Wahka II, and Ibu. The best preserved of these belonged to Wahka II, the brother of Ibu, and according to his titles the highest official of this family. The initial part of the ascending causeway of his tomb complex is now unfortunately lost, so we may only speculate that a brick structure similar to those discovered in the complexes of Wahka I and Ibu originally stood here. It consisted of a rectangular chamber, the ceiling of which was supported by four pillars. The opening in the rear wall of the room gave way to the roofed ascending causeway, which was also built of bricks and cased on the inside with limestone slabs. The course of the causeway was traced approximately at the point where it turned west, and where it could also be entered by a small structure in the east. From this point the causeway ascended directly to the columned court, which it reached after 152 m. The court itself was divided from the causeway by a large pylon-like structure made of bricks. The court, approximately square, was lined with eighteen columns. In its centre there was a stairway leading to the platform where the tomb itself was located. A rectangular chamber with two rows of four columns each led to the rooms cut into the rock massif. The visitor first passed through an oblong chamber with 10 pillars, which opened into a large offering hall with an altar in the middle. Its slightly vaulted ceiling was decorated with colourful geometrical ornaments arranged in regular rectangles. The side walls of the room contained niches for the statues of the deceased, which enabled the tomb owner to take part in the offering rituals conducted in the hall. The walls were originally decorated with bright paintings, of which, however, only poor traces remain, originally published by William Flinders Petrie in 1930. One of the recorded scenes depicted priests performing offering rituals, another female dancers and acrobats. This room gave way to a rectangular chamber with niches for the statues of the tomb owner. Along the sides of the room were small chambers, from which shafts led to the burial chambers of Wahka II and his wife Kemu. The large stone sarcophagus of greyish limestone in the burial chamber of Wahka contained a wooden coffin, which had once held his mummy. The opening in the floor contained canopic jars with the mummified viscera of the deceased. The walls of the chamber were plastered and originally inscribed with the Coffin Texts.

Most of the objects coming from these tombs – decorated stone sarcophagi, tomb statues or fragments of stone decoration – can now be seen in the recently reconstructed galleries of the Egyptian Museum in Turin.

A prominent place among the masterpieces of Middle Kingdom architecture and painting undoubtedly belongs to the tombs which can still be visited at the southern frontier of Egypt at the city of Elephantine, on the rock spur of Qubbet el-Hawa on the western bank of the Nile, and the tombs built in Middle Egypt at the village of Beni Hassan. These groups of tombs are interesting, since a large part of their decoration is still preserved, and enables us to get a glimpse of their original appearance.

The Middle Kingdom tombs of Elephantine continue the tradition of local rock-cut tombs from the end of the Old Kingdom (this site is the burial place, among others, of the famous commander Harkhuf). Their owners traditionally supervised the trade and security in this frontier area of Egypt. Elephantine was the starting point of numerous Egyptian military and trading expeditions, and through Elephantine, African goods entered Egypt. The tomb of Sarenput I (No. 36) dates to the time of Senwosret I. Sarenput I was the mayor of Elephantine, nomarch of the 1st nome of Upper Egypt, overseer of royal ships, overseer of foreign countries and of interpreters. His rock-cut tomb was accessible by a stone stairway leading from the quay to a large open court cut into the rock massif in front of the entrance of the tomb itself. The western side of the court contained a portico with six pillars. The walls of the court and the façade of the tomb were decorated with inscriptions and scenes executed in sunk relief. The scenes depict Sarenput, either seated or standing, with the attributes of his power – the *kherep* sceptre and a staff, wearing a long white skirt and carefully finished headdress. Most scenes are located in the western façade of the court, where the tomb owner is depicted spear-hunting in a boat, accompanied by his favourite dog. The opposite scene shows Sarenput seated, holding a sceptre and a staff, receiving four women of his family, headed by his wife. The accompanying legends describe them as 'his beloved wife, mistress of the house Sattjen, his beloved daughter Satethetep, his beloved daughter Sattjen.' The longer inscription above their heads refers to the offering rituals for the spirit of the deceased:

'The offering which the king gives and Osiris, lord of Busiris, great god, lord of Abydos, may an offering (bread, beer, cattle, and fowl) be offered at all places, consisting of a thousand of pieces of cloth, a thousand of god's offerings and all good things from which god lives, for the ka of the noble and overseer of priests, Sarenput.'

Over and flanking the entrance to the inner parts of the tomb is the so-called ideal biographical inscription, which records some details from the life of

Fig. 4.28 Sarenput I with insignia of his office, detail

Sarenput. Beside his titles and functions, we learn for example the fact that during one of the religious festivals, Sarenput spent a night in the temple – this practice resembles the much later custom of staying overnight in the 'sanatories' built in the immediate vicinity of Graeco-Roman temples, which were considered places of magical healing. Sarenput's inscription begins as follows:

'The noble and prince, chancellor of the king of Lower Egypt, the sole friend, priest of Satet, mistress of Elephantine, justified before Anubis, born of Sattjeni, speaks as follows:

O you who live on earth, who shall pass along this tomb faring downstream or upstream, if you love your goods, praise your god by a funerary offering for the ka of the justified noble Sarenput.

He says: I am the one who fills the heart of the king in the temple, speaker of Nekhen in the temple of Satet, Nekhbi in the sanctuary of Buto, overseer of priests, chancellor of the king of Lower Egypt, the sole friend, herald of the king in the army. He who hears as the only one, he to whom the entire land comes … on the place of the defeat of the king's enemies. Privy to the king …

Seal-bearer of all affairs of the land of Kush of kings' wives, he to whom the tribute of the Medjay, the rulers of the foreign lands, is announced.

He who spends the night in the temple at the time of the great festival, who accepts costly gifts that the ruler gives in the palace. Chief of the joyful ones in the divine barque of the god performing all miracles of the Nubians in the whirlpools. Privy to the people on the dikes, great overseer of ships in the royal house, he who keeps both treasuries in order, commander of the settlements in Nubia, under whose supervision is he who sails as well as he who lands.

The noble and overseer of priests Sarenput says:

I built my tomb in the favour of the king. His Majesty distinguished me in the land, so that I was elevated over (the other) nomarchs. I am … law codes of old times. I reached the sky in a single moment. I commissioned stone workers with works on my tomb and His Majesty praised me greatly on account of it in the presence of the officials and of the queen. He equipped it with gifts from the royal house, he secured all its needs, he filled it with jewells, equipped with offering and everything that was destined for it.'

The inner rooms of the tomb consist of a hall with four pillars, from which a narrow passage led to the cultic chapel of an almost square ground plan. The roof of the chapel was supported by two pillars and the western wall contained a niche, where the offering stele once stood. Two shafts opening in the floor of this room led to the burial chambers of Sarenput and the members of his family.

The most typical tomb in terms of architectural design is that of Sarenput II (tomb no. 31). The entrance remained unfinished – it consisted of an open court giving access to the inner rooms which reached more than 31 m into the rock massif. A narrow passage led from the court into the rock and opened into a large pillared hall, the ceiling of which was supported by three pairs of large pillars. Between the two westernmost pillars was the entrance onto the stairway leading into a long, narrow passage, each wall of which was decorated with three

Fig. 4.29 Interior of the tomb of Sarenput II at Qubbet el-Hawa (Assuan)

niches containing bound Osirid statues of the tomb owner. The passage gave way into the cultic chapel with four pillars. In its western wall was a niche with an offering stele and originally also a statue of the deceased. The overall architectural design of the tomb expresses the Egyptian concept of the journey to the other world. The gradually rising floor of the individual rooms as well as the sinking ceiling create the impression of a journey to the west, the voyage to the blessed afterlife existence and ascent to the sky.

The idea of the journey to immortality also dominates the composition of the individual rooms. The southern pillared hall of 12 × 8.55 m is divided by pillars into three naves, the central and largest of which leads further into the tomb interior. The height of its ceiling decreases gradually towards the west: while in the beginning the height of the nave reaches 4.85 m, at the end it is 4.45 m. A stairway leading to the corridor which gives access to the cultic chapel adjoins the western part of the hall. The corridor is over 9 m long, the height of its ceiling reaches 2.60 m and its floor rises towards the west. The cultic chapel was of an almost square ground plan, its side measuring 4 m. Its western wall contained a niche, the western part of which was closed by a double-winged door and contained a granite seated statue of the tomb owner, now in the British Museum. Offering rituals were conducted in the entrance hall, in the western corner of

Fig. 4.30 Tomb of Sarenput II, detail of the offering niche in the westernmost part of the tomb (Qubbet el-Hawa)

which there originally stood a large offering table of red Assuan granite. Its upper part was decorated with the motif of an offering mat laden with loaves of bread and *hes*-vessels. Its placement is reminiscent of the location of altars in the *wesekhet* courts of the pyramid temples of the Old Kingdom, where ceremonies of burnt offerings were conducted. In stark contrast with other tombs of comparable type and importance, the tomb of Sarenput contains almost no painted decoration, which is limited to the offering chapel and the niche for the statue of the tomb owner. Undoubtedly, the decoration of the western wall, almost entirely preserved, was the most important. It was the centre of the tomb and together with the statue also the centre of the funerary cult. In the middle of the scene stands an offering table laden with offerings and to the left of it the tomb owner, dressed in a pleated skirt and adorned with armbands and a necklace, seated on a chair with lion paws. His son Ankhu approaches him from the right to offer him a lotus flower. Over them there is a hieroglyphic inscription connected with the tomb owner:

'One justified in front of Satet, mistress of Elephantine, and Nekhbet, the noble Nubkaurenekhet. One justified in front of Khnum, lord of the cool water at Elephantine, the noble Nubkaurenekhet.'

The inscription accompanying his son runs as follows: *'His son of his own body, whom he praised and loved every day, Ankhu.'*

The right wall of the niche is immediately connected to the offering scene. In its western part we see Sarenput's mother Satethetep, seated on a chair. Satethetep is wearing a tight white dress with shoulder-straps, in her left hand she is holding three lotus flowers, and her right hand is extended to the offering table. To her right Sarenput is depicted as if striding towards the visitor. He is dressed in a short skirt with long straps of cloth and he is holding a long staff and the *kherep* sceptre. His chest is adorned with a large necklace of pearls and he is wearing the ritual beard. The accompanying inscriptions contain an appeal for offerings for the spirit of the deceased. The opposite side is reserved for three people. Besides the similarly dressed tomb owner, we can also see the smaller figures of his son Ankhu and his wife Khnumdedet. Corresponding inscriptions appear over their heads. The longest contains an appeal for the burial of the tomb owner:

'An offering which the king gives and Geb, an offering which Anubis gives and Imiut, an offering which Osiris, lord of the Westerners gives, a beautiful offering for the spirit of the deceased, prince and noble, chancellor of the king of Lower Egypt, the sole friend, noble, the one who refreshes the heart of the king of Upper Egypt, the overseer of frontier guards, speaker of the gate of the southern mountains, noble, overseer of priests of Satet, mistress of Elephantine, overseer of troops, Sarenput, justified.'

Fig. 4.31 Façades of the rock-cut tombs of Beni Hassan

Undoubtedly the most splendid tombs of Middle Egypt are those at Beni Hassan, which belonged to the dignitaries who ruled the Sixteenth, Oryx, nome of Upper Egypt. This nome is mentioned already on the stone vessels from the underground passages of the Djoser pyramid, and on the walls of the so-called White Chapel of Senwosret I. Even its length along the Nile is recorded – 46 km. The tombs at Beni Hassan were cut into the rocks of the eastern bank of the Nile, where the ancient funerary estate *Menat Khufu* (meaning 'Khufu's Wetnurse') was also located, while the capital on the west bank of the Nile consisted of two sites, Harwer and Nefrusi. The duties of the nomarchs also included guarding the Eastern Desert, which was a frontier area of Egypt. The high rank and power of these local rulers find precise and eloquent expression in their tombs. One of the most important of these is undoubtedly that of Khnumhotep II (Tomb BH 3) from the time of Amenemhat II and Senwosret II. His titles inform us that Khnumhotep II was the mayor of the estate Menat Khufu and overseer of the eastern desert. He had two wives, Kheti and Tjat. His tomb consisted of a 7.2 m wide and 2.2 m deep entrance hall with a vaulted ceiling, which was supported by two columns with fluted shafts. The hall gave way into the main room of square ground plan, the sides of which measured 9.60 m, the height of its ceiling reached almost 6 m. The vault was supported by four fluted columns, which divided the room (in the east-west direction) into three naves. The niche in the western wall of the room originally contained a seated statue of the deceased tomb owner.

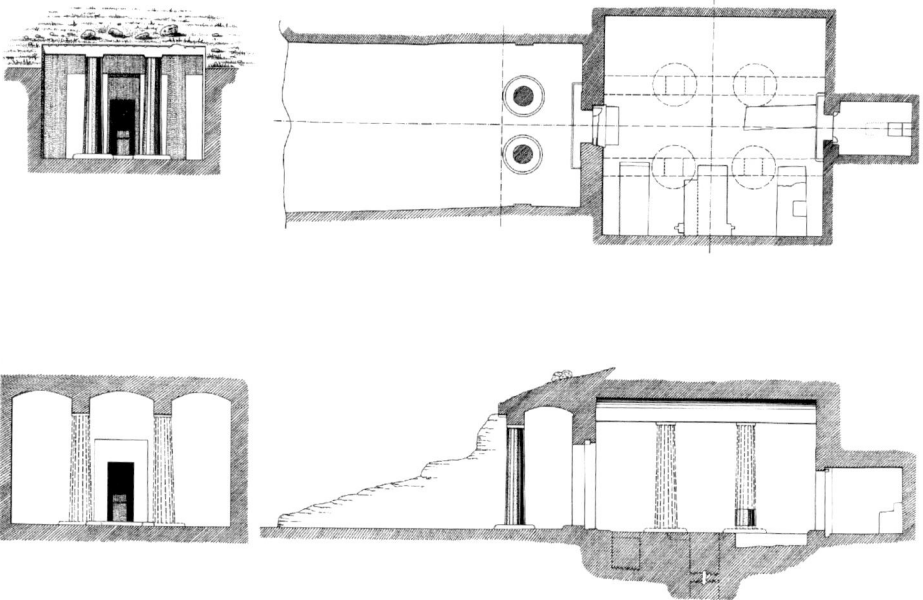

Fig. 4.32 Groundplan of the tomb of Khnumhotep II at Beni Hassan

The tomb of Khnumhotep II and others similar to it illustrate the new artistic methods which were used in the Middle Kingdom. Artists often preferred painting on plaster to pure relief. They thus had at hand a much larger variety of modes of expression, using not only the six basic colours – black, white, red, blue, green, and yellow – but also their hues. This period also witnessed the development of the art of complex compositions and scenes, which are only rarely divided with lines. The individual scenes merge into one another, phasing appears, scenes are now presented from various points of view, the scenes abound in dynamics and vividness. Of no small importance was also the fact that painting on plaster was more economical and faster. The highest level of development can be seen in the complex compositions and variations of individual scenes. The artists employ methods of space division, merging and overlapping, optical distortion and the effects of light and shade. The painting and reliefs are also rendered more naturalistic by making use of the irregularity and imperfections of the surface of the decorated walls, expressing motion and stability by capturing apparently arbitrary details of composition.

Besides the above-mentioned aspects of decoration, the already described tomb of Sarenput II at Assuan also contains unique evidence of a new way of encoding the proportions of human figures, which became more common in the art since the Twelfth Dynasty, namely, the use of an auxiliary square net executed in red. It was found on several places in the cultic chapel, on the pillars supporting the ceiling of this room, and in the niche in the western wall, serving the proportioning of the figures of Sarenput and his wife Khnumdedet. An important aspect of the use of the net was that fact that in case of large-scale and complex compositions, it allowed the artists to make model drawings of the individual parts of the scene. The net developed from the so-called axis crosses. The latter method was used in Old Kingdom times for the proportional depicting of human figures, which were divided vertically into two halves and horizontally into seven parts. The net developed in the Middle Kingdom was based on the basic unit of the human fist. The human figure was divided into nineteen equal parts horizontally and eleven parts vertically. From the feet to the waist at the point of the knot of the skirt there were ten units, from the feet to the shoulders sixteen, etc. This method remained basically unchanged for the following thousand years.

In the individual inscriptions in his tomb, Khnumhotep II emphasizes above all his noble origin. His mother Baket was the daughter of the Great Chief of the Oryx nome and the wife of Neheri, the governor of the capital of the nome. Khnumhotep II was appointed to his office, which he inherited from his grandfather, by Amenemhat II in the nineteenth year of his reign. Khnumhotep's eldest son succeeded him in his office in the seventeenth year of the reign of Senwosret II.

The motifs of decoration in this and most other tombs of that period are more or less the same as those that we know from the Old Kingdom. Their main aim is to provide the tomb owner with everything he needs and equip him with

Fig. 4.33 Khnumhotep II fowling

material possessions for an undisturbed life in the other world. In the First Intermediate Period just as in the Middle Kingdom, the main themes thus concentrate on cattle breeding, fieldwork, crafts, hunting, fishing, and scenes of offering and cult. A new religious motif appears, the so-called scene of the journey to Abydos, which shows the deceased sailing to the cult place of Osiris in Abydos. This ritual became very popular in the Middle Kingdom, and to undertake it at least on a symbolical level (i.e. recording it on the walls of the tomb of the deceased) was among the several conditions of a successful and peaceful afterlife.

Most of the scenes on tomb walls depict concepts of the afterlife. Even so, as in the case of Old Kingdom reliefs, we can form from them an idea of everyday contemporary life and even of some individual events in the life of the tomb owner. He is depicted as if communicating to the visitor of his tomb, conveying information on himself and on his high social rank during his lifetime through the impressive decoration and content of the individual scenes.

The same conventions can be clearly seen in the tomb of Khnumhotep. The western wall is dedicated to the motifs of cultic journeys on boats to Abydos. Further we can see scenes of fishing, grape harvest, garden irrigation, seasonal fieldworks – ploughing, harvest, loading donkeys with grain and sieving grain on the threshing floor, cloth weaving and pottery firing, shipbuilding and the filling of granaries under the scrutiny of scribes controlling quantities of grain with a measure. Over the entrance to the niche in the western wall are two horizontal bands of scenes depicting the bringing of funerary offerings and transporting the statue of the deceased to the necropolis, and the filling of granaries. Many scenes are surprisingly dynamic, capturing the movement. We can see for example a fisherman angling for a fish, a sailor sounding the depth of water under the ship, a ploughman and a man cutting down a tree the leaves of which are being eaten by a goat. The northern wall, which is probably the most famous in this tomb, is also full of movement. It shows Bedouins entering Egypt being led by their chieftain Abishay. According to the accompanying inscription, there are thirty-seven Bedouin bringing black paint to Egypt. It has already been noted above that numerous high officials buried at Beni Hassan were also guardians of the Egyptian eastern frontier. It is therefore not surprising that Khnumhotep appears here in this role and receives the Bedouin, who are being led to him by the scribes of the royal documents, Neferhetep and Kheti. Khnumhotep is depicted in more than actual size – his height spans three registers of decoration. He is accompanied by his son, the herdsman Khnumhotep, and his three dogs. No less imposing is the scene in the upper part of the wall, where he is depicted hunting gazelles and lions in the desert. Khnumhotep is captured in motion, his body leaning forwards at the moment of shooting an arrow. He is wearing a long skirt and in one hand, he is holding several spare arrows. Khnumhotep assisted by his four sons, who are also shooting from bows – Nakhti, Khnumhotep, Neheri, and Netjernekhet. The lower part of the scene contains scenes of bird tending, and cattle and gazelle feeding. Finally the lowermost register depicts the bringing of cattle for registration and control, perhaps also for tax collection. The whole action takes place under the scrutiny of the over-

Fig. 4.34 Khnumhotep II engaged in a desert hunt and supervising offering procession

seer of cattle, Meri, and three scribes headed by the scribe of the royal documents and chief of the nome council, Imeni.

The southern wall is slightly more monotonous, but from the point of view of the tomb owner even more important: it is dedicated to offering rituals. In the centre of the scene, Khnumhotep is seated behind an offering table laden with bread loaves. Above his head, his most important titles are recorded next to the list of offerings including the seven sacred oils used in the course of funerary rituals. To the right of the table are offerings, consisting of food and drinks and some objects used for offering and acts of purification. Behind them are bearers of funerary equipment. There are seven priests conducting offering rituals for the spirit of the deceased, headed by the funerary priest pouring pure water into the bowl on a stand, the *sem*-priest wearing a panther skin, and the lector priest. The entire scene is closed by a priest wiping off the traces of human presence in the chapel. In the upper right corner we see the wife of the tomb owner in a similar position, enjoying numerous offerings for her spirit dwelling in this world. The lowermost registers are reserved for a long procession of men bringing cattle for slaughter, and butchers who successively bind, slaughter and cut up cattle. The climax of these sequences finds expression in the lower left corner, where the burnt offering is depicted. We see three tall stands, on two of which meat is being burnt. A man brings the meat from the butchers on the right. It is placed on a large plate (we can see two calves and a head). The offering process itself is directed by three men. The first one, named Kheret, is the overseer of the place of incense and he is regulating the process of burning by means of a fan. The other two are identified by the accompanying inscriptions as the overseer of the residence Kheti and scribe Mentuhotep.

Most vivid of all is the scene on the eastern wall of the tomb, which is divided by the entrance. Immediately over the entrance, Khnumhotep is depicted seated on a stool while fowling with a net. He is accompanied by his son and the chancellor Baket. The inscriptions are focused on the offering for the spirit of the deceased. To right and left of the entrance, the tomb owner is enjoying the favourite pastimes of the upper levels of Egyptian society. On the left, he is sailing on a papyrus boat through a thicket, fowling by means of a throwing stick; he is already holding some birds in his left hand. Other birds, as well as butterflies, are flying in the air around him. Khnumhotep is wearing a simple short skirt. The safety of his sail is guaranteed by the magical *wedjat*-eye, painted on the front of the boat which is cutting its way through the thicket. The water swarms with fish, but we can also see a crocodile and an hippopotamus. Khnumhotep is accompanied by his son Khnumhotep and *'his beloved wife, the priestess of Hathor, daughter of a count, mistress of the house Kheti.'* Below this main scene there is a smaller register showing fishing by means of a net with floats. It must have been a demanding activity, since ten men are involved. The whole scene is supervised by the overseer of ships Mentuhotep.

To the right of the entrance of the tomb is a similar scene. Khnumhotep, this time dressed in a long kilt reaching to his mid-calves, is fishing with a large

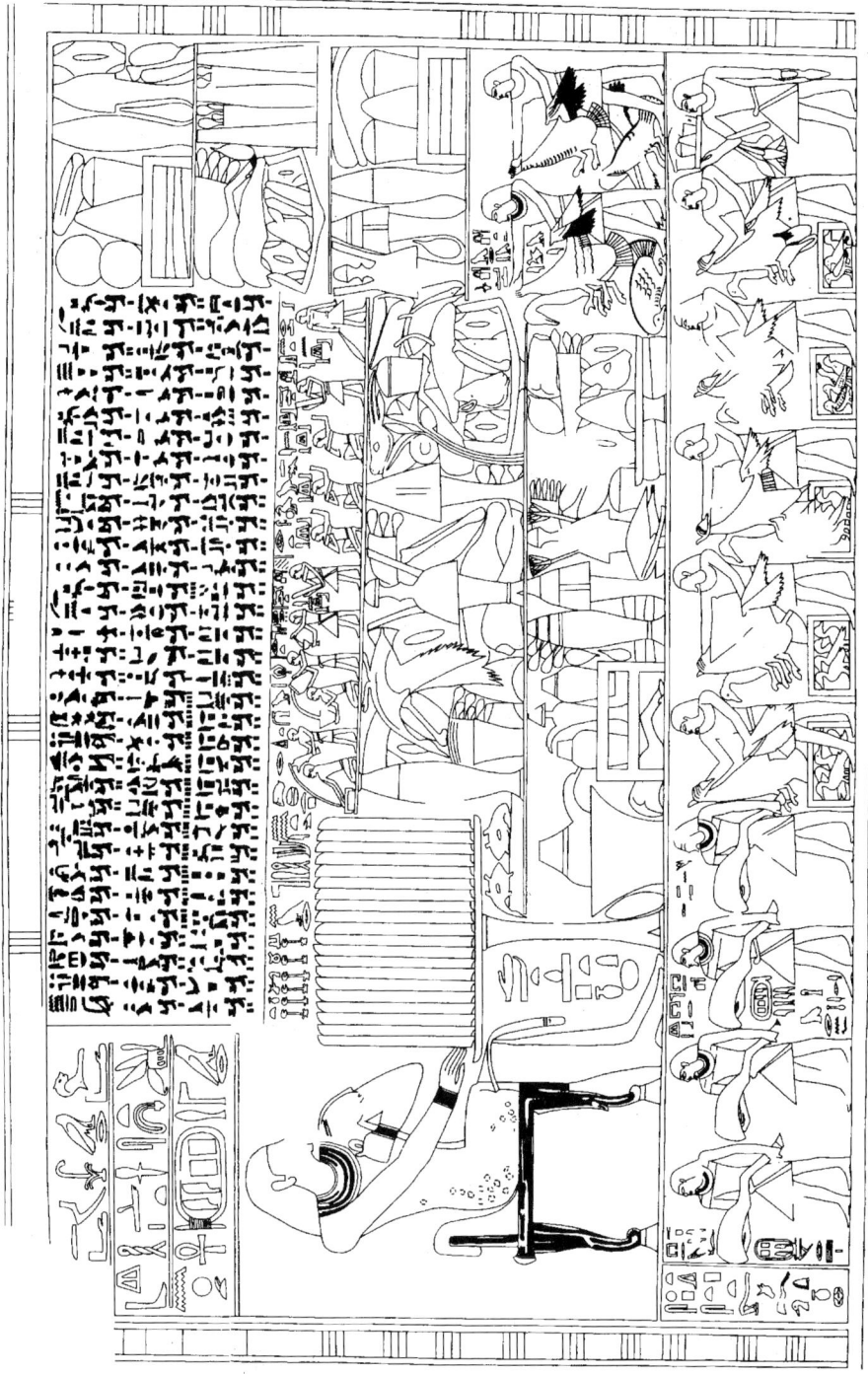

Fig. 4.35 Pepiankh Kem receiving offerings in his chapel in Meir (A. M. Blackman, M. R. Apted, *The Rock Tombs of Meir, Part V*, London 1953, pl. 34)

harpoon. He is again accompanied by his son Khnumhotep, who is holding the reserve harpoon for his father. The scene below them depicts three fishing boats with crews striving for the day's catch.

Relatively most poorly preserved is the decoration of the offering niche. The lower part of the walls is covered with an ornament depicting the motif of a palace façade, which is broken at regular intervals by closed double-winged doors. They are thirteen in number, as in the case of the eastern side of the enclosure wall of Djoser's pyramid complex. This decoration symbolised Khnumhotep's afterlife existence, his eternal life after death. These gates formed the connection between this world and the next. As Khnumhotep's spirit passed through them, the members of his family brought him offerings and said goodbye. To the north we can see his four sons led by Nakhti, who is bringing offerings. He is depicted standing at the offering table covered with vessels and bringing fowl to his father. His three brothers are striding behind him: Khnumhotep, Neheri, and Nekhtinetjer. The other three figures are a lot smaller. The first is another son called Khnumhotep, followed by the chancellors Baket and Khnumhotep. The composition is closed by a priestly ritual. The accompanying inscription underlines the importance of the entire scene:

'An offering which the king gives and Osiris, lord of Djedu, great god, lord of Abydos, an offering consisting of cattle, fowl, alabaster vessels and cloths, to the spirit of the noble and prince, Khnumhotep, justified, son of Neheri.'

The opposite wall is analogous, but instead of the sons we now see three women, the wives of Khnumhotep.

These examples clearly show that painted tombs are an exception in the First Intermediate Period. Poorly decorated tombs prevail, their decoration is mostly (both in the case of rock-cut tombs and of small mud brick mastabas) limited to an offering stela located at the western wall of the chapel. The central place of the cult, the stela, is thus preserved, and placed at the end of the tomb, in its westernmost part, as close as possible to the 'beautiful west', the realm of the dead. This trend continues into the Middle Kingdom in the residential cemeteries around Memphis. The walls of the above-ground rooms are basically undecorated. In most cases the only decorative and inscribed element is a stone ritual stele, which thus becomes a parallel to the so-called false doors common in the tombs of the Old Kingdom.

The stele with the offering scene represented the minimal equipment indispensable for the existence of any tomb. It encoded three elements which were fully sufficient for the maintenance of the afterlife existence. There was above all the text containing offering formulae listing all the basic needs necessary for a satisfied afterlife, prayers, the name and titles of the deceased, the dating formula, and geneaological data. The second important element was the figure of the deceased, thus, his idealised form was traced and preserved for eternity. Finally, the third important element was the offering table laden with many of-

Fig. 4.36 Statue of the vizier Mentuhotep from the reign of Senwosret I (Luxor Museum)

ferings to satisfy the needs of the deceased. Often the closest family members were depicted on the stelae or on the adjoining tomb walls – the sons, wives, or parents. Some of the stelae form a kind of microcosm – they include offering formulae, name and titles of the deceased, the offering scene, family members, butchers ritually slaughtering cattle, offering bearers, craftsmen, women making flour, kneading dough and baking bread, beer brewing and even the deceased on a bed involved in sexual intercourse with his concubine in the other world.

Just as in the Old Kingdom, in the Middle Kingdom statues form an indispensable part of tomb decoration. The basic difference lies in the fact that while in Old Kingdom times the statues of the tomb owner were hidden from the sight of the visitor in closed rooms *(serdabs)*, they now become an integral part of the architecture of tomb chapels and are mostly placed in niches, which belong to the main cult places. The statue is now directed to the eyes of the visitor and becomes an independent part of the tomb. At the same time it retains its ancient function – it depicts the deceased tomb owner, is his alternate form, and as such it can also accept offerings. It is, however, almost the rule that the preserved statues were not discovered in their original places. In most cases it is even impossible to determine which statue comes from which tomb. Most are small, relatively carelessly executed, with little or no details and tendency to schematism, and it seems that they were being mass-produced for those who could not afford more costly pieces. Most often they are based on models known from Old Kingdom times. The seated statue represents the deceased tomb owner as a man of a high rank, while the standing type emphasizes above all his active conduct and his role in state administration.

Besides the tomb itself, a burial according to strict rules was indispensable for the afterlife existence of the deceased. The bodies were placed into wooden coffins, which were considered to be the dwellings for the eternal life of the deceaed, as the nature and content of their decoration indicate. Most of the cofins are made of joined planks. They are rectangular in shape and decorated on the outside with motifs representing the individual architectural elements of house. In the course of the Middle Kingdom, the inner, anthropomorphic coffin appears for the first time. It is painted to resemble a mummy wrapped in bandages. They are placed in tombs with their heads towards the east. A pair of *wedjat*-eyes is painted on the surface of the coffin in the place of the head or in its immediate vicinity to enable the deceased to look out. There is even a representation of the so-called false door as a symbolic gate through which the spirit of the deceased could pass between this and the other world. The significance of the symbolic 'window' was based on three basic concepts: the deceased could watch the conduct of the daily cult in the tomb and take part in it, he could observe the rising of the sun and thus the rebirth of the sun-god Ra, and finally

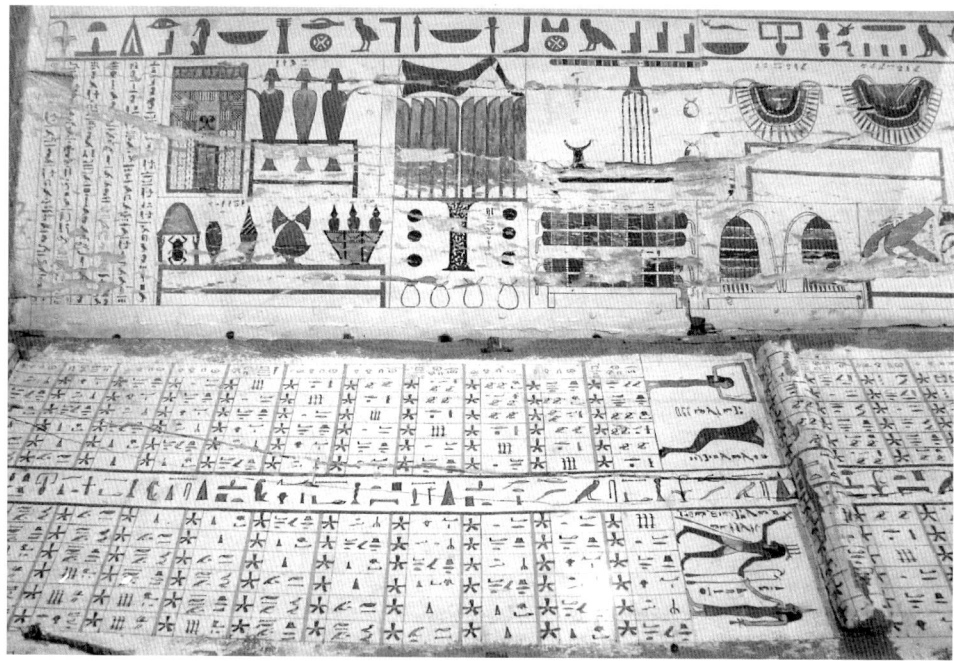

Fig. 4.37 Detail of the inner coffin decoration, including the false door, coffin of Nekhet (Roemer- and Pelizeus Museum, Hildesheim, c. 2000 BC)

he could take part in his daily journey over the sky. Of other elements of decoration we may particularly mention the frieze, which was basically the depiction of a row of objects, which were part of the funerary equipment and thus were always at the disposal of the tomb owner.

The inner walls of the coffins contained pre-eminently offering formulae and lists of offerings, accompanied by the so-called Coffin Texts, a collection of spells that helped the deceased on his journey to the other world and magically protected him. Their name derives from the fact that since the First Intermediate Period they were inscribed especially on coffins. They may, however, appear also on tomb walls, mummy masks, and papyri. They were based on the Pyramid Texts from the pyramids of the Old Kingdom rulers, which were further augmented and modified. Usually they are inscribed on the inner walls of coffins, and they focus on the journey of the deceased through the other world.

The Egyptians imagined that the afterlife was just like their life on earth, with its fields and waterways, gates and cities. The attainment of bliss and regeneration were imagined to be the result of the journey through the hereafter. As an example of this concept of resurrection and afterlife existence, we may mention the literary work called 'Book of the Two Ways' (from the Coffin Texts), which gives a detailed description of the topography of the other world and that which comes after death. The entire composition begins with the first hours after death:

> *'Trembling falls on the eastern horizon of the sky at the voice of Nut, she makes free the paths of Ra before the Great Ones when he goes around.'*

This introduction mentions the everyday rising of the sun on the eastern horizon. According to ancient Egyptian beliefs, the sky was the body of the goddess Nut, who every day gave birth to the sun god Ra just to swallow him again in the evening, at dusk. During the night, Ra travelled the netherworld filled with enemy demons and adversary gods, to be born again in the morning in the eastern horizon. The above-quoted passage further describes the deceased becoming a member of the crew of the boat of Ra, in which he sails the day sky. The deceased then enters the other world through a gate, which is guarded by the netherworld demons. The netherworld itself is black, dark and deep, lit only by the flames of fires. It is characterised as a road, which the deceased has to travel and whose numerous gates he has to pass. At the end of the journey is a building, the royal palace and seat of the lord of the netherworld, Osiris. It is here that the resurrection of the deceased takes place, in which even the sun god Ra takes part. In the subsequent phases the soul of the deceased travels the netherworld and overcomes numerous traps set by its demons. He joins the suite of Ra and becomes Osiris – 'the resurrected one'.

The deceased passes two other main locations during his journey: Rasetau, the semi-mythical burial ground where Osiris was buried, and the 'field of offerings', which is commonly equated to the mythical paradise where the well-equipped deceased dwells and where he spends his afterlife existence. This is probably the place that Sinuhe wants to reach, when, towards the end of his story, he speaks about his desire to be properly buried. At the end of his journey, the deceased enters the 'secret places' of Ra where the blessed dead dwell, where Ra is re-born in splendour and where the world came into being. Four deeds of the Lord of the Universe are celebrated here – the creation of the air and of the Nile flood, the maintenance of the existence of mankind on earth and the creation of the other world for the deceased.

At the end of the composition, the relationship of light and darkness to life and death is defined. The former qualities are represented by the sun god Ra, the latter by the lord of the hereafter, who is Osiris. One cannot exist without the other, life and death are intertwined and death is followed by resurrection. It remains to be said that as far as the location of the other world is concerned, Egyptian beliefs were not unanimous. According to one of these conceptions, the other world could either be within the necropolis, where the souls of the deceased dwelt (this place is often called 'the beautiful west') or, according to other beliefs, the other world was the tomb itself, where the body of the deceased was buried. Still other conceptions allow us to identify the other world with the sky, through which the sun god Ra travels daily in his barque.

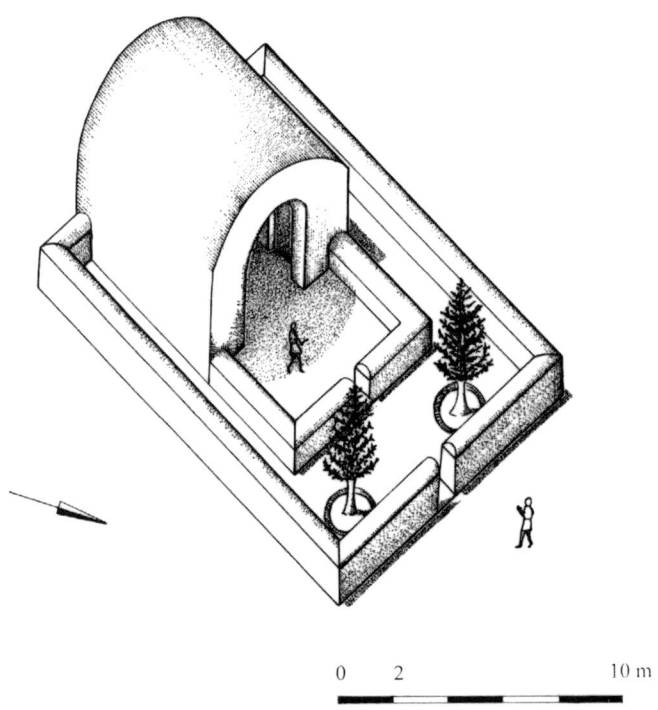

Fig. 4.38 Reconstruction of a cenotaph (symbolic grave) of a wealthy official at Abydos, the mythical burial place of Osiris (after D. O'Connor, Mélanges G. E. Mokhtar II, Cairo 1985, pp. 174 and 176, pls. 5 and 6)

The wish to reach a blessed afterlife existence, as Henenu expressed it in the time of Mentuhotep II, corresponds well to these conceptions. Henenu sums up his wishes for the afterlife as follows:

'May (Henenu) cross heaven, travel the sky,
Come to the Great God,
And join with the earth in peace in the beautiful west,
As one blessed in front of Osiris.
May he sail to the western horizon where Osiris is.
May the desert open its arms toward him,
May the West give him its hands.
May he open the ways of his liking,
May he walk on the roads of the necropolis together with the followers of Osiris.
May the West open its doors for him,
May Hapi bring him his offerings.
May he eat with his mouth and see with his eyes,
May he know himself among the souls.
May hands be given to him in the neshemet barque on the ways of the West.
May he be told "Come in peace" by the Great Ones of Abydos,
May he steer the oars of the night barque,
May he unite with the earth in the day barque of the sun!
May the great ones tell him: "Travel in peace in front of Ra in the sky!"'

From the beginning of the Middle Kingdom, *ushabti* became part of the funerary equipment. The first specimens of these figures were the so-called spare mummies, which had the form of miniature nude human bodies made of wax or clay, wrapped in bandages and buried in small coffins. Thus a spare mummy of the deceased could be supplied should his real body be damaged or destroyed. Often *ushabti* bear inscriptions with the name and genealogy of the tomb owner; from the Twelfth Dynasty even offering formulae appear here. Today it is generally presumed that in the course of the Middle Kingdom, *ushabti* replaced the servant statuettes and models of workshops, which enjoyed high popularity in the end of the Old Kingdom, in the First Intermediate period, and at the very beginning of the Middle Kingdom.

Statuettes of servants performing various activities and models of estates were very common in the beginning of the Middle Kingdom. Their basic function was to secure an undisturbed afterlife of the tomb owner, supplying various types of food and beverages, and, last but not least, to entertain him.

The deceased was provided with models even when his tomb was decorated. The broad range of themes and motifs covered all his needs in the afterlife. We find fieldworks, tending cattle, filling granaries, preparing of meals, making items of everyday use, work in slaughterhouses, and crossing the river on boats for both secular and religious reasons, such as sailing with the mummy of the deceased to the necropolis or the ritual journey to Abydos.

Fig. 4.39 Funeral mask of an unknown man (Roemer- and Pelizaeus Museum, Hildesheim, about 2000 BC)

In the course of the Middle Kingdom it was usual to place these models in a shaft or underground chamber, where they were undoubtedly much safer from potential tomb robbers. They were discovered mainly in Middle and Upper Egypt; the production of these figures largely ceased at the beginning of the Middle Kingdom. The individual figures in the models do not represent any particular personage. They remain anonymous and their only function is to ensure and realise the afterlife of the tomb owner and to satisfy all his potential needs. In this respect they are very clearly distinguished from the statues of the tomb owner and his family. Models and statuettes of servants are attested from many provincial cemeteries. One of the most numerous assemblages comes from the tomb of the nomarch Djehutinakhte at el-Bersha, where forty-five statuettes and models of estates and fifty-five model boats were discovered. The most famous discovery comes from the Theban tomb of the dignitary Meketre. The models from this tomb are now part of the exhibitions of the Egyptian Museum in Cairo and of the Metropolitan Museum of Art in New York.

The tomb of Meketre, found in Western Thebes, comes from the era that approximately corresponds to the supposed lifetime of Sinuhe, namely from the time of the reign of Amenemhat I. A closer look at the objects from this tomb offers perhaps the most detailed picture of funerary beliefs in this period.

Meketre was a high official, only a little older than Sinuhe himself. His tomb became famous at the beginning of this century, thanks to the excavations that H. E. Winlock of the Metropolitan Museum of Art in New York carried out on the western bank of Thebes, close to Deir el-Bahri where lie the funerary temples of Mentuhotep II and Hatshepsut. Two kilometres to the northwest lies the Valley of the Kings with tombs of New Kingdom rulers.

The tomb of Meketre became famous due to the discovery of the greatest collection of wooden models found so far. These had been placed in the tomb as part of his funerary equipment. Meketre was an important historical personality, well attested from other sources. He accompanied his ruler to the valley of Shatt el-Righal, where he met with the returning expedition led by Inyotef and the chancellor Kheti. Meketre is mentioned in Shatt el-Righal as 'the overseer of the Six Great Courts', which means that he was engaged in supervising the judiciary. The fragmentary decoration in his tomb provided us with evidence that he was a 'hereditary noble and prince, treasurer of the king of Lower Egypt, hereditary prince at the gate of Geb, the sole friend and overseer of the Great House (of the king)'.

The tomb of Meketre was originally one of the most beautiful non-royal tombs from the beginning of the Twelfth Dynasty. Its architectural plan is typical of the developing Theban tradition of tomb-building, which profoundly influenced

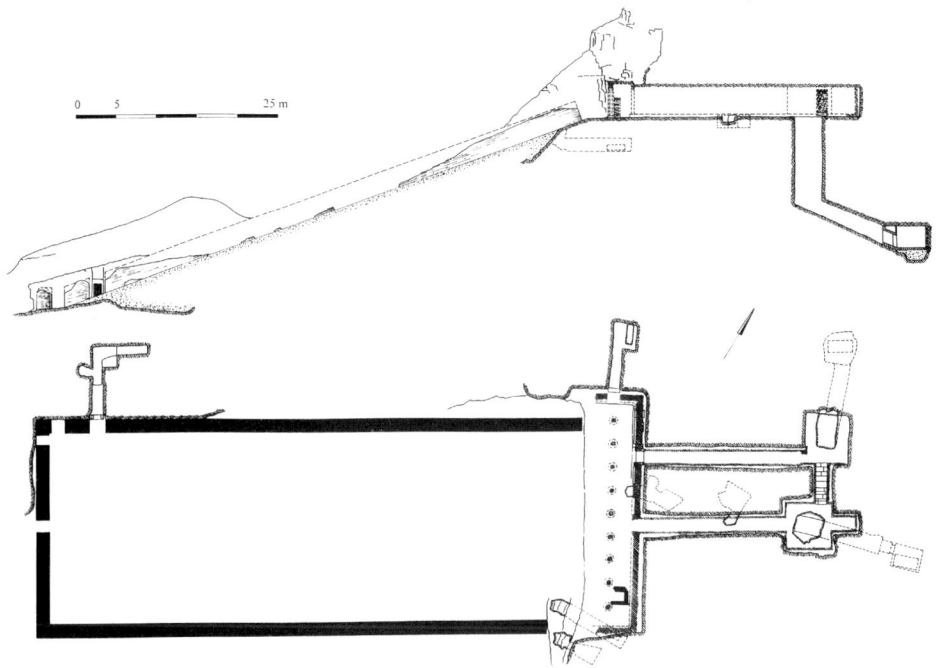

Fig. 4.40 Groundplan of the tomb of Meketre at Thebes (after H. E. Winlock, Models of daily life in ancient Egypt, New York 1955, pl. 54)

tomb development in the whole area. It was built on a southward incline, at the foot of which stood the entrance gate, which gave way to a large 25 m wide and 70 m long courtyard that rose rather steeply towards the tomb entrances. The western side of this courtyard contained entrances to four tombs: those of Wah, Meketre, Inyotef and an unknown occupant. Its façade was decorated by a row of rock-cut columns. The columns were painted black to imitate granite, a very valuable material coming from the quarries at the southern tip of Egypt at Assuan. The right and left corners of this part of the court were each occupied by one tomb: on the north was that of an official from the time of Meketre. The owner of the tomb to the south, which had a small brick cult chapel, was Wah. Next to this smaller tomb, another underground room was discovered, which contained the remains of a mummification ritual equipment connected perhaps with Meketre himself.

Meketre's own tomb had a 20 m long corridor originally decorated with limestone reliefs, which led into a rectangular room, his cult chapel. In its western wall was a niche containing a statue of the deceased, the 'home' to which Meketre's *ka*-soul returned every time offerings were brought. In the floor of the chapel was the entrance to the corridor leading to Meketre's burial chamber. The tomb of his son Inyotef was built nearby. This did not differ in any significant way from that of his father. At the western end of the tomb, a transverse corridor connected the chapels of father and son, both to facilitate the movement of funerary priests maintaining the funerary cult of both men and to enable the son's soul to visit his father.

In a small niche cut into the floor of the corridor of Meketre' s tomb a discovery was made that astonished the archaeologists – even now, it belongs to one of the most popular collections of the Metropolitan Museum in New York and the Egyptian Museum in Cairo. The find included wooden models of eight houses and workshops, twelve boats and barques, a large collection of offering bearers, and a giant model representing Meketre with his officials taking a census of cattle. The reason why these models were placed in his tomb was because the Egyptians wanted to maintain the funerary cult for the soul of the deceased. Models of boats, Meketre's residences and workshops were at the disposal of their lord even after his death, and would readily serve him at the moment when the individual magical formulae would be recited to give life to the individual figures. They enable us to draw a fairly precise picture of Meketre's way of life.

Although the two models of his palace are very simplified, they do show with great precision the typical features of a high official's house. Such houses were spacious, decorated with architectural details, and could even be multi-storeyed, as is shown also by other models from this time. Meketre's own houses are clustered around a water container, a pond, the banks of which are flanked with trees and bushes, which would provide their owner with cool shadow and resting-places. Sailing in a boat and hunting or fishing, either accompanied by his wife or alone, was one of the favourite pastime activities of an Egyptian official. The boat was not just a source of entertainment for the ancient Egyptians: it was

Fig. 4.41 Offering bearers from the tomb of Meketre (Metropolitan Museum of Art, New York)

also the main means of transport. With its help it was possible to ferry across from one bank of the Nile (which at that time still swarmed with crocodiles and hippopotami) to another. Boats enabled people to travel hundreds of kilometres up the Nile (aided by sails) or downstream, floating along with the currents or rowing with oars. The boat was also used for fishing. Fish belonged to the main staple of the ancient Egyptians (beef was not affordable for the majority of the population) and dried fish were used as a part of the salary for workers and artisans.

Every day, the sun god Ra also travelled the sky in a boat, which was called *mandjet*. At night he sailed through the netherworld in a barque called *mesektet*, together with a suite of guardian deities who protected him against impure powers. Egyptians also made religious journeys by boat to Abydos, one of the main cultic centres of Middle Kingdom Egypt. According to legend, Osiris was murdered here under the *aru* tree by his brother Seth, and here in Abydos he was also buried. In Middle Kingdom times, the tomb of one of the First Dynasty rulers, the reformer Den, was identified with the grave of Osiris. This tomb became the destination of annual pilgrimages for worshippers, who left behind numerous stone stelae dedicated to Osiris. This expression of religious humility bears in many ways a strong resemblance to contemporary religious piety. This religious pilgrimage in the south also had its counterpart in the north. Here, the destination was the city of Buto, where the sacred palm grove was supposed to hide the graves of the legendary Lower Egyptian rulers from the times before Egyptian unification.

Fig. 4.42 Model of Meketre's residence (Metropolitan Museum of Art, New York, Rogers Fund and Edward S. Harkness Gift, 1920)

Fig. 4.43 Reconstruction of the house of a wealthy Egyptian official (after G. Perrot, Ch. Chipiez, Histoire de l'Art dans l'Antiquité. L'Égypte - Assyrie - Perse - Asie Mineure - Grèce - Etrurie - Rome. Paris 1882, p. 483, fig. 267)

Fig. 4.44 Meketre sailing on his yacht (model from the tomb of Meketre, Metropolitan Museum of Art, New York, Rogers Fund and Edward S. Harkness Gift, 1920)

Even the king travelled through Egypt in a large barque. In Middle Kingdom times, he left his residence in Itj-tawy every winter to move together with his suite of servants and officials 600 kilometres to the south to Thebes, where he spent the winter season, which can be very cold in the north. And it was on boats too that the ancient Egyptians transported their dead to the necropolis. No wonder Meketre, while preparing for 'immortality', took extreme care to have enough boats at his disposal!

A significant part of Meketre's collection contains models of agricultural units, such as slaughterhouses, granaries, breweries and bakeries, a weaving mill and a joinery, where wooden household and tomb items, including the coffin, were made. All these models bear direct testimony about what the ancient Egyptian considered important in life and after death. As a rich dignitary, Meketre considered it essential to ensure that his wealth would be at his disposal even after death. This wealth was mainly the result of annual Nile floods which brought with them the nutrient-rich fertile soil that gave Egypt its generous harvests.

The height of Nile flood was measured by the so-called *Nilometres*, which enabled the Egyptians to predict the poor crops and famine that could result from low Nile floods. Immediately after the waters receded, Egyptian scribes set out to their assigned districts, measured the extent of the fields and estimated future crops. This act was of great importance, for the state administration lived mainly from taxes collected from the peasants who were the economic generators of agricultural wealth. In Egypt, all land was formally in the hands of the king, but in practice it was divided between the king, the temples and high-ranking individuals. It was estimated that in the Ramesside period (Nineteenth Dynasty) Egypt had over one and a half million hectares of cultivated land, which was worked by the majority of the population. We know that, for example, the average yield of a field of 1 aroura (0.275 ha) was 10 sacks of corn, half of which had to be handed in as taxes.

This is the reason why one of the models shows a granary approached by Egyptian peasants who carry corn on their shoulders as taxes due to the state treasury. To the left, immediately behind the entrance, sits the 'guardian of the gate' wrapped in white cloth, and the scribes who meticulously record the value of the collected taxes, sit behind him. The scribes sitting along both sides of the room formed a path through which every peasant had to pass and have his corn measured. Only behind the scribes could one enter the granary, into which the now measured corn was poured from above.

Emmer wheat and barley were the basic ingredients of Egyptian bread and beer, the making of which can be seen in another of Meketre's models. This model again shows several rooms, with the entrance watched by a guardian in

Fig. 4.45 Registering grain and filling granaries (model from the tomb of Meketre, Metropolitan Museum of Art, New York, Rogers Fund and Edward S. Harkness Gift, 1920)

white gown. His role was to guarantee that none of the produce would be taken away illegally. The individual rooms show men grinding grain and preparing dough, while the women are forming bread cakes similar to modern ones. In the corners of the room, other men control the baking in the bread ovens. Brewing takes place in the largest of these rooms. This activity was wholly dependent upon bread baking. Egyptian beer was made out of barley bread dough. This dough was lightly baked, broken into small pieces and put in water with some date juice. After fermentation, the liquid was filtered, and the finished beer was poured into the so-called beer jars and sealed with Nile-mud sealings in order to secure the contents of the vessels. From the most ancient times, bread and beer production were among the commonest scenes depicted on tomb walls, since bread and beer were the basic staples not just of peasants but also of officials and priests.

Similar themes of food preparation can be observed in the slaughterhouse scenes, which depict butchers slaying cattle, cutting meat into portions and drying meat. This model is closely related to Meketre's funerary cult, since it depicts the preparation of meat, which was presented to the spirit of the deceased in his offering chapel. Unlike bread and beer, meat was mostly a prerogative of the highest echelons of society, and thus even this model represents Meketre's social position. Two other can be understood in a similar way – models of a workshop for making cloth and a workshop for wooden items of funerary equipment, including the coffin and models of maid-servants.

Fig. 4.46 Tax collection (model from the tomb of Meketre, Egyptian Museum, Cairo)

By far the most explicit testimony about Meketre's social position is provided by yet another model, one showing him accompanied by other officials while collecting taxes in the form of cattle. Apart from agriculture, cattle breeding had played an important role in Egypt ever since the beginnings of the unified state. The cattle census was so important that it originally even served as the basis for the method of measuring the length of reign for the individual kings. Once every two years, there was a census of 'small and big cattle' in the entire country. Based on detailed evidence for the size of the herd, taxes were then collected in the form of a given number of cattle. It is precisely this activity that Meketre is depicted performing while seated on a stool under an airy shelter. Scribes are seated on the ground to his right, meticulously recording the number of cattle on their papyrus scrolls. Meketre's eldest son sits to his left and takes part in the tax collection, together with his father. The cattle is brought in front of Meketre in small groups driven by individual herdsmen, who step forth in front of him, bowing slightly in respect. Once inspected, the cattle are being led to the state stalls. This model captures the true position of Meketre as 'one in charge of the (royal) seal' and 'overseer of the Great House', a title which would in our contemporary terms correspond closely to the Chancellor of the Exchequer. As such, Meketre was mostly in charge of the country's economy, the estimation of harvest and cattle taxes and, above all, their collection. As one of the highest officials in the country, Meketre was subordinate only to the vizier – the highest official of the land who represented the king – and then to the king himself. This model can be considered as a kind of summary of Meketre's career as a court official, which began under King Mentuhotep II and ended in the reign of Amenemhat I.

With all this equipment for life in the hereafter, Meketre hoped that he would be properly buried and that in case of need the individual workshops but above all the servants would be at his disposal and would perform all physical work for the king on his behalf. In ancient Egypt, manual labour was inconsistent with the position of a high official. The magical spells that brought to life the wooden figures of servants called *ushabti* are attested already among later Middle Kingdom texts. We may conjecture that Meketre's wooden models were brought to life in a very similar manner:

'Look at him, gods and blessed spirits and dead,
Whether he is in the sky or on earth. He attained his power.
He took up his seats (i.e. official functions).
He ruled with the sceptres, which had been made for him (the deceased)
According to the will of the gods.
If this (deceased) is called for any compulsory work
On a kato(?) land, to remove a segment,
To bridge over (?) the soil around the banks, to cultivate new fields for the king,
[Say] "Here I am!" and] volunteer to every summoner who shall come for this (deceased) as his substitute.

Take your picks, your hoes, your poles for carrying loads, your baskets, lo,
Just as everyone does for his master.
.... say Lo, here I am.
If this (deceased) is called for (a job) which is done there,
To cultivate new fields, strengthen riverbanks, ferry to the west the sand that had been blown to the east, and in reverse,
Lo, here I am, record it for him.
Words spoken to the likeness of the owner, as he was upon earth, made out of tamarysk or zizimus wood and placed in the funerary chapel of the blessed dead.'

The first chapter of this book mentioned that Sinuhe's account bears characteristic signs of the style and structure of Old and Middle Kingdom autobiographical inscriptions. If he had existed, his own tomb would not have lacked such a biographical inscription: it was considered to be no less important for the existence in the hereafter than mummification or the funeral. In his biography, an official would list all the important titles and functions that he had held during his lifetime, as well as his deeds for the benefit of the king. A lucky coincidence allows us to cite an inscription that is a representative example of this genre and comes from the time of the reign of King Senwosret I, namely the in-

Fig. 4.47 Detail of a female offering bearer (model from the tomb of Meketre, Metropolitan Museum of Art, New York, Rogers Fund and Edward S. Harkness Gift, 1920)

scription preserved in the rock tomb of the noble Amenemhat (I) in Beni Hassan. This inscription provides us with a detailed testimony about the career of a high official in royal service. It begins by recording the year in which the inscription was carved, including the royal titulary, i.e. the enumeration of all five names of the king. Then it turns to the passers-by with a request for prayer and offering in favour of Amenemhat's soul and continues with the description of the important events of his life. In the case of Amenemhat, they include mostly military campaigns and expeditions for gold and other mineral resources, in which he earned the king's confidence and the office of governor of the Gazelle Nome. When his career at the royal court was over, Amenemhat settled down as a prince of his nome and was mostly concerned with its management and development. His main duties included the collection of cattle and land taxes for the state, respectively for the King of Egypt. Amenemhat does not hesitate to mention a string of misdeeds from which he was exempt (repressing widows and the poor, peasants and herdsmen). The fact, that he considers it worthwhile to include this list enables us to assume these deeds were the most commonly committed transgressions by the Egyptian nobility. The biography ends with a description of years of bad harvests, during which Amenemhat proved to be a good governor of his people, sustaining them in need. Let us now have a look at a typical example of an ancient Egyptian autobiographical inscription:

'Year 43 under His Majesty Horus Ankhmesut, King of Upper and Lower Egypt, Kheperkare, may he live eternally, Two Ladies Ankhmesut, Golden Horus Ankhmesut, son of Ra Senwosret, may he live for ever and ever; corresponding to (regnal) year 25 in the Gazelle Nome as a noble, prince, the good one, Amenemhat, justified.

Year 43, second month of the Inundation season, day 15:

O you who love life and hate death! Say: a thousand of bread and beer, a thousand of cattle and fowl for the soul of the noble and prince, the good one, the great chief of the Gazelle Nome, chamberlain, the warden of Nekhen, the warden of Nekheb, chief priest, Ameni, justified.

I followed my lord when he sailed to the south to conquer the enemies in four foreign countries. I sailed southward as a son of the prince, seal-bearer and army general, great (chief) of the Gazelle Nome, as a man who substitutes his old father because of his good name in the royal offices and the love of him in the royal palace. I have passed the land of Kush sailing southward, and I have reached the border of the land and brought all products, and the praise of me touched heaven.

Then His Majesty set out in peace and defeated the enemies in the vile country of Kush, I returned in his suite with an experienced spirit, and my army suffered no loss.

I sailed south to bring gold ore to His Majesty, King of Upper and Lower Egypt, Kheperkare, may he live for ever and ever. I sailed south together with the prince and noble, the eldest son of the king of his own body, Ameni, may he live, prosper and be healthy. I sailed south together with 400 choicest troops from my army. I returned in peace, my army suffered no loss. I brought the gold as had been ordered to me. I was praised for it in the royal offices and the king's son thanked me for it.

Then I sailed south to bring ore from the harbour of Coptos together with the noble and prince, the overseer of the city, the vizier Senwosret, may he live, prosper and be healthy. I sailed south in the company of 600 troops, the bravest of the Gazelle Nome. I returned in peace without any loss to my army. I did everything that had been commanded to me.

I was friendly, continually beloved, a governor whom his city loved. Then I spent years as a sovereign of the Gazelle Nome and all duties of the royal offices were performed by me personally. Then the overseers of the departments of cattle breeding administration, the herdsmen of the Gazelle Nome, brought 3000 bulls from their herds. I was praised for it in the royal offices every year of the census of cattle. I turned in all their dues for the royal offices. In no royal office were there any debts in taxes recorded against me. The entire Gazelle Nome worked for me with great efficiency.

I abused no poor man's daughter, I oppressed no widow. I did not punish any peasant, I refused no herdsman. There was no overseer of workmen, whose men I brought to do (other) work. There were no poor in my time. There were no hungry [people] under my rule. When hungry years came, I cultivated all fields of the Gazelle Nome all the way to its southern and northern frontier. I kept its inhabitants alive, I secured nourishment for them, no one was hungry there. I gave to the widow as to the married woman. I did not favour the strong over the weak in anything I commanded.

Then high Niles came, rich in corn and wheat, rich in all things. I, however, did not collect dues in land taxes.'

Fig. 4.48 Offering stela of Chancellor Neferyu in front of a large pile of offerings (Metropolitan Museum of Arts, New York, Gift of J. Pierpont Morgan, 1912)

The natural desire of every Egyptian was to reach an undisturbed and eternal afterlife existence. If the ancient Egyptian dignitary succeeded in building himself a tomb, equipping it and finding means for mummification and the burial ceremony, only one thing remained after the successful journey to the other world: to be found innocent at the last judgement. The court proceedings with the deceased had been an integral part of the afterlife concepts in the Old Kingdom, at least since the Fourth Dynasty. Inscriptions on the walls of the non-royal tombs from this time and from the two subsequent dynasties attest the existence of a concept of an afterlife judgement of those who would in any way do harm to the tomb owner or to the tomb itself. Already at this time, the offering formulae include the idea that the deceased becomes 'justified' in front of Osiris, lord of the Netherworld.

Later, in Middle Kingdom times, the so-called Coffin Texts include whole passages indicating that at least by this time the canonical concept of the afterlife judgement was established. Its main elements were the heart of the deceased, which as the centre of human thoughts and actions was reponsible for a man's deeds, a tribunal of judges (their number is not mentioned yet, later they were forty-two), the scheme of the defense of the deceased based on the questions of the judges, and finally even the idea of a set of scales, on which the deeds of the deceased were weighed.

Having attained an afterlife existence, it was desirable to provide for the regular funerary cult. The care for his deceased father and mother belonged to the basic duties of the eldest son who had to make sure that their souls would receive offerings on a regular basis. Often, however, a wealthy official would sign a contract about the maintenance of his funerary cult with professional funerary priests. He assigned to them a part of his property, large enough to support the cult and provide an appropriate salary to the priests. From the Old Kingdom, these contracts had been inscribed on tomb walls in order to preserve their eternal validity. The tomb of the nobleman Djefahapi (III) in Asyut comes exactly from the time of the reign of Senwosret I. He signed several contracts concerning his funerary cult. One of them runs as follows:

'The contract concluded between the noble, overseer of the priests, Djefahapi, justified, and the personnel of the temple of Wepwawet, Lord of Asyut: that they give him one white bread every day, to his statue which is in the care of his funerary priests, namely in the first month of the inundation season, the first day, on New Year's Day when the house is given to his lord after the lamp has been lit in the temple; together with a procession all the way to the northern corner of the temple, as they do when they celebrate their own noble ones on the day of the lighting of the lamp. What he gave them for it: 1 hekat (i.e. 4.8 l) of northern barley out of every field (in his property), from the first harvest of the noble's estate, as every common inhabitant of Asyut does with his first harvest.'

Like Sinuhe, who concludes his story by mentioning that the king secured his funerary cult in his tomb, we too shall now part from the world of this early

Middle Kingdom official. The world in which his story is set did indeed exist much as he describes it. On the basis of our current state of knowledge on the time 4000 years ago, we are able to partially understand not only Sinuhe's thoughts but also the environment in which he lived. We will probably never know whether Sinuhe, the hero of our story, truly existed. This is not very important, however, since similar destinies may have marked the lives of many of the dignitaries who lived in this period. They, above all, were the focus of this book.

Afterword

The story of Sinuhe is now almost four thousand years old. Nonetheless, it may in many respects interest the modern reader and this was indeed my main motivation for writing this book. The vanished societies and states of antiquity are only apparently dead, and it is our task to search the roots of our own cultures by looking back – often several thousand years to the past. The tale of Sinuhe reaches beyond the frame of ancient Egypt: the hero finds himself in a kind of 'exile' in foreign territories, although he left Egypt of his own accord. Sinuhe spends most of his life in the area of today's Syria. In the end, however, he returns back to Egypt, his homeland, since in his mind only the Egyptian religion and belief in the other world can guarantee him an undisturbed existence in the afterlife.

We will probably never know what was the main motivation for the writing of this story. Perhaps there was no single reason, but rather many different factors that stimulated its creation. One reason may have been political – the legitimisation of the reign of King Senwosret I after the violent death of his father, Amenemhat I. The narrative may have also been an attempt to formulate as a specific example the relationship between the ruler and his officials, a demonstration of the loyalty of the Egyptian official to his sovereign, who mainly rewarded his supporters by providing them with all their needs for their afterlife existence. This relationship between the ruler and his officials was, in the first half of the Twelfth Dynasty, particularly fragile, since the chief officials of various provinces of the country had been largely independent of the king from the First Intermediate Period. It is possible that the work was supposed to be read aloud for the entertainment of the hearers, and at the same time to gradually condition them to understand and accept the ideal setup of the Egyptian state: the king is the patron of the afterlife of his subjects, whose main task is to maintain loyalty to him. Finally, we today learn many valuable details concerning the shape of the world at that time, the world of the Egyptian gods, religious ideas and beliefs in the afterlife, the lifestyle of the nomads in Syria-Palestine, and many others, though the intention of the author may not have been to create a record for posterity.

The story also gives us valuable information concerning the relationship between ancient Egypt and her Near Eastern neighbours, which had been in the process of evolving from prehistoric times. At approximately the time of Sinuhe's stay in Syria-Palestine, Abraham (Abram until his covenant with God) with his followers also migrated all the way to Egypt, and he thus became one of the first known individuals of this area who had stayed there.

If we thus were to identify the special importance of Sinuhe's account (despite the fictitious nature of its main protagonist), it would be its contribution to the knowledge of the history, lifestyle, and thinking of this area in the beginning of the second millennium BC, that is at a time that has left a lasting imprint on the modern world.

Selected Bibliography

(The following abbreviations of series and journals are used throughout the text: ACER – The Australian Centre for Egyptology Reports, Sydney; ArOr – Archív Orientální, Praha; ÄA – Ägyptologische Abhandlungen, Wiesbaden; ÄAT – Ägypten und Altes Testament, Wiesbaden; ÄgFo – Ägyptologische Forschungen, Glückstadt; BASOR – Bulletin of the American Schools of Oriental Research, New Haven; CdÉ – Chronique d'Égypte, Bruxelles; GM – Göttinger Miszellen, Göttingen; JAOS – Journal of the American Oriental Society, New Haven; JARCE – Journal of the American Research Center in Egypt, Boston; JEA – Journal of Egyptian Archaeology, London; JNES – Journal of Near Eastern Studies, Chicago; MDAIK – Mitteilungen des Deutschen Archäologischen Instituts, Abteilung Kairo, Mainz; MMJ – Metropolitan Museum Journal, New York; OBO – Orbis Biblicus et Orientalis, Fribourg, Göttingen; SAK – Studien zur Altägyptischen Kultur, Hamburg; ZÄS – Zeitschrift für ägyptische Sprache und Altertumskunde, Leipzig).

Sinuhe's narrative and its background

Bar-Yosef, O., Khazanov, A., *Pastoralism in the Levant. Archaeological Materials in Anthropological Perspectives*, Madison, Wisconsin, 1992;

Behrens, P., 'Sinuhe B 134 ff oder die Psychologie eines Zweikampfes,' *GM* 44, 1981, 7–11;

Blumenthal, E., 'Zu Sinuhes Zweikampf mit dem Starken von Retjenu,' *Fontes atque pontes. Eine Festgabe für Hellmut Brunner*, ÄAT 5, 1983, 42–46;

Bolshakov, A. O., Soushchevski, A. G.; 'Hero and Society in Ancient Egypt,' *GM* 163, 1998, 7–25;

Bonnet, H., *Reallexikon der ägyptischen Religionsgeschichte*, Berlin 1952;

Cribb, R., *Nomads in archaeology*, Cambridge 1991;

Goedicke, H., 'The Route of Sinuhe's Flight,' *JEA* 47, 1954, 77–85;

Goedicke, H., 'Sinuhe's Duel,' *JARCE* 21, 1984, 197–201;

Goedicke, H., 'Where did Sinuhe stay in «Asia»,' *CdÉ* 67, 1992, 28–40;

Gomàa, F., *Die Besiedlung Ägyptens während des Mittleren Reiches. II. Unterägypten und die angrenzenden Gebiete*, Beihefte zum Tübinger Atlas des Vorderen Orients, Reihe B, Nr.66/2, Wiesbaden 1987;

Green, M., 'The Syrian and the Lebanese Topographical data in the Story of Sinuhe,' *CdÉ* 58, 1983, 38–59;

Greenwood, N., *The Sinai. A Physical Geography*, Austin 1997;

Hart, G., *A Dictionary of Egyptian Gods and Goddesses*, London 1986;

Hobbs, J. J., *Bedouin Life in the Egyptian Wilderness*, Cairo 1990;

Lanczkowski, G., 'Die Geschichte vom Riesen Goliath und der Kampf Sinuhes mit dem Starken von Retenu,' *MDAIK* 16, 1958, 214–218;

Levy, T.E. et al., 'Early Bronze Age metallurgy: a newly discovered copper manufactory in southern Jordan,' *Antiquity* 76 (292), June 2002, 425–437;

Malamat, A., 'Mari and the Bible: Some Patterns of Tribal Organisation and Institutions,' *JAOS* 82, 1962, 143–150;

Mazar, A., *Archaeology of the Land of the Bible. 10,000 – 586 B.C.E.*, New York, 1992;

Parkinson, R. B., *The Tale of Sinuhe and Other Ancient Egyptian Poems 1940 – 1640 B.C.*, Oxford 1997;

Parkinson, R. B., *Poetry and Culture in Middle Kingdom Egypt. A dark side to perfection*, London New York 2002;

Posener, G., 'À Propos des Graffiti d'Abisko', *ArOr* 20, 1–2, 1952, 163–165;

Rainey, A. F., 'The World of Sinuhe,' *Israel Oriental Studies* 2, Tel Aviv 1972, 369–409;

Schenkel, W., *Memphis-Herakleopolis-Theben. Die Epigraphischen Zeugnisse der 7.–11. Dynastie Ägyptens, ÄA* 12, Wiesbaden 1965;

Staubli, T., *Das Image der Nomaden im Alten Israel und in der Ikonographie seiner sesshaften Nachbarn, OBO* 107, Freiburg 1991;

Tregenza, L. A., *Egyptian Years*, London 1958;

Vandier, J., *Mo'alla. La Tombe d'Ankhtifi et la Tombe de Sébekhotep*, Le Caire, 1950;

Egypt in the time of Sinuhe's flight

Allen, J. P., 'Some Theban Officials of the Early Middle Kingdom,' Der Manuelian, P. ed., *Studies in Honor of William Kelly Simpson*, Boston 1996, 1–26;

Altenmüller, H., Moussa, A. M.; 'Die Inschrift Amenemhets II. aus dem Ptah-Tempel von Memphis. Ein Vorbericht,' *SAK* 18, 1991, 1–48;

Anthes, R., 'Eine Polizeistreife des Mittleren Reiches in die westliche Oase,' *ZÄS* 65, 1930, 108–114;

Arnold, D., 'Amenemhat I and the Early Twelfth Dynasty at Thebes,' *MMJ* 26, 1991, 21–32;

Berlev, O. D., 'The Eleventh Dynasty in the Dynastic History of Egypt,' Young, D. W. ed., *Studies presented to Hans Jakob Polotsky*, Massachusetts 1981, 361–377;

Bourriau, J., *Pharaohs and Mortals. Egyptian Art in the Middle Kingdom*, Cambridge 1998;

Callender, V. G., *Egypt in the Old Kingdom. An Introduction*, Melbourne 1998;

Grimal, N., *A History of Ancient Egypt*, Oxford 1992;

Habachi, L., 'King Nebhepetre Mentuhotp: Place in History, Deification and Unusual Representations in the Form of Gods,' in *MDAIK* 19, 1963, 16–52;

Hayes, W. C., *The Scepter of Egypt. Part I: From the Earliest Times to the End of the Middle Kingdom*, New York 1953;

Hayes, W. C., *The Middle Kingdom in Egypt*, Cambridge Ancient History, Vol. I, Chapter XX, Cambridge 1961;

M. Lehner, *The Complete Pyramids*, Cairo 1997;

Lichtheim, M., *Ancient Egyptian Autobiographies Chiefly of the Middle Kingdom. A Study and an Anthology*, OBO 85, Freiburg 1988;

Malek, J., *Egyptian Art*, London 1999;

Peet, T. E., *The Stela of Sebek-khu. The Earliest Record of an Egyptian Campaign in Asia*, Manchester 1914;

Schneider, T., *Lexikon der Pharaonen*, München 1996;

Shaw, I. ed., *The Oxford History of Ancient Egypt*, Oxford 2000;

Stadelmann, R., *Die ägyptischen Pyramiden. Vom Ziegelbau zum Weltwunder*, Mainz 1991;

Strudwick, N. and H., *Thebes in Egypt*, New York 1999;

Vandersleyen, C., *L'Égypte et la vallée du Nil. Tome 2. De la fin de l'Ancien Empire à la fin du Nouvel Empire,* Paris 1995;

Vercoutter, J., *L'Égypte et la vallée du Nil. Tome 1. Des Origines à la fin de l'Ancien Empire,* Paris 1992;

Verner, M., *Pyramids, the mystery, culture and science of Egypt's great monuments,* Cairo 2002;

Wildung, D., *Sesostris und Amenemhet. Ägypten im Mittleren Reich,* München 1984;

Wilkinson, T. A. H., *Early Dynastic Egypt,* London 1999;

Winlock, H. E., *The Slain Soldiers of Nebhepetre Mentuhotpe,* New York 1945;

Winlock, H. E., *The Rise and Fall of the Middle Kingdom in Thebes,* New York 1947;

Egypt and Syria-Palestine in the time of Sinuhe's flight

Albright, W. F., *The Archaeology of Palestine,* London 1949;

Ben-Tor, A. (ed.), *The Archaeology of Ancient Israel,* New Haven and London 1992;

Burns, R., *Monuments of Syria. An Historical Guide,* London 1994;

Bietak, M., *Avaris. The Capital of the Hyksos. Recent Excavations at Tell el-Dab'a,* London 1996;

Černý, J., 'Semites in Egyptian Mining Expeditions to Sinai,' *ArOr* 7, 1935, 384–389;

Cohen, S. L., *Canaanites, Chronologies, and Connections. The relationship of Middle Bronze IIA Canaan to Middle Kingdom Egypt,* Winona Lake, Indiana, 2002;

Der Königsweg. 9 000 Jahre Kunst und Kultur in Jordanien, Mainz 1987;

Dever, W. G., 'The EB IV – MB I Horizon in Transjordan and Southern Palestine,' *BASOR* 210, 1973, 37–63;

Dever, W. G., 'New Vistas on the EB IV ('MB I') Horizon in Syria-Palestine,' *BASOR* 237, 1980, 35–64;

Flammini, R., 'The 'ḥȝtyw-ꜥ' from Byblos in the Early Second Millenium B. C.,' *GM* 164, 1998, 41–61;

Goedicke, H., 'Abi-Sha(i)'s Representation in Beni Hasan,' *JARCE* 21, 1984, 203–210;

M. Haiman, 'Early Bronze Age IV Settlement Pattern of the Negev and Sinai Deserts: View from Small Marginal Temporary Sites,' *BASOR* 303, 1996, 1–32;

W. Helck, *Die Beziehungen Ägyptens zu Vorderasien im 3. und 2. Jahrtausend v. Chr.,* ÄA 5, Wiesbaden 1962;

Hobbs, T. J., *Bedouin Life in the Egyptian Wilderness,* Cairo 1990;

Jidejian, N., *Byblos through the Ages,* Beirut 1986;

Kempinski, A., Reich, R., *The Architecture of Ancient Israel from the Prehistoric to the Persian periods,* Jerusalem 1992;

Kenyon, K. M., *Archaeology in the Holy Land,* London 1960;

Kurth, A., *The Ancient Near East c. 3000 – 330 BC,* London 1998;

Land des Baal. Syrien – Forum der Völker und Kulturen, Mainz 1982;

Levy, T. E., 'Egyptian-Canaanite Interaction at Nahal Tillah, Israel (ca. 4500–3000 B.C.E.): An Interim Report on the 1994 – 1995 Excavations,' *BASOR* 307, 1997, 1–51;

Levy, T. E., ed., *The Archaeology of Society in the Holy Land,* London, New York, 1998;

Mark, S., *From Egypt to Mesopotamia,* London 1998;

Matthiae, P., *Aux origines de la Syrie. Ebla retrouvée,* Paris 1996;

Mazar, B., 'The Historical Background of the Book of Genesis,' *JNES* 28,2, 1969, 73–83;

Meyers, E. M. (ed.), *The Oxford Encyclopedia of Archaeology in the Near East*, Oxford 1997;

Montet, P., *Byblos et l'Egypte: Quatre campagnes à Gebeil 1921–1924*, Paris 1929;

Murphy-O'Connor, J., *The Holy Land*, Oxford 1992;

Negev, A., (ed.), *Archäologisches Bibel-Lexikon*, Neuhausen-Stuttgart 1991;

Rainey, A. F. (ed.), *Egypt, Israel, Sinai. Archaeological and Historical Relationships in the Biblical Period*, Tel Aviv 1987;

Redford, D. B., 'Egypt and Western Asia in the Old Kingdom,' *JARCE* 23, 1986, 125–143;

Redford, D. B., *Egypt, Canaan and Israel in Ancient Times*, Cairo 1993;

Rothenberg, B., *The Egyptian Mining Temple at Timna*, London 1988;

Ryholt, K. S. B., 'Hoteibre, a Supposed Asiatic King in Egypt with Relations to Ebla,' *BASOR* 311, 1998, 1–6;

Stadelmann, R., *Syrisch-palästinensische Gottheiten in Ägypten, Probleme der Ägyptologie*, Leiden 1976;

Valbelle, D., Bonnet, Ch., *Le sanctuaire d'Hathor, maîtresse de la turquoise. Sérabit el-Khadim au Moyen Empire*, Paris 1996;

Sinuhe's Afterlife

Assmann, J., *Tod und Jenseits im alten Ägypten*, Munich 2001;

Barta, W., *Aufbau und Bedeutung der altägyptischen Opferformel*, ÄgFo 24, Glückstadt 1968;

D'Auria, S., Lacovara, P., Roehrig, C. H., *Mummies and Magic. The Funerary Arts of Ancient Egypt*, Boston 1988;

Faulkner, R. O., *The Ancient Egyptian Book of the Dead*, London 1985;

Hermsen, E., *Die zwei Wege des Jenseits. Das altägyptische Zweiwegebuch und seine Topographie*, OBO 112, Göttingen 1991;

Ikram, S., Dodson, A., *The Mummy in Ancient Egypt. Equipping the Dead for Eternity*. Cairo 1998;

Kamrin, J., *The Cosmos of Khnumhotep II at Beni Hassan*, London 1999;

Kanawati, N., Hassan, A., *The Teti Cemetery at Saqqara. Vol. II. The Tomb of Ankhmahor*, ACER 9, Sydney 1997;

Koch, K., *Geschichte der ägyptischen Religion. Von den Pyramiden bis zu den Mysterien der Isis*, Stuttgart 1993;

Möller, G., *Die beiden Totenpapyri Rhind des Museums zu Edinburg*, Leipzig 1913;

Parkinson, R. B., *Voices from Ancient Egypt. An Anthology of Middle Kingdom Writings*, London 1991;

Quirke, S., *Ancient Egyptian Religion*, London 1992;

Quirke, S., Forman, W., *Hieroglyphs and the Afterlife in Ancient Egypt*, London 1996;

Settgast, J., *Untersuchungen zu altägyptischen Bestattungsdarstellungen*, Glückstadt 1963;

Shafer, B. E. (ed.), *Temples of Ancient Egypt*, London 1997;

Shedid, A. G., *Die Felsgräber von Beni Hassan in Mittelägypten*, Mainz 1994;

Schulz, R., Seidel, M., *Ägypten. Die Welt der Pharaonen*, Köln 1997;

Spencer, A. J., *Death in Ancient Egypt*, London 1982;

Taylor, J. H., *Death and the Afterlife in Ancient Egypt*, London 2001;

Wilson, J. A., 'Funeral Services of the Egyptian Old Kingdom,' *JNES* 3, 1944, 201–218;

Winlock, H. E., *Models of Daily Life in Ancient Egypt from the Tomb of Meket-Re at Thebes,* Cambridge 1955;

Afterword

Foster, J. L., 'Sinuhe: The Ancient Egyptian Genre of Narrative Verse,' *JNES* 39, 2, 1980, 89–117;

Hess, R. S., Satterthwaite, P. E., Wenham, G. J. (eds.), *He Swore an Oath. Biblical Themes from Genesis 12–50,* Cambridge 1993;

Hoffmeier, J. K., *Israel in Egypt. The Evidence for the Authenticity of the Exodus Tradition,* New York 1996;

Tobin, V. A., 'The Secret of Sinuhe,' *JARCE* 32, 1995, 161–178.

Chronological Table
(down to the Twelfth Dynasty)

(The following list contains the names and dates for the kings relevant to Sinuhe's story. It is based on J. Baines, J. Malek, *Atlas of Ancient Egypt,* Oxford 1980).

Predynastic period
(down to c. 3000 BC)

Early Dynastic period (3000–2575 BC)
First Dynasty (3000–2770 BC)
Hor-Aha, Djer, Wadj, Den, Adjib, Semerkhet, Qaa

Second Dynasty (2770–2649 BC)
Hetepsekhemwy, Raneb, Ninetjer, Peribsen, Khasekhemwy

Third Dynasty (2649–2575 BC)
Nebka, Djoser, Sekhemkhet, Khaba, Huni

Old Kingdom (2575– 2134 BC)
Fourth Dynasty (2575–2465 BC)
Sneferu, Khufu (Kheops), Radjedef, Khafre (Khephren), Menkaure (Mycerinus), Shepseskaf

Fifth Dynasty (2465–2323 BC)
Userkaf, Sahure, Neferirkare, Shepseskare, Raneferef, Neuserre, Menkauhor, Djedkare, Unas

Sixth Dynasty (2323–2150 BC)
Teti, Pepi I, Merenre I, Pepi II, Merenre II, Neitokret

First Intermediate Period (2150–2040 BC)
Seventh/Eighth Dynasty (2150–2134 BC)
about 20 ephemeral kings

Ninth/Tenth Dynasty (2134–2040 BC)
about 18 rulers, several of them called Khety

Eleventh Dynasty (2134–2040 BC)
Inyotef I (2134–2040)
Inyotef II (2118–2069)
Inyotef III (2069–2061)

Mentuhotep II (2061–2010)
Mentuhotep III (2010–1998)
Mentuhotep IV (1998–1991)

Middle Kingdom (2040– 1640 BC)
Twelfth Dynasty (1991–1783)
Amenemhat I (1991–1962)
Senwosret I (1971–1926)
Amenemhat II (1929–1892)
Senwosret II (1897–1878)
Senwosret III (1878–1841)
Amenemhat III (1844–1797)
Amenemhat IV (1799–1787)
Sebeknofru (1787–1783)

Credits

Photographs
All photographs were provided by the author; those enumerated below were published with a kind approval from the following institutions and individuals:

1.1 Archives of the Czech Institute of Egyptology, M. Zemina
1.3 Archives of the Czech Institute of Egyptology, M. Zemina
1.4 Inv. Nr. 3896a, Kunsthistorisches Museum, Wien
1.7 Archives of Set Out, R. Míšek
1.19 © Thomas E. Levy and Wadi Faynan Project, University of California, San Diego
2.6 Archives of the Czech Institute of Egyptology, M. Zemina
2.14 Archives of the Czech Institute of Egyptology, M. Zemina
2.22 Archives of the Czech Institute of Egyptology
2.33 Courtesy Jaromír Málek, Oxford
2.24 Louvre, Egyptian Collection
2.26 Egyptian Museum, Cairo
2.32 Louvre, Egyptian Collection
2.43 Egyptian Museum, Cairo
2.49 Egyptian Museum, Cairo
3.29 Archives of the Czech Institute of Egyptology, M. Zemina
3.30 Archives of the Czech Institute of Egyptology, M. Zemina
4.1 Archives of the Czech Institute of Egyptology, M. Zemina
4.2 Louvre, Egyptian Collection
4.3 Archives of the Czech Institute of Egyptology, M. Zemina
4.6 Drawing by P. Vlčková
4.7 Archives of the Czech Institute of Egyptology, M. Zemina
4.8 Archives of the Czech Institute of Egyptology, M. Zemina
4.19 Archives of the Czech Institute of Egyptology, K. Voděra
4.37 Inv. Nr. 5999, Roemer- und Pelizeus Museum, Hildesheim
4.39 Inv. Nr. 6226, Roemer- und Pelizeus Museum, Hildesheim
4.41 Acc. No. 20.30.8, Metropolitan Museum of Art, New York
4.42 Acc. No. 20.3.13, Metropolitan Museum of Art, New York
4.43 Courtesy of the Metropolitan Museum of Art, Expedition to Dahshur
4.44 Acc. No. 20.3.4, Metropolitan Museum of Art, New York
4.45 Acc. No. 20.3.11, Metropolitan Museum of Art, New York
4.46 Egyptian Museum, Cairo
4.47 Acc. No. 20.3.7, Metropolitan Museum of Art, New York
4.48 Acc. No. 12.183.8, Metropolitan Museum of Art, New York

Maps
All maps were prepared by Petra Vlčková

Line drawings
Jolana Malátková: 2.21, 2.45, 3.2, 3.25

Lucie Vařeková: 1.3, 1.25, 1.28, 1.33, 1.34, 1.35, 2.10, 2.16, 2.17, 2.29, 2.31, 2.36, 2.43, 3.6, 3.10, 3.13, 3.19, 3.24, 3.26, 3.27, 3.30, 3.34, 4.9, 4.10, 4.14, 4.15, 4.16, 4.25, 4.32, 4.38, 4.40, 4.43

Petra Vlčková: 4.6.

Index

1. Names

Abishay *180, 181, 249;*
Abraham *9, 10, 38, 43–45, 161, 163, 164, 177, 182, 192, 273;*
Ahmose *56, 91;*
Akhenaten *9;*
Albright, W. F. *46;*
Altenmüller, H. *114, 116;*
Amenemhat I *9, 10, 13, 17, 32, 35, 36, 64, 67, 70, 99–103, 105–107, 109–111, 165, 180, 186, 187, 223, 258, 267, 273;*
Amenemhat II *112, 114, 115, 117, 119, 120, 192, 246;*
Amenemhat III *11, 12, 17, 77, 132–137, 155, 163, 185, 191;*
Amunenshi *15, 20, 36, 37, 43, 49;*
Ankhmahor *219, 221;*
Ankhtify *51, 52, 79–81, 83, 234, 235;*
Arieh, B. *147;*
Arnold, Di. *94, 95;*
Arnold, Do. *89;*
Ashayit *94;*
Baket III *86–88;*
Bietak, M. *188, 189;*
Borchardt, L. *160, 168;*
Callender, V. G. *94;*
Darnell, D. *11, 12, 83;*
Darnell, J. C. *11, 12, 83;*
David and Goliath *9, 49, 50;*
Dedusobek *11, 12;*
Den *200, 201, 261;*
Djefahapi III *271;*
Djehutihotep *126, 127, 184;*
Djoser *129, 133, 134, 202, 208, 218, 246, 251;*
Emery, W. B. *68, 69;*
Fakhry, A. *32, 67;*
Franke, D. *127;*
Gardiner, A. H. *65, 168;*
Gilgamesh *159;*
Gophna, R. *143;*
Habachi, L. *89;*
Hardjedef *199;*
Harkhuf *53, 55, 240;*
Hatshepsut *89, 259;*
Hawass, Z. *204, 219, 220;*

Hekaib *85;*
Henenu *97, 183, 257;*
Herodotus *125, 128, 129, 134, 214, 215, 217;*
Hyksos *55, 56;*
Iah *91;*
Ibu *236, 239;*
Inti (Deshasha) *167, 170;*
Inyotef I *81, 83, 84, 91, 93;*
Inyotef II *83–5, 91, 93;*
Inyotef III *85, 91, 93;*
Inyotefiker *101, 102, 110, 223, 224;*
Ipuwer *77, 172;*
It *120, 121;*
Itakait *111;*
Kai *87, 88;*
Kawit *93, 95;*
Kenyon, K. *42;*
Khafre *32–4, 219, 220;*
Khebded *190, 191;*
Kheti I *79;*
Kheti III *81, 82;*
Khnumhotep I *101;*
Khnumhotep II *180, 181, 231, 246–52;*
Khufu *33, 101, 109, 155, 156;*
Khusobek *127, 128;*
Lapp, P. W. *46;*
Lepsius, K. R. *11;*
Levy, T. E. *47;*
Lot *43–46;*
Manetho *79;*
Mazar, A. *146, 150, 152, 173;*
Meketre *258–62; 264–8;*
Meki *25, 64;*
Menes *91;*
Menkaure *33;*
Mentuhotep I *83;*
Mentuhotep II *31, 54, 59, 77, 81, 84–6, 88–97, 109, 183, 211, 212, 257, 259, 267;*
Mentuhotep III *97, 99;*
Mentuhotep IV *101;*
Merenre *125;*
Mereruka *233;*
Merikare *79, 81, 82, 85, 178, 179;*
Mesekhti *88;*
Morgan, J. de *121, 130;*

Moussa, A. *114, 116;*
Narmer *141–5;*
Neferkare VII *79;*
Neferti *34, 35, 100;*
Nesmontu *103–5;*
Newberry, P. E. *87, 126, 181;*
Niankhpepi *232;*
Oren, E. *67, 73;*
Pepi I *234;*
Pepi II *234;*
Pepiankh *218, 221, 222;*
Peribsen *146;*
Petrie, W. M. F. *122, 123, 136, 239;*
Qar *220, 228;*
Ramesses I *65;*
Ramesses II *27, 59, 187;*
Rast, W. E. *46;*
Sahure *61, 155, 160, 168, 178, 203–5;*
Sarenput I *238, 240–2;*
Sarenput II *242–5, 247;*
Saul *50;*
Sebekhotep *57;*
Sennedjem *15;*
Senwosret I *9, 10, 12, 13, 22, 23, 31, 32, 36, 57, 58, 65, 70, 106–12, 114, 197, 209, 213, 223, 224, 240, 246, 253, 268, 269, 271, 273;*
Senwosret II *112, 119, 120, 123–6, 163, 180, 246;*
Senwosret III *125, 127–32, 134, 184, 187;*
Sethi I *59, 65–7, 72;*
Schaub, T. R. *46;*
Sinuhe *9, 10, 12, 13, 15, 22, 24, 28, 31–9, 41–3, 49–52, 54, 55, 57–60, 62–5, 67, 74, 77, 99, 106, 107, 112, 136, 139, 140, 155, 157, 163, 171, 180, 182, 186, 190–2, 197, 199, 201, 213, 217, 221, 225, 229, 256, 258, 259, 268, 271–4;*
Sithathoriunet *124;*
Smendes *158, 159;*
Sneferu *33, 100, 168, 191;*
Stadelmann, R. *96, 110, 112;*
Tefib *85;*
Teti *78, 79, 212;*
Thutmosis III *102;*
Tjehemau *54;*
Tubb, J. N. *149;*
Unas *206–8;*
Upuautaa *55;*
Vachala, B. *78, 83, 180;*
Wahka I *236, 239;*

Wahka II *239, 240;*
Waltari, M. *9;*
Wenamun *157–9;*
Weni *125, 167, 171, 183, 199;*
Winlock, H. E. *89, 90, 259;*
Yarim-Addu *37;*
Žába, Zb. *101, 102;*

2. Sites

Abgig *108;*
Abisko *54;*
Abu Simbel *101;*
Abusir *61, 77, 160, 168, 178, 203, 220, 226, 228, 229, 233, 235;*
Abydos *55, 83–85, 103, 105, 127, 129, 131, 142, 199–202, 223, 240, 248, 252, 256, 257, 261;*
Afridar (Ashkelon) *144, 186;*
Aleppo *166;*
Aniba *112;*
Arad *142, 143, 147–9, 153;*
Armant *80, 82, 83, 103;*
Assuan *53–55, 99, 120, 133, 235, 237, 238, 240, 243, 247;*
Asyut *81, 82, 86, 238, 239;*
Avaris *55, 165;*
Ay *147, 153, 183;*
Ayin Zik *173, 175;*
Bab el-Dhra *46, 47, 147;*
Bahr el-Litani *36;*
Beit Shean *146, 172, 176;*
Beit Yerah *146, 147;*
Beni Hassan *86–88, 101, 127, 180, 231, 238, 240, 245, 246, 249, 269;*
el-Bersha *126, 127, 184, 238, 258;*
'En Besor *144, 145;*
Biahmu *136;*
Bir Resisim *173, 174;*
Bitter Lakes *35;*
Bubastis *103;*
Buhen *68–70;*
Buto *62, 139, 190, 208, 242, 261;*
Byblos *15, 36, 61, 64, 65, 81, 153–9, 161, 167, 172, 183–6, 193, 194;*
Coptos *83, 97, 98, 270;*
Cyprus *159, 162;*
Dabenarti *70;*
Dahshur *33, 77, 119, 121, 128–31, 133, 134, 222, 233;*
Dakhla Oasis *83, 90;*
Damascus *43–5;*

Dead Sea *43–6;*
Deir el-Bahri *59, 84, 89, 91, 92, 94–7, 109, 183, 212, 259;*
Deir el-Medineh *12, 15;*
Dendera *103;*
Deshasha *167, 170;*
Dor *158, 159;*
Ebla *163, 164, 172;*
Edfu *80, 81, 91;*
Ehnasya el-Medina *79;*
Elephantine *25, 64, 81, 83–5, 91, 100, 169, 171, 240, 242, 244;*
Fayyum Oasis *60, 79, 108, 120, 132–4, 136;*
Gaza *66, 67, 142;*
Gebel el-Akhmar *34;*
Gebelein *88, 89, 235;*
Gerf Hussein *101;*
El-Girgawi *101;*
Giza *31–33, 77, 109, 156, 217, 219, 220, 233, 235;*
Gomorrah *44, 45, 176;*
Halif Terrace *144, 145;*
Har Yeroham *173, 174;*
Harubah *70, 72, 73;*
Hatnub *87, 108, 125, 127;*
Hawara *133–135;*
Hazor *172, 176, 190;*
Heliopolis *62, 103, 108, 209, 210;*
Helwan *145, 184;*
Herakleopolis *79, 81, 88;*
Hierakonpolis *52, 79–81;*
Illahun *120, 123, 124;*
Island of Sneferu *14;*
Itj-tawy *26, 27, 67, 264;*
Jericho *42, 146, 167, 172, 176, 177, 190;*
Jerusalem *161, 186, 187;*
Kaneferu *13;*
Karnak *58, 59, 66, 67, 72, 96, 102, 103, 108;*
Kashu *25, 65;*
Kemwer *14, 35;*
Kerak *42, 46;*
Kharga Oasis *83;*
Khenemisut *13;*
Khirbet Hamra *47, 48;*
Lakhish *147, 176, 177, 187, 190;*
Lebanon *114, 117, 118, 154, 155, 157–9, 193;*
Lisht *17, 23, 103, 107, 109–112;*
Luxor *51, 59, 63, 84, 235, 253;*
Mari *37, 155, 165, 166, 188;*
Medamud *213;*

Megiddo *36, 146, 149, 150–2, 172, 176, 184;*
Meir *218, 221, 222, 232, 251;*
Memphis *60, 79, 103, 114, 115, 119, 226, 252;*
Mirgissa *70, 120, 184, 185;*
Mo'alla *51, 52, 80, 81, 234, 235;*
Numeira *147;*
Ombos *81;*
Qaw el-Kebir *84, 235, 236, 238, 239;*
Qedem *15, 22, 25, 36, 63, 64;*
Qubbet el-Hawa *237, 238, 240, 243;*
Rafah *65, 66, 173;*
Retjenu *9, 15, 19, 20, 22, 25, 36, 41, 49, 50, 52, 55, 188, 190;*
Saqqara *77–9, 109, 133, 134, 185, 202, 207, 218, 220, 221, 226, 233, 235;*
Sehel *125;*
Semna *70, 101, 125;*
Serabit el-Khadim *106, 116, 132, 188, 190–4;*
Sileh *65–7;*
Sinai *37–9, 43, 55, 61, 62, 66, 72, 73, 91, 103, 106, 108, 114, 115, 120, 125, 132, 142, 143, 147, 150, 166, 168, 172, 173, 176, 177, 179, 188, 190–3;*
Sodom *44, 45, 176;*
Tanis *158, 159, 195;*
el-Tarif *84, 91;*
el-Tel (Hai) *161;*
Tel Azeka *49;*
Tel Dan *45, 146;*
Tell el-Daba'a *186–90;*
Tel el-Far'ah *147, 149, 150;*
Tell es-Sa'idiyeh *147, 149, 150;*
Tel Erani *144, 145;*
Tel Ma'ahaz *144, 145;*
Tel Malhata *143;*
Tel Tanakh *149;*
Tell Abu Seipha *65;*
Tell el-Rataba *35;*
Tell el-Yehudieh *27, 34;*
Tell Hebua *65;*
Tell Hezi *65;*
Thebes *11, 12, 26, 58, 59, 79–81, 88, 91, 94, 103, 105, 112, 137, 212, 259, 264;*
Thinis *81, 84–6;*
Timna *143;*
Timsakh (Lake) *35;*
Tjehenu *13, 15;*
Tod *103, 112, 113;*

Toshka *101, 120, 133;*
Tura *133, 157, 199;*
Tyre *36, 41;*
Ugarit *107, 112, 162, 163, 172, 184;*
Uronarti *125;*
Wadi Arabah *143, 147;*
Wadi el-Hol *11, 12;*
Wadi el-Hudi *99, 108, 120, 125, 193;*
Wadi Faynan *47, 48, 175, 176;*
Wadi Gasus *97;*
Wadi Gawasis *119, 120;*
Wadi Hammamat *97–99, 101, 108, 120, 125, 133;*
Wadi Maghara *166, 168;*
Wadi Natrun *31, 32, 67, 70, 216;*
Wadi Shatt el-Righal *90, 91, 214, 259;*
Wadi Tumilat *34, 35, 180;*
Walls of the Ruler *14, 34, 35, 99;*
Waset *24, 57;*
Ways of Horus *26, 35, 65–7, 70, 72, 141, 142, 176;*
Yaa *18, 26, 39;*
Yarmut *149, 153;*
Yebu *16;*

3. Gods and goddesses

Amun *24, 57–59, 62, 63, 83, 84, 102, 103, 109, 158, 159;*
Amun-Ra *58, 96, 108, 212;*
Anat *56;*
Anubis *216, 220, 229, 242, 245;*
Astarte *56;*
Atum *24, 57, 62, 63, 193, 206, 210;*
Atum-Khepre *210;*
Baal *162, 194, 195;*
Geb *61, 62, 210, 245, 259;*
Hapi *257;*
Harwer-Ra *25, 57, 63;*
Hathor *24, 26, 33, 57, 60, 61, 63, 64, 93, 94, 106, 153, 154, 157, 165, 191–195, 250;*
Horus *24, 26, 57, 60–63, 65, 100, 101, 193, 208, 210–213, 216, 228, 239;*
Horus-Min *57, 62, 63;*
Ishtar *161, 164–6;*
Isis *60, 62, 210, 222, 230;*
Khnum *244;*
Khons *58, 218;*
Khontamenti *105;*
Min *62;*
Montu *20, 24, 26, 50, 52, 54, 57–9, 63, 83, 96, 103, 105;*
Montu-Ra *95, 99;*
Mut *58;*
Nephthys *62, 210, 222;*
Nekhbet *100, 204, 212, 244;*
Nun *123;*
Nut *25, 33, 57, 61–3, 156, 157, 208, 210, 255;*
Osiris *60, 62, 93, 95, 105, 127, 129, 131, 200, 201, 210, 212, 222, 223, 228, 229, 234, 240, 242, 245, 248, 252, 255–7;*
Ptah *23, 114;*
Ra *22, 24–6, 28, 58, 61, 63, 64, 203, 206, 208, 209, 212, 227, 229, 254–7, 261;*
Ra-Atum *108;*
Ra-Harakhte *156;*
Satet *242, 244;*
Sebek *135, 165;*
Sebek-Ra *24, 57, 60, 63;*
Sekhmet *16, 64;*
Seth *56, 60–3, 100, 101, 123, 193, 195, 210–3, 231, 239, 261;*
Shu *61, 62, 210;*
Sopdu *24, 57, 61–3, 106, 191;*
Taiet *24;*
Tefnut *61, 210;*
Thoth *88, 193, 206, 229;*
Wadjet *62, 63, 100, 204, 212, 239;*
Wepwawet *82, 271;*
Wereret *17, 25, 57, 62, 63.*

Miroslav Bárta
SINUHE, THE BIBLE, AND THE PATRIARCHS
Foreword by Thomas E. Levy
Published by SET OUT – Roman Míšek
Tyršova 11, 120 00 Prague, Czech Republic
1st edition Prague 2003
Text © Miroslav Bárta, Thomas E. Levy
Translation © Renata Landgráfová
Photos © Photographers and Institutions as indicated
Drawings and maps © Jolana Malátková, Lucie Vařeková, Petra Vlčková
Cover design Roman Míšek
Editor Hana Navrátilová
Printed by ÚJI Zbraslav, Prague
Printed in Czech Republic